Praise for
Finding Peace in the Promised Land

"A ***must-read*** for anyone who wants to understand the A
Israel conflict and the path for **peace** and **coexisten**
– **Khaled Abu Toameh**, noted Muslim Arab Israeli journa

"In *Finding Peace in the Promised Land* Aryeh Green bravely st
to succeed where countless others have failed by seeking to
the Middle East conflict. His **formula is unique** and his **ideas
fresh**. For all those passionate about the search for Middle East
peace, Green offers **a new and compelling perspective**."
– **Michael Oren**, former Israeli deputy minister and ambassador
to the United States

"These days, it's far too easy to despair. Fortunately, Aryeh
Green is too **optimistic**, too **energetic**, and too **wise** to
succumb. Juggling between the philosophical, the theological,
and the pragmatic, he makes the convincing case that the **path
to peace** is through the mosque and the synagogue - the power
of our **shared Abrahamic faiths**. Most surprisingly, this
compelling book does an impressive job of both wielding
sources and finding contemporaries who do just that."
– Professor **Gil Troy**, author, *The Reagan Revolution, Moynihan's
Moment, Never Alone, To Resist the Academic Intifada*, and *The Zionist
Ideas*

"Drawing on his personal experience, Aryeh Green proposes
five 'hard, practical' steps to end the 'Palestinian-Israeli' conflict:
humility, acceptance, gratitude, forgiveness, and purpose. He
offers these not as immediate solutions but 'as the first steps on
a long hike [that] will make the destination possible.' I personally
hold to a tougher approach but **hope he is right**; his
contribution to the public discussion and policy debate is
both **timely** and **important**." – **Daniel Pipes**, founder of the
Middle East Forum and prominent analyst and commentator

"While I may not agree with some of his narratives, arguments, and perspectives, **I applaud Aryeh Green's efforts** to bring together the disparate elements of religion, politics, history, philosophy, and logic **in service of the essential cause of peace** and of our **shared goals of coexistence and reconciliation**. Our differences highlight the gap between the three narratives – the Israeli, the Palestinian, and the peacebuilders' narrative. We do not have to agree with each other, but we should avoid the three negative Ds when promoting each narrative: Demonization, Delegitimization, and Denunciation. This way, the three narratives would contribute positively to public debate and policymaking in the realm of moderation and peacebuilding. I see these differences as a **vital part** of our ongoing interfaith dialogue to bring a genuine, lasting peace to our region." – Professor **Mohammed S. Dajani Daoudi**, founder of the **Wasatia** moderate Islamic movement in Palestine committed to the advancement of peace and humanity

Finding Peace
~ in the ~
Promised Land

From Hatred to Humanity:
Five Transformative Steps to Resolve
the Arab-Israel Conflict

Aryeh Green

GreenHouse Press

San Francisco, CA

ISBN 13:
979-8-9950255-0-4 (Hardback)
979-8-9950255-1-1 (Paperback)
979-8-9950255-2-8 (eBook)

Published by GreenHouse Press, an imprint of Skylake Associates, Ltd.

LIBRARY OF CONGRESS CATALOGING-IN-PUBLICATION DATA

Names: Green, Aryeh, 1963- author.
Title: Finding Peace in the Promised Land / Aryeh Green.
Description: Middle East policy analysis; includes bibliographical
references.
Subjects: LCSH: Green, Aryeh, 1963--- Arab-Israeli conflict – Peace | Peace-building – Middle East | Judaism – Relations – Islam | Conflict management – Middle East

Cover design by Rebecacovers © 2026 Aryeh Green

Printed in the United States of America

1 0 9 8 7 6 5 4 3 2 1

For my grandchildren – Noga, Alma, Adam, Aviv, Ben, Erel,
Ivri, Amiaz, and Yarden – and for all the children and
grandchildren in our region who deserve to live in peace.

———————— ✴ ————————

Dedicated to the memory of "The Beautiful Six" – Alex, Eden,
Hersh, Ori, Almog, and Carmel – taken hostage, tortured and
murdered by Hamas. May their memory be a blessing, and may
their families, and the families of all those killed and injured on
Oct. 7th and after, be comforted by the attainment of real peace
in our region.

———————— ✴ ————————

*"And [Abraham's] sons Isaac and Ishmael [together]
laid him to rest in the cave of Machpelah...."* (Genesis 25:9)

Finding Peace in the Promised Land

From Hatred to Humanity – Five Transformative Steps
to Resolve the Arab–Israel Conflict

By Aryeh Green

Contents

Prologue 9

Introduction – The Background and Conceptual Framework . 17

Chapter One: A Brief History of it All in Three Parts 28

Chapter Two: The Five Elements of Peace 67

Chapter Three: Humility 75

Chapter Four: Acceptance 85

Chapter Five: Gratitude 102

Chapter Six: Forgiveness 120

Chapter Seven: Purpose 135

Chapter Eight: From Vision to Blueprint 175

Chapter Nine: Conclusion – Putting it All Together 200

Acknowledgments 211

Prologue

This book has been over four years in the writing, but some forty years in the making. Like the children of Israel wandering for forty years in the desert, I have been meandering through various intellectual paths while living in Israel. But like the children of Israel with their singular focus of arriving in the promised land, I have journeyed within a consistent conceptual framework throughout; one which, when distilled to its essence, calls for mutual respect, tolerance, understanding, love and acceptance.

I learned this approach to life, and to overcoming differences and disagreements, from many sources: on the knees of my liberal American Jewish parents and grandparents in the US, in my studies of Gandhian methods of conflict resolution at UC Berkeley, in my student trip to the former USSR, in my studies at (Reform Jewish) rabbinical school and at (Orthodox Jewish) yeshivas/study halls, in my master's program in international relations at Hebrew University, and in over four decades of public and private activism promoting freedom, democracy and peace in the Middle East.

That mindset was challenged by the events of October 7th '23 in the South of Israel – the barbaric Shmini Atzeret/Shabbat Hamas massacre – and by the ensuing years of war, pain, death, devastation and struggle; and in no small part by the attitude and policies of much of the leadership of the free world.

The Hamas terror group in Gaza as well as its close cousin Hezb'Allah* in Lebanon, their sponsor Iran and their supporters Qatar, Turkey and others, were tolerated, sympathized with, and often actually supported – including in news media and academia, in parliaments and places of worship. This, in spite of the murderous outrage carried out by Hamas 'activists' and 6000 other Gaza civilians, including gruesome and now well-documented acts of heinous torture, rape and the murder of parents in front of children and children in front of parents.

Meanwhile, Israel and the Jews were castigated for defending themselves, and even more disturbingly, maligned for using

---

* This spelling is closer to the name of this terrorist organization – "Party of God" – than the usual "Hezbollah".

'disproportionate force' and even for pursuing a supposed 'genocide'. The facts point clearly to the opposite conclusion, as noted by urban warfare expert John Spencer and the former commander of British forces in Iraq and Afghanistan, Colonel Richard Kemp, among other leading western military strategists and historians

Israel's defensive military operations were and are shining examples of restraint and morality, protecting civilian lives and property more successfully than any military force in history, using tactics not employed by the US or the UK or any other western power in its military operations. (And all at the cost of losing its own soldiers, the majority of whom are reservists called away from family and work to defend their country and people against brutal, horrific terror regimes.)

Although many of the ideas in this book were cultivated during a long contemplative trek, their genesis lies in a number of premises advocated by Gandhi – among them non-violence, sensitivity, and seeking a Truthful solution.

For Mahatma Gandhi, Truth (Satya) is the ultimate reality, synonymous with God, an absolute principle governing the universe that must be experienced through humility, self-realization, and rigorous adherence in thought, word, and deed. This formed the basis for his philosophy of Satyagraha (truth-force) and non-violence (Ahimsa). Gandhi famously declared, "Truth is God" (or "God is Truth"), seeing Truth as the fundamental reality, the essence of existence, and the ultimate goal. He saw Truth as a journey, a constant search and striving for perfection, requiring immense humility.

These ideas have permeated my thinking and writing about the Arab-Israel conflict for these past four decades, after learning them from Prof. Mark Juergensmeyer at Berkeley (*Fighting with Gandhi*). But one of the primary features of most conflict-resolution paradigms, including Gandhi's, has now been shattered. It is the insistence that both sides to a conflict have a recognized 'narrative', or their own 'truth', which must be taken into account if one wishes to achieve a resolution. That theoretical framework for resolving this conflict simply no longer applies.*

It must be said clearly: An ideology which promotes the rape of innocent young women and the murder of babies – in fact the ripping of unborn babies from the wombs of their young mothers, as documented on October 7th – has no place in our modern and free world, nor in the Middle East, nor, as will be discussed, in normative Islam.

An ideology which denies historical reality, accepting a false 'narrative' whereby the people of Israel have no historical connection with the land of Israel (as Yasser Arafat told President Clinton, claiming there had never been a Jewish Temple in Jerusalem) has no place in efforts to bring peace to our region.

Such a political ideology (which is what Islamist interpretations of Islam and Arab nationalism are) is fascism at its worst, where a combination of ignorance and intolerance based on religious fervor and propaganda have created a culture of hatred and a cult of death-worship. This simply cannot be seen as a legitimate part of civilized

---

* Throughout this work, we refer to the "Arab-Israel conflict". Others refer to a "Palestinian-Israel" struggle, or even a Jewish-Muslim civilizational battle. Considering that (1) the original opponents of Zionism and invaders of Israel were Arab states and leaders, and (2) the "Palestinian" Arabs are not the only or even the leading opponents of Israel, we use the term "Arab-Israel conflict" for convenience. Though Israel has formal peace treaties already with six Arab countries, and non-belligerence with at least a few others, there is still a majority of Arab countries which are not at peace or even non-belligerence with Israel. Perhaps more important, the people of the region, including in Jordan and Egypt and Palestinian society, are among the most antisemitic and anti-Israel Jew-haters on the planet. That's hardly peace.

For the record, Persian Iran, though not Arab, is included in our broadly-meant terminology, as are the opponents of Israel and Jews elsewhere (Boko Haram, Al Qaeda, Taliban and others). Similarly, though much of our argument here points to a need for reform in Islamic thought, our Middle East conflict is not so much between Jews/Judaism and Muslims/Islam as much as it is between western ideas of acceptance and compromise and Islamist rejectionist political ideology, so it is not a "Muslim-Jewish" conflict.

As will be described, there are of course millions of more moderate Muslims around the world – however we define "moderate" – as well as moderate Arabs. The shorthand serves us well, however simplistic it may be; and I apologize to Arabs who do not seek to promote the conflict.

dialogue as we search for a resolution to this conflict. Nazi Germany's aggression against Europe, and its vile ideology, were not just another conceptual framework to engage with in respectful debate; their 'narrative' was rejected as false and odious. And there are many Muslim and Arab thinkers and leaders who now agree with this approach regarding Islamist ideology.

It is evident that after the Oct. 7th massacre, extremist Islamist fascism, or Islamo-fascism for short, has no claim to any 'truth', and the 'narrative' of Jews stealing Arab/Muslim lands has no place in discussion of resolving the Arab-Israel conflict. The unambiguous understanding of this insight creates a new climate in which these conversations are taking place.

Which in fact has made this book somewhat easier to write, and to publish. In previous years and decades there was at least a façade, accepted and even celebrated by many in the West, that Arabs who self-identified as "Palestinian" since the 1960s were interested in a combination of justice and freedom and in the establishment of an independent "Palestine". Their opposition to certain Israeli policies or actions, and the antagonism towards Israel of Arab and Muslim leaders in general (and others), was presumed to have noble intentions.

Today, post-Oct. 7th, that pretense has been ripped away. And not only for Israelis. Many Muslim/Arab leaders and thinkers – including those interviewed for this book and quoted in these pages – agree that Oct. 7th represents a watershed in the emergence, and the exposure, of the anti-Israel, anti-West, anti-Christian, anti-freedom and antisemitic dogma which permeates too many of the Arab and Muslim institutions and societies in the region and around the world.

This book is dedicated to the thesis that such concepts as acceptance, forgiveness and a sense of purpose must form the basis for accommodation between Arabs and Israelis. Prior to Oct. 7th, such a proposal would probably not have been welcomed enthusiastically. The idea that such concepts could bring about peace between Muslims and Christians and Jews might have once been seen as overly idealistic or too simplistic for such a complex conflict. Works focused on solving the conflict were written in a standard format: laying out the historical and philosophical underpinnings of each 'side' and its perspective, outlining the failures of each party and reviewing the many mistakes made by them and the international community over the past century, and presenting a form of 'compromise' bringing the two sides together.

But following Oct. 7th and the ensuing years, including the war to prevent Iran from developing nuclear weapons and halt its support for terror, it is clear that we need to re-evaluate our assumptions and the parameters of a resolution to this centuries-old conflict. Or it is clear at least to those observers who still pride themselves on independent thought and careful, fact-based analysis, and who are actually interested in finding a Gandhian, Truthful solution.

Those who continue to call for a "Two-State Solution" after Arafat's ruining the Oslo Process with the "2nd Intifada", the Palestinian response to Israel's disengagement from Gaza, and the massacre of Oct. 7th (and Arab/Muslim/Palestinian support for it) are intellectually sterile. Just as the US and its allies did not and would not seek compromise with the Nazis or Al Qaeda or others seeking their destruction, neither will Israel and the Jewish people. And this consensus will remain strong for at least a generation.

Thus, when beginning to put these ideas on paper in the years prior to Oct. 7th, I was very cautious in my criticism of Islamism (as an ideology and political creed), and careful to be extremely 'balanced' in making demands of both Arab and Israeli leaders and societies, both Muslim and Jewish thinkers and communities. After Oct. 7th I am now less concerned with politically-correct balance and more concerned with that Truth which Gandhi so rightly focused on as the fundamental source of lasting resolution of any conflict.

Yet it is not only the horrific violence of Oct. 7th which has rendered the thesis of this book more plausible. The initiation and success so far of the Abraham Accords have also made publishing these ideas seem more realistic. That these peace agreements were signed between Israel and the UAE, Bahrain, Morocco and Sudan is of course encouraging. More important, as we'll discuss, the foundations were laid at every level of society for true acceptance and real peace.

As important, it has become ever more clear to policy makers that one of the motivations for the timing of the Oct. 7th attack was the progress made in bringing Saudi Arabia into the Abraham Accords and "normalization" with Israel. Perhaps paradoxically, Oct. 7th has now motivated even more rigorous soul-searching and public discussion of extremist Islamist ideology – including condemnations from those previously seen to espouse similar Islamic thinking, from the Wahhabis of Saudi Arabia and other Salafists to the scholars at Islamic seminaries from Egypt to Iraq.

So, however naïvely optimistic my original contemplations were back in '14 when I was hiking the Israel Trail, the last few years have confirmed the soundness of this approach. And more recent events involving Iran, including the revolt of the Iranian people against the Islamist oppression of their Shiite tyrants, similarly vindicate this sort of thinking.

There is much to criticize in Israeli policy and actions, and there are demands to be made of Israel, its government and people and supporters. But to be honest, as we must be, most of the demands, the criticism, and the need for change in behavior, in ideology, in attitude and education and policy and action, are directed at the leadership and societies of the Arab and Muslim world, and their supporters.*

If that strikes you as one-sided, so be it. If that prevents you from reading this book, I would humbly suggest that this makes you part of the problem, demonstrating a close-mindedness you probably wouldn't embrace; and that such an unwillingness impoverishes your understanding of the complexities of the issues. And it limits your ability to evaluate alternatives and to effect change in any meaningful way.

So there are no apologies for what is a simple but radical approach to bringing peace to the promised land: Promoting an outright revolution, or reformation, in the hate-filled societies and

---

* The small minority of Jewish fanatics in Israel and elsewhere must also be opposed – but they are neither the acknowledged leaders of the Jewish world nor of the state of Israel, and their ideologies, while repugnant, are neither genocidal nor supported by the vast majority of Jews.

ideologies which gave birth to and then supported the savage raping and murdering of innocents on October 7th in southern Israel. Repelling evil, as the Quran demands. As noted, there are Arabs and Muslims who agree; sadly, too few are willing or able to say so out loud, and fewer still are in positions of power in their society or supported by a majority of their brethren.

As incongruous or even seemingly arrogant as it appears for an Israeli/American Jew to encourage a transformation in Arab or Muslim society, it may well be necessary for an outsider – without condescension, without being patronizing – to point the way or endorse such reform. But ultimately it must come from within Muslim/Arab societies – and many have begun this process, thankfully.

For true coexistence to be possible, such change is essential and must emerge. Our responsibility, as outsiders – politicians in the free world, heads of civil society organizations, leaders of the UN and other international bodies, regional democracy activists, Israelis and all others – is to support and promote these processes in every possible way.

In this land, history does not lie buried. It lives in the stones, in the streets, in the faces of those who walk them. Every hilltop carries a memory; every olive tree could tell a story. Here, biblical miracles, ancient wounds and modern headlines share the same soil.

To speak of peace in such a place is not naïve – it is necessary. But it cannot be peace as a slogan, a fragile handshake in front of cameras. An actual end to a state of war must be implemented, tested in daily encounters, and grounded in principles that endure beyond political fashion.

Both the Quran and the Hebrew Bible call for this deeper peace.

The Quran teaches: "*And if they incline to peace, then incline to it [also], and rely upon Allah.*" (Quran 8:61)

The Hebrew Bible echoes: "*Seek peace and pursue it.*" (Psalm 34:15)

In Jewish thought, we are taught that all humans are created בצלם אלקים *b'tzelem Elokim* – in the image of God.

In Arab and Islamic tradition, the same principle appears in the teaching that humility is a virtue tied to justice. Imam Ali ibn Abi

Talib said: *"People are of two types: your brothers in faith or your equals in creation."*

One presumes you've picked up this book as it piqued your interest in new ways of thinking about this centuries-old clash of civilizations in the Middle East, and that you might be interested in exploring the subtleties of the history and ideologies which have contributed to the ongoing battle for the soul of this region. In these pages you'll find some history, some philosophy, and many perspectives on the culture, religion and beliefs of the people of the Levant. And you'll find a clear and moral, values-based path to genuine reconciliation, with no holds barred and no sacred cows left standing.

It may make you uncomfortable… but as Michael Huffington has said, "*…growth comes from adversity.*"

"Between stimulus and response there is a space. In that space is our power to choose our response. In our response lies our growth and our freedom." — Viktor E. Frankl (attributed).

Even with some disquiet, I hope you'll read on, with the memory of all those killed and injured on October 7th (and since) foremost in your mind, and with the understanding that from such discomfort may emerge the seeds of genuine peace.

Introduction – The Background and Conceptual Framework

Three days and about 20 miles into my 2014 hike on *Shvil Yisrael,* the Israel National Trail, I ascended some 2000 feet to the top of Ma'ale Amram, the third of dozens of peaks in the mountains of the southern Negev just outside Eilat, Israel's southernmost port city at the tip of the Red Sea. I was already exhausted, almost beaten by the heat and the loneliness, the steep ascents and descents and more ascents, and the overwhelming silence of the desert. Reaching the summit, in a whirl of triumph and with a whoop of victory, I spun around a few times.

What I saw made me stop, and think, and wonder. Looking back the way I'd come, the panorama was glorious: dark and light brown mountains spread out beneath me, with the hills of biblical Moab, today's Jordan, across the valley and the Red Sea shimmering in the late afternoon light in the distance. Had I actually come that far? Did I really climb Mt. Shlomo and Mt. Shekhoret already and now Mt. Amram, all alone – with this 50-pound pack on my back?

Standing there I had an epiphany which would stay with me for the rest of my two-month solo trek across Israel, and thereafter; a realization which would help me to recover from my devastating divorce (the reason I embarked on the trek at age 51). It certainly was not an eternal truth never before articulated; but it was, for me, a significant part both in my personal healing and in the development of this model for resolving problems on a much larger scale.

That view was spectacular not only as a vista; and not only as it made tangible the results of my hiking efforts over the preceding days. It offered a completely different *perspective* on the scenery I'd passed through only hours before. I had been constantly heading north, offering one view of the hills and valleys, sky and rocks and trees and distant mountains (and mostly looking down at the immediate steps in front of me). At the top of Ma'ale Amram I turned and looked south, and it was like gazing on a new landscape; it could have been an entirely different hike.

That's what gave me pause. Sometimes we have to stop; turn around; and look how far we've come. Sometimes we need to put our baggage aside, and to re-evaluate our position, as I wrote in a different context in my book describing the experience. Reconsider our assumptions; reassess our goals and approaches to whatever challenges we're facing; look at things from another angle.

My previous book, _My Israel Trail_, is a personal tale of one man's struggle to come to terms with a divorce he hadn't looked for and which turned his life upside down. The book describes not only walking along the 650-mile _Shvil Yisrael,_ from the border with Egypt to the border with Lebanon, but the lessons learned along the way.

Those lessons I learned on this trek – as part of the physical act of hiking, day in, day out, on my own; over deserts, mountains, forests, towns, valleys and beaches – enabled me to find a way out of the morass of despair and anger, resentment and sorrow in which I found myself. In _My Israel Trail_ I describe the transformative experience of the hike, and reflect on five elements that brought with them insight and lessons enabling me to move on with my life – five concepts which have also been helpful to others facing their own personal challenges.

Those five elements that are critical to meeting personal challenges can be applied also to much larger situations, such as national and international discord. These concepts offer new approaches, methods and ideas for conflict resolution. And these five elements – humility, acceptance, gratitude, forgiveness and purpose – can have far-reaching applications, and implications, for the Arab-Israel conflict.

For well over a hundred years, well-meaning (and some not-so-well-meaning) diplomats, politicians, religious leaders and academics from the West and East – Arabs and Jews, Americans and Europeans and Egyptians and others – have tried to find a peaceful resolution to our conflict here. They have all failed. Others are endeavoring even now to do so. Dozens of "plans" – from the "Partition Plan" through the "Rogers Plan" to the "Road Map" and Oslo Accords and so many others, including the "Peace to Prosperity" plan publicized in January 2020 by the first Trump administration – have been proposed, only to be shattered in the face of intransigence, intolerance, hatred and hostility.

Hundreds of books have been written, analyzing those plans and the people and interests behind them, examining the cultural and psychological, national and religious motivations guiding the protagonists and antagonists in our conflict. Some propose solutions, based on maps or history, justice or 'rights', law or religion. Some probe the details of previous proposals seeking wisdom or guidance. Few – if any – offer new ideas or innovative directions; those that do, like Daniel Pipes' insistence on victory, Mordechai Kedar's "Emirates" proposal for clan-based government or Josef Avesar's "Israel-Palestine Confederation", unfortunately remain on the fringes of public policy debate.

It must be said that many of the proposals and some learned analyses over the years come from a standpoint of *arrogance*. Outsiders have even been quoted that where others have failed, *they* will succeed – because of their smarts, or connections, or personal history, or negotiation skills. The failure is shared across the board, between liberals and conservatives, Americans and Europeans and Russians, the League of Nations (more a gaggle than a league) and the [non-] United Nations and its Security Council, which offers little security and even less wise counsel. And it has been equally true of the many – some even well-intentioned – efforts by Jews and Arabs, Israelis and Palestinians.

The starting point of this work is *humility*: those who aim to assist, and those who lead a process of conciliation and conflict resolution in Arab and Jewish societies, must approach their task with open-mindedness and the understanding that they do not have all the answers, or all the truth, or all the wisdom. The ending point of this work is an application of Gandhi's understanding, and teaching, that there is a Truth which can be arrived at by dispassionate exploration of the history, the reality on the ground, the factual legal parameters and the foundations of belief by all parties to the conflict. And the truth of that solution is, I believe, staring us in the face.

The Israel Trail winds through Jewish towns, Arab villages, Christian monasteries, and Druze and Bedouin communities. I strode past markets thick with the scent of cumin and cardamom, vineyards with budding grapes and fields where farmers waved as I went by. In each place, I was offered tea, bread, or shelter – sometimes from people whose politics I might never share, but whose kindness I will never forget.

Walking in Israel is a lesson in contrasts. On one hilltop, a *mikveh*

(Jewish ritual bath) from millennia ago, among 2,000-years-old later Roman ruins. In one valley, a centuries-old mosque; in the next, a synagogue built within the last decade. Children playing soccer in one language, shouting to each other in another. The same sun warming both.

It struck me that this is what peace, if it ever comes, must look like: not erasing the differences, but learning to live with them without fear.

The Quran says: *"O mankind, indeed We have created you male and female, and made you peoples and tribes that you may know one another."* – Quran 49:13

The Talmud offers a similar vision, a radical, unequivocal statement of theological acceptance: one does not need to be Jewish to be beloved by God: *"The righteous of all nations have a share in the world to come."* (Tosefta Avodah Zarah 9:4)

These are not abstract ideals; they are instructions.

As I walked, I thought about how often peace efforts here fail because they focus only on the political top layer – leaders, negotiations, borders – without changing the deeper story people tell themselves about the other. Treaties without trust are like buildings without foundations: they stand only until the next storm.

This book is my attempt to address both levels at once. It is rooted in years of policy work, interfaith dialogue, and personal encounters across the divides. It draws equally on Arab and Muslim thinkers, Jewish and Israeli voices, and the real experience of ordinary people.

It recognizes that underlying the politics and the killing, the trauma and history are two fundamental and still influential religious systems that are super-powered because they address the personal, the political and the communal as well as the theological and spiritual. Most efforts towards peace ignore – or explicitly deny – the religious and cultural ideologies at the core of the conflict. Acknowledging this fundamental truth enables us to discover new paths for transformation.

The journey ahead will explore not only *what* must change, but *how.*

- In governance, where decisions shape the structures of coexistence;
- in media, where rhetoric can heal or inflame;
- in communities, where small acts of generosity can break cycles of suspicion; and
- in the human heart, where humility, acceptance, gratitude, forgiveness, and purpose take root – or do not.

I learned on the trek that you cannot see the entire horizon from where you start. But you can see enough to take the next step. And each step changes the landscape just a little – until one day, perhaps, the horizon itself begins to move closer.

With few exceptions, the approach proposed here has never been attempted; certainly not in this combination, nor with the mindset suggested in these pages. "Something's gotta give", as the saying goes, and this could not be more true in our tragic and explosive situation in the Middle East. And the conviction we bring to the undertaking reflects the famous aphorism attributed to Einstein that doing the same thing and expecting different results is a definition of insanity.

Our region often seems insane, with its violence and entrenched enmity and repeated attempts to square the circle of this ongoing conflict with tired phrases and written "peace" agreements. New ideas are necessary, given the life-and-death nature of our conflict and our region, as the October 7th '23 massacre and the war it provoked have only served to demonstrate in the most horrific and incandescent manner. New thinking, new approaches, new attitudes are in fact possible, not least with the advent of social media and modern means of transnational communications as well as a new generation in the region which sees the conflict through a different prism – or which can do so, if encouraged. Recent events demonstrate this truth, with an ever-growing number of Arab states choosing to make peace and normalize relations with Israel, based on their own interests and values.

What's offered here is an insider/outsider's perspective on the conflict, its causes and consequences, and its potential resolution. Great demands will be made of the reader, let alone of those who might actually carry out these plans. We will have to be humble, indeed; and forgiving; and focused on a future which does not include all our desires or even much of what we know we are entitled to. We will have to relinquish our focus on our own perspective, and recognize others' perspectives, even while aware that they may be warped by time and confusion, propaganda and politics – what some call "narratives".[1]

I don't pretend to have answers to all the major issues related to our conflict (see above re: arrogance). I do, actually, have experience discussing with Arab leaders and activists many of the "usual" issues – borders, security, water, refugees (Arabs and Jews), Jerusalem, independence, coexistence and all the rest. And I must note that some of us largely managed to resolve those issues, in just a few hours' effort over strong Mediterranean coffee and sweet baclava in the basement conference rooms of various hotels in Jerusalem, years ago. That sounds absurd, admittedly. The reason it was possible, and the reason those solutions never were implemented, is that the men and women of good will taking part in those back-channel discussions were not, by definition, the leaders of their countries or in positions of authority.

Yet it is that familiarity with the real moderates of our region which continues to fill me with optimism about the possibility of real peace between Arab and Jew in this small strip of land on the eastern Mediterranean. After earning my bachelor's degree at UC Berkeley, focusing on psychology with side pursuits exploring

---

[1] As my friend Yossi Klein HaLevi has noted (here, for instance), there are competing perspectives that define this conflict. But the term "narrative" is an unfortunate one, overused in discussing Jews' and Arabs' claims in the region. Terminology and language are such crucial elements of the situation here and create fundamental misunderstandings about the nature of our struggle. "Narratives" are stories, or myths, but in common parlance the term implies legitimacy with a patina of objectivity. "Perspectives" are by definition subjective: how one views something, from one's own history or belief system or cultural lens. By using the term "perspective" we can at one and the same time acknowledge that the two sides come from very different places, while not providing legitimacy to the ahistoric, propaganda-based and untruthful "narratives" which affect - or infect - public discourse. Hence my refusal to use the term "narrative" when comparing differing perspectives on history and values. I use it sparingly when referring to how writers or societies present these perspectives.

conflict resolution and religious studies, I spent five years studying international relations in Jerusalem, earning a master's degree from Hebrew University with an emphasis on our region's conflict(s) and the psychological processes of decision-making in foreign affairs. I've worked over the past four decades in education, in government, in high-tech and other business ventures, as well as with the international media – and my academic and professional experience inevitably included extensive interaction with Muslim and Christian Arabs, Druze and Bedouin, Jews/Israelis of all stripes, as well as others across the region.

Moreover, my work with Natan Sharansky (the former Soviet human rights leader who was imprisoned there for nine years and who became Israel's deputy prime minister a decade after he was released and immigrated to Israel) immersed me in the world of democracy activists. My connections with prominent freedom advocates in Egypt, Saudi Arabia, Iran, Syria, Jordan and of course Palestinian society give me a much different perspective – to use the term which is one of the foundations of our discussion – than that of most decision-makers, pundits and even academics, whether they sit in America, Europe or here in Israel. The same can be said for the relationships created through my work in renewable energy in our region and in Africa, and at MediaCentral, the Jerusalem-based project I ran for over a decade providing services for journalists based in or visiting the area from around the world, including many Muslim and Arab nations.

It is my deeply-held belief, based on over forty years living in the eastern Mediterranean and grounded in countless interactions, formal and informal, with Arabs and Jews from all walks of life, all religious persuasions, all shades of the political spectrum, and virtually all countries of the area, that harmony between our peoples, coexistence between our societies, and peaceful relations between our states, is indeed possible. I am also convinced it will only come if preceded by a prolonged, genuine, and broad cultural and educational transformation founded on humility, acceptance, gratitude, forgiveness, and a sense of national and communal purpose which transcends individual grievances and parochial interests.

The present work is divided into sections reflecting the five elements from the trek which were crucial to my healing process, applying those lessons to the national, religious and ethnic communities in the region, with reference to history, theology, psychology and politics as appropriate. Unlike my previous book, which was a personal story, a trekking tale offering these tools as something of a self-help guide, this is admittedly an intellectual argument and policy prescription. It is an impassioned case and plea for a radically new tactic or paradigm to engender real peace between the Arabs of the region and the people of Israel, the Jews.

The penultimate chapter includes practical steps which our leaders in the region and supportive leaders in the international community can take to realize our shared objective: genuine reconciliation between our peoples and nations. We are witness in our times to a number of further attempts to resolve the Arab-Israel conflict, with an expansion of the Abraham Accords, eradication of terrorist groups and punishment of their sponsors (and rejection of their supporters), and efforts at opposing and eliminating the hateful ideologies of Islamism and anti-Zionism. Chapter eight offers specific, tangible proposals to complement and augment these current efforts, reflecting the book's approach. And it is my fervent hope that this methodology can become a blueprint for other conflicts in the region as well.

As with *My Israel Trail*, nothing proposed here is original in concept; what is innovative is both the notion of starting over, renouncing the worn-out arguments of the past century, and the combination of these elements into a unified structure and methodology, applying them to international sphere rather than only the personal realm.

The ideas presented here have been shared and discussed with dozens of Arab and Muslim civil society leaders, academics, activists, religious authorities and political leaders. Where I can, I quote them by name; unfortunately, as noted, many were not willing to go on record with their agreement, as calling for a reformation of Muslim theology and Arab society is not conducive to good health or freedom in any Arab or Muslim country, even today. Which perhaps most unambiguously presents the case being made.

And one caveat to the reader, regarding the many quotations of text and statements made: As a non-Muslim, non-Arab, I am not attempting to convince Arabs and Muslims to modify their beliefs or behaviors. They alone can effect transformation. My goal in this work is to make a compelling case for two logical assertions, for policy-makers and others interested in achieving a resolution of this civilization conflict between Arabs and Israelis, Muslims and Jews:

1. There will never be real peace without a change in Arab and Muslim attitudes leading to acceptance, forgiveness and a new sense of purpose which includes peace and coexistence; and
2. There exist normative and traditional Arab and Muslim thinkers/leaders who support such a change.

Proof for these contentions can be found not only in rational arguments, but more persuasively by quoting those Arab/Muslim scholars and intellectuals verbatim. A careful reader will notice that very few quotations – from the Quran, Hebrew Bible or Christian Bible, from the Talmud and Hadiths, from earlier or modern philosophers and theologians and statesmen – are repeated. Mindful of the strain on attention, I have not included many credible citations substantiating these ideas, nor cited many of the influential scholarly works analyzing the history of Muslim and Arab culture and society. But I have tended to include more quotations than perhaps necessary, to address the casual, inaccurate, but widely-held belief that these are isolated, exceptional opinions.

Although the cogent nature of the argument(s) made here can stand alone, sources from Arab democracy activists and leaders of civil society are also included extensively, to demonstrate the universal appeal of the approach as well as its grounding in Arab and Muslim culture and thought. (And not incidentally, to preempt those looking for simple solutions who might claim that it's inappropriate for an Israeli/American Jew to speak so openly and clearly about resolving our conflict.) Similarly, though we include many citations from religious sources and leaders, the program outlined here is pertinent irrespective of the religious or secular nature of the reader or policy-maker.

The path to peace in the Middle East – and throughout much of the world – goes through the mosque (and church and ashram and synagogue). The role of imams, ayatollahs, priests, popes, rabbis, and other religious scholars and leaders of all faiths cannot be minimized. And this applies to those commenting on this conflict from positions of authority outside the region – including Christian leaders across Europe, Asia, Africa and South America. It is crucial for national and transnational religious leaders to guide and educate their flocks in the paths of peace, rather than promoting hatred and intolerance, violence and war.

This is a call for moderation and pragmatism; for reason and logic; for truth and justice and the use of humanity's moral compass. It is a call echoed by the real moderates in our region – including Muslim and Christian Arabs – many of whom are indeed quoted in these pages. And we already are seeing some implementation of these ideas, with the opening of diplomatic relations and business and cultural ties between the Gulf states and others and Israel as part of the Abraham Accords. As Mohammed bin Zayed Al Nahyan, Crown Prince of Abu Dhabi, has said: *"Tolerance and coexistence are fundamental to the stability of our society and the wider world."*

As the Hebrew Bible has it in another context, "כי יכול נוכל לה – *ki yachol nuchal la"* – *"We can surely achieve this"* (Numbers 13:30).

As the Christian Bible says, *"For all things are possible"* (Mark 10:27).

And as the Quran says, *"Good and evil deeds are not equal. Repel evil with what is better. Then you will see that one who was once your enemy has become your dearest friend"* (Quran 41:34).

"Faith is taking the first step even when you don't see the whole staircase." – commonly attributed to Martin Luther King Jr.

A personal note:

I hesitated to write this book, as who am I to recommend to those greater and wiser than I, sharper and more experienced in security and politics, diplomacy and negotiations, that they consider new methods and tactics? However, based on the requests and encouragement of many others whom I admire and respect, I submit the ideas here for the consideration of the new generation of leaders who sincerely are seeking a way forward out of our quagmire, whether they are Arabs or Jews; Christian or Muslim or Jewish; Israeli, Arab, European or American.

Chapter One: A Brief History of it All in Three Parts

The Arab-Israel Conflict – 3500 years in less than 35 pages

In 1725, Miguel Pacheco da Silva was expelled from Portugal, along with his wife and teenage son. They were Conversos, or *Marranos*, the derogatory term used to describe Jews who had converted to Christianity under the Spanish Inquisition, but remained secretly Jewish. He brought his family to Amsterdam, and from there to London; once having escaped the Iberian Peninsula, he became known as Abraham Mendes Seixas. In 1730, Abraham and his wife Abigail were remarried in a Jewish ceremony at London's Bevis Marks Spanish/Portuguese Jews' synagogue – as their *Ketuba*, or Jewish marriage contract, in the archives of the synagogue, attests.

Their son Isaac Mendes Seixas was one of earliest Jews to arrive in America circa 1740, and his son – Abraham and Abigail's grandson – Gershom Mendes Seixas was born in 1746 in New York. Gershom Mendes Seixes became known during the American War of Revolution as the "Patriot Rabbi", for his support of the revolution, and was one of the clergy who participated in the inauguration of President George Washington. Seixas served on the board of Kings College, precursor to Columbia University (the first and then only Jew to do so, appointed by Alexander Hamilton), and was a fierce proponent of religious and personal liberty. He was the first leader of American Jewry to have been born in America.

This writer is a direct descendent of Abraham, Isaac and Gershom Mendes Seixas. As an eighth-generation American-born Jew, I chose to make my home and live my life these past 40 years in Israel, the ancestral homeland of the people of Israel – the first of my extended family to do so in hundreds if not thousands of years. And though it may seem to be a strange way to begin a discussion of the history of the Arab-Israel conflict, it seems a fitting starting point for this chapter, as our discussion is a personal one. There are many excellent histories of Israel, the Arab world and the Middle East and this is not meant to be exhaustive. Rather, this is a more intimate (and brief) review of what Israel and the Jewish people, and Muslim/Arab society, and the conflict itself, are all about.

Most discussions of the Arab–Israel conflict begin in the last century – with the Balfour Declaration of 1917, the United Nations Partition Plan of 1947, or the Six-Day War of 1967. But these are only recent chapters in a history which spans millennia. To grasp the roots of the dispute, we must step back – far back – to the birth of two peoples, the Israelites and the Arabs; two faiths, Judaism and Islam; and two claims to the same land.

This chapter is my attempt to walk with you through 3,500 years of that story – not as an academic exercise, but as a journey through the roads and roots that brought us here. It is compressed, but it is not rushed. Like my hike from the southern desert to the northern hills, it moves steadily, pausing at places that shape the view ahead.

In the pages below, we'll explore the history of Israel – the land, the people, the civilization. And we'll explore, similarly, the history of Arabia – the land, the people, and the culture. Then, connecting the two themes, we can begin to understand how we reached the current impasse.

Part I: Israel & Judaism

Jewish history in the promised land is not something recent; it is an ancient thread that has endured both unbroken presence and long dispersal. From Abraham's initial arrival some 4000 years ago, through the First and Second Temples in Jerusalem over 2000 years ago, to the synagogues of Tiberias and Safed 1000 years ago and until the modern re-establishment of Jewish sovereignty in the Land of Israel, Jewish life has ebbed and flowed with tribal and national working of the land, conquest, exile, and return.

Even after the Roman expulsion in 70 CE and the later dispersions, Jewish communities remained in Jerusalem, Tiberias, Hebron, and Safed. Prayer and pilgrimage bound those abroad to those who stayed and to each other. As Rabbi Yehuda Halevi wrote from medieval Spain: *"My heart is in the East, though I am in the West."*

That longing was not abstract; it was carried in daily ritual. Every day, at prayer three times a day and after every meal, Jerusalem and the Land was and is central. Every Passover, Jews declare(d): *"Next year in Jerusalem."* Every Jewish wedding ceremony, wherever performed across the planet, ended and still ends with the breaking of a glass to recall the destruction of the Holy Temple in Jerusalem. These were not simply traditions – they were a way of keeping the map home alive.

3500 years ago a man named Abraham was told to "leave your land, your birthplace, the house of your father" and to go to "the land that I will show you" – as recorded in the book of Genesis in the Bible. These two themes have been repeated throughout the history of his family, our people: connection to the land, and wandering.

His family, through his son Isaac and grandson Jacob, became first a **tribe** and then a **nation** called Israel (Jacob's other name); and the history of this family and nation is the history of this the modern nation-state of Israel, and of the Jews – the People of Israel.

How can we condense 3,500 years of history into a few pages? Wherever we look there are familiar names, nations and stories, each of which could take up full chapters to describe sufficiently.

Most of us are familiar with the Biblical episodes of family dynamics of the tribe: Isaac & Ishmael, Jacob & Esau, Joseph & his brothers, the matriarchs Sarah, Rebecca, Rachel & Leah. Most western readers are also familiar with the national and religious epics of the Exodus, Moses and the Giving of the Torah at Mount Sinai, the wandering in the desert for forty years, entering the promised land. Some may recognize accounts of the wars of conquest, the battles of defense and freedom, nations arising and falling – Edomites, Hittites, Canaanites, etc. – described in the Bible and contemporaneous literature.

People of the western world are well acquainted with the prophets of hope, praise and salvation – Samuel, Isaiah, Ezra & Nechemia – and those of criticism and disaster – primarily Jeremiah and Ezekiel. Many are familiar with the epic stories relating to the people manifesting Israel's sovereignty in the Land of Israel in the thousand or so years before the common era, with all its challenges – including its great, less-great, and terrible leaders, from King Saul and Kings David and Solomon to the lesser-known Rechavam, Jerocham, Achav, Queen Jezebel, Hezekiah (good), and Menasseh (not so good).

The Israelites built a kingdom, established Jerusalem as their capital under King David around 1000 BCE, and constructed the First Temple under his son Solomon. This was not merely a religious center. It was the political and cultural heart of a sovereign nation. Archaeology supports much of this biblical account: ancient Hebrew inscriptions, the remains of city walls, and artifacts such as the Tel Dan Stele refer to the "House of David."

There were many foreign conquerors, periods of lost and regained and lost again or partial independence; "autonomy" with oppression under the Babylonians, Persians, Greeks, Assyrians, and Romans; and various periods of real independence (the latest under the Maccabees, commemorated in the celebration of Chanukah). The people of Israel, the children of Jacob, endured destruction, devastation, degradation – but never fell into despair nor abandoned our dedication to our homeland.

We lost our sovereignty twice, with the razing of our two Temples – the seat and holy site of God's presence manifest on earth. These led to two expulsions – first by the Babylonians in 586 BCE, to return just 45 years later (some of the tribe but not the majority, with the blessing of Cyrus, King of Persia) and then by the Romans in 70 CE (by Vespasian & Titus, as commemorated in the Arch of Titus in Rome), leading then to nearly 2000 years of a wandering, insecure existence in the Diaspora.

It was in that second dispersion – over these past 2000 years – that the people of Israel, otherwise known as "Hebrews" or "Israelites", became known as "Jews", as they were expelled from JUdea, the last holdout of the tribes of Jacob. (For a short while a separate area of then-"Israel" was distinct from "Judea", but the tribe and region of Judea was the final remnant of the once expansive Kingdom of David and Solomon.) It is a curious matter of language and cultural development that today the terms "Judaism" and "Jewish" tend to be used to describe a religion or belief system, as if similar to Christianity or Islam or Buddhism; whereas Jews are more of a civilization (according to anthropologists and sociologists[2]), a united people from a specific

---

[2] See, for instance, Marcy Brink-Danan, "Anthropology of the Jews", Oxford Bibliographies, 2012.

region with historical ties to that area (Judea) and a distinct language, culture etc. which are all intertwined with their unique set of religious beliefs and faith practices.[3]

Similarly, it is a curious matter of language and history that the Romans' unsuccessful attempt to divorce the people of Israel from the land of Israel – the Jews from Judea – ended up in the modern era with two contradictory uses of the term "Palestine".   Rome renamed the territory "Palestina" in reference to the Philistines of the biblical era, trying to erase the connection between the conquered land of Israel from its people.   The name stuck for cartographers, historians and theologians alike, though "Palestine" was of course nothing more than a geographical designation.

From the late 1800s through 1948, it was *Jews* (i.e. the people of Israel) who returned to Palestine, raised funds for the Palestine Endowment Fund, established the Palestine Bank (now Bank Leumi) and the Palestine Post (now Jerusalem Post) and the Palestine Symphony Orchestra (now the Israeli Philharmonic). Official documents and graphic images from that period always used the Hebrew "ארץ ישראל" (*Eretz Yisrael* or the Land of Israel, literally) alongside the English name "Palestine" – on stamps, official documents, maps and the like.   It was as the foundation for the establishment of a Jewish home that Britain was given the "Palestine Mandate" by the international community.   But then it was the Arabs resident in Mandatory Palestine and then in TransJordan (and Gaza) who began to adopt the moniker as part of their 'resistance' to the establishment of Israel.   We will return to this theme in a later chapter.

In this quick overview, we'll skip over the last 2000 years of vibrant communal, religious and social life, the incredible volume of scholarship, the continued and constant remembrance (Tisha B'Av, the national day of mourning for our loss of self-government in our land and the destruction of the Temples, on the 9th of the month of

---

[3] Which is why in this work they are referred to more frequently as the 'people of Israel' than as 'Jews', though the two can be used interchangeably. Sometimes, for clarity, the term is repeated to accentuate the diverse nature of the identity, as in "Arabs & Jews, Muslims & Jews", the former highlighting the national/ethnic aspect, the latter the religious/faith element.

Av in the Hebrew calendar), the ongoing development of our culture, and the never-ending commitment and identity. Those two thousand years included a dedication to that identity, as well as to the Land of Israel, unrivaled in human history (as noted by John Jacques Rousseau and the Dalai Lama[4]), with Zion/Jerusalem and the Land central elements in song and prayer expressed multiple times a day and in all four annual holiday festivals and at the end of the holiest day in the Jewish calendar, Yom Kippur.

Without going into detail, we'll note simply that throughout two millennia of exile, Jewish communities persisted across the land in cities like Jerusalem, Hebron, Tiberias, and Safed – whether invaded and ruled by Roman, Byzantine, Arab/Muslim, Crusader, Ottoman/Muslim, or British empires and colonialism. Jewish poets from medieval Spain wrote of Jerusalem's beauty as if they had just walked its streets. Maimonides, the great philosopher of the 12th century, visited the city and prayed at the Temple Mount. Similarly, without itemizing, we can recognize the past 2000 years of contributions by the people of Israel to philosophy, science, the arts, medicine etc., with the likes of Maimonides and Freud, Spinoza and Einstein and even Spielberg almost household names, but much of which is simply not known.

Crucial to even this cursory review is that these are historical facts, not myths or stories, fables or 'narratives'; the brief description above describes the historical record, based on archeology, contemporary reports and historical analysis. One cannot understand the people or State of Israel without understanding this history; and none of this is a "political" statement.

The history of the return of the people of Israel to our ancestral homeland and the founding of the modern nation state of Israel is a chronicle which has captured the imagination of millions. The international support for its establishment, its rejection by the Arab world and attacks by Arab marauders and then Arab countries, its

---

[4] Jean-Jacques Rousseau, *The Social Contract and other later political writings*, Cambridge University press, 2010, 180; Roger Kamanetz, *The Jew in the Lotus*, HarperOne, 2007.

efforts to make peace, its struggle for survival, the absorption of millions of Jews – refugees from Arab countries and Europe and Africa as well as by-choice immigrants from western nations – are elements of our history which are also well known.

What is often missing from the telling, though – and in particular among those hostile to Israel or Zionism or the idea of the assertion of national identity in general – is the basic understanding that Zionism is the national liberation movement of the Jewish people, and that the State of Israel is the modern embodiment of the return of the nation of Israel, as the only extant indigenous people connected to this land, to the Land of Israel.[5]

The modern Zionist movement, founded in the late 19th century by Theodor Herzl and others, was not the creation of a "new" Jewish identity but the political expression of an ancient commitment and aspiration of a people to return to its ancestral homeland. The 1917 Balfour Declaration, in which Britain pledged support for a "national home for the Jewish people" in Palestine, was explicit recognition of that reality, and its incorporation into the League of Nation's "Mandate" given to Great Britain following WWI to establish that national home reflected the ubiquitous acknowledgment of this by the international community. Obviously, this acknowledgment of the legitimacy of the connection of the people of Israel to the land of Israel predated the Holocaust, and undeniably refutes any contention that 'Israel was created as a result of the Holocaust'.

Israel's development as a modern nation-state is nothing short of miraculous: from making the desert bloom with agricultural innovations, through unsurpassed contributions to high tech, medicine & science, to providing aid around the world, and with its multicultural, multi-ethnic democratic society (including its various challenges) – including providing refuge and defense for the Jewish

---

[5] Nothing in this statement, nor anywhere in this book or argument, negates a potential claim by others to some form of independence in the territory once called the "Mandate for Palestine", as will be seen. This is merely a factual statement, according to the accepted scholarly definition of "indigenous" – the earliest known continual inhabitants of a land, whose distinct culture, language, history and civilization were created there and are expressly and uniquely connected to the area.

people everywhere – Israel has exceeded all expectations and succeeded in ways never imagined… except perhaps by its founders and earlier prophets.

Israel continues to work towards a future of peace in the region and benefit to the world, as articulated in its founding documents and as expressed by its leading figures. Israel's first Prime Minister, David Ben-Gurion, often stressed that Israel would ultimately be judged not by its wealth or military strength, but by its moral character and its commitment to peace.

We extend our hand to all neighboring states and their peoples in an offer of peace and good neighborliness. – Israel's Declaration of Independence (1948)

Let us make peace, a true peace, and plant its seeds in the soil of our land; No more wars, no more bloodshed. – Prime Minister Menachem Begin (Camp David Accords, 1978; and speech in the Knesset, after peace treaty signed with Egypt, 1979)

Enough of blood and tears. Enough. – Prime Minister Yitzhak Rabin (Oslo Accords signing, 1993)

We are leaving behind us the era of belligerency and are striding together toward peace. – Foreign Minister Shimon Peres (Nobel Peace Prize lecture, 1994)

I am willing to make painful compromises to achieve this historic peace. – Benjamin Netanyahu (U.S. Congress, 2011)

Part II: Arabia and Islam

The biblical narrative of the Hebrews' Exodus from Egypt and wandering the desert for 40 years finally reaching the promised land of their forefathers captured the imagination of the people of the West (and informed many of the founding principles of Western democracy and society). So too have the history and stories of the Arabian peninsula found a treasured place in the pantheon of Western thought and literature – from the Arabian Nights to images of swashbuckling pirates to traders' camel trains to the oil barons and Sheiks of recent centuries.

Without even knowing some of the details, most Westerners are aware of the multifaceted nature of Arab culture and Islamic thought, from notions of medieval assassins and Caliphates to tribal warfare, Muslim/Arab empire(s), pilgrimage to Mecca, Bedouin-style lifestyles and polygamy. Part caricature, part romanticizing, combining storybook fantasy with rumour and media hype and not a little ignorance, public perceptions of the nature and depth of Arab and Islamic culture are often warped and twisted, if they have any resonance at all.

The present work does not pretend to offer an extensive review of the complex 1400 years of Arab and Islamic history. What is presented here, similar to the section above on Israel, is a succinct perusal of some of the main themes which are relevant to our later thesis.

The Arab nation, or *Umma*, comes from Arabia, as the linguistic parallel makes clear. The religious faith called Islam – or the Islamic civilization if you will – began in Arabia, and still looks to Mecca and Medina as its holiest sites. In the early 7th century, the prophet Mohammed unified much of Arabia under Islam, a faith that combined spiritual guidance with political governance, resulting according to Muslim tradition from a visit by the angel Gabriel to Mohammed in a cave in 610 CE.

Within decades of Mohammed's death, Muslim (Arab) armies had conquered vast territories – from Spain in the west to India in the east. In 635 CE, the city known as Aelia Capitolina (Jerusalem) was captured by the Caliph Umar ibn al-Khattab. Islamic jurisprudence classified conquered lands as part of *Dar al-Islam* – the House of Islam – and thus, in theory ideologically and religiously, under Muslim rule forever.

As scholars have documented, the adoption of the modern concept of a unified Arab "nation" is relatively recent, championed by Nasser and others in the early to mid-20th century. The Muslim Umma, comprised of all believers, is an expression of identity and unity of the community of faith, and includes all those who identify as Arab as well as all other nationalities. The 14th-century Arab scholar Ibn Khaldun explained the centrality of the concept of *'Asabiyyah* (social solidarity or group feeling), mainly within the context of clans and nomadic tribes. More recently, as has been noted by Middle East experts like Bernard Lewis, Mordechai Kedar, Ephraim Karsh and many others, the primary identification and focus of loyalty in the "Arab" world has been and continues to be to the tribe or clan – as an old Arab proverb has it, "Me against my brother; my brother and I against our cousin; our clan against other clans; our tribe against other tribes; our nation against other nations...."

When the Arab Muslim leaders extended their rule by conquering other areas in the region – including today's Iran, Iraq, Turkey, North Africa, and of course the Levant (the eastern Mediterranean crescent including modern Lebanon, Syria, Israel, Jordan and Egypt) – they expanded the reach of Islam as well, often through forced conversions, and settled Arabian/Islamic clans in conquered areas in classic, traditional colonialist fashion. As noted, within Islamic religion doctrine, an area conquered and held by Islamic forces must remain under Islamic control, an issue we'll return to in the next chapter, which applies not only to present-day Israel including Jerusalem but much of southern Europe and North Africa as well.

There remain small but important non-Muslim religious communities throughout the Middle East which identify as "Arab", not least various Christian sects (Copts in Egypt, Melkites and Circassians and others in Israel and Lebanon) as well as Druze and others. And yet, the conflation of Arab identity and Muslim religious affiliation has affected the attitudes of the adherents of other faiths as well, leading them to adopt some Islamic principles as applying to their Arab identity – not least the insistence on the "Arab" nature of the holy land and some antisemitic tropes.

Thus religion – Islam – plays a central role in Arab society and of course politics. This is not the place for an extensive exploration of the development of Islamic thought over the past millennium, but as will be detailed below, the overt radicalization of Islamic thought and theology over the recent decades has affected the goals and aspirations, let alone public policy, of every Arab or Muslim country in the region (and perhaps the world).

And though Islam, by tradition, demonstrated over its first 1000+ years more respect for and connection to Jews and Judaism, in ideology and practice, than Christendom did, the myth of "tolerance" for Jews and Christians as "People of the Book" under

Arab and Islamic rule has taken on an unrealistic position in western views of Islam. Treated as second-rate citizens with *"Dhimmi"* status, Jews (and Christians) were subject to discrimination and harassment consistently whenever and wherever they lived under Islamic or Arab rule.

Though acts of violence against Jews were carried out over the previous centuries in the region, it wasn't until the insistence of the people of Israel to return to their ancestral homeland in the land of Israel and the international community's support for the establishment of a modern nation-state for the Jews there that more violent aggression and attacks became the norm (and the ideal) in Arab and Muslim society.

The infiltration of Medieval Christian-style violent antisemitism into Arab and Islamic culture started in the early 20th Century, coinciding with the emergence of the modern Zionist movement advocating Jewish sovereignty in the holy land. This animosity was expressed, among other ways, by the adoption of traditional Christian tropes of Jews[6] as the enemy of God and rejectors of the 'true faith' (delegitimization), depictions/descriptions of Jews as rodents or monkeys or other animals (dehumanization), as the devil incarnate (demonization) – and was intensified by alliances with Hitler's Germany. Post-WWII antisemitism, the expulsion of Jews from Arab countries, and anti-Israel hostility resulting from the very public enmity of their leaders to the establishment of the modern state of Israel, meant that a central aspect of Arab and Muslim dogma in the modern era has included hatred of Jews and Israel as a matter of social and cultural identity.[7]

Unfortunately, the more radicalized Islamist ideologies – political creeds based on religious interpretations, now known as "Islamism" (distinct from Islam, the religion) – have become ever more popular among the region's leaders as well as populations, as can be seen from any news media reporting from the ground in the Middle East (and elsewhere) and as documented by independent and objective

---

[6] Based on Natan Sharansky's 3Ds of the new antisemitism; for more, see here, here and here.
[7] Unfortunately, this is still the norm; see Kill a Jew, go to Heaven and here, and next chapter.

academic researchers (Arab and Muslim scholars as well as others).

One example will perhaps suffice among far too many. On January 17th, '09 on Egypt's Al-Rahma television, Sheikh Muhammad Hussein Yaqoub said explicitly: *"If the Jews left Palestine to us, would we start loving them?… The Jews are infidels – not because I say so,… but because… Allah who said that they are infidels…. They are enemies not because they occupied Palestine. They would have been enemies even if they did not occupy a thing…. Our fighting with the Jews is eternal…, until not a single Jew remains on the face of the Earth"*[8]

These sentiments are shared among the fanatics known well to western societies, such as Al Qaida, ISIS, Hamas, Boko Haram, Hezb'Allah, Islamic Jihad and of course the Muslim Brotherhood and other groups, let alone the leadership of Iran, Qatar, Turkey, Saudi Arabia, Yemen and other Islamist states. Yet they are also shared among the wider societies in Muslim-majority countries affected by Salafist and other radical interpretations of Islam, and in Muslim communities in western countries as well, as documented by George Washington University, Pew, ADL and other polls in recent years.[9]

Fortunately (for Muslims and Jews, and for Israelis and Arabs and in fact for the world), there are many Muslim and Arab thinkers and leaders who have come to accept both Israel and more moderate interpretations of Islam – interpretations which can be seen as actually more in line with traditional and normative Islam.

As will be seen, these include those early peace-makers in the region like President Anwar Sadat of Egypt and King Hussein of Jordan, as well as more recent leaders including Sheikh Mohammed bin Zayed Al Nahyan, President of the UAE, King Mohammed VI of Morocco, and Bahrain's King Hamad bin Isa Al Khalifa – the earliest members of the "Abraham Accords" establishing normal relations and peace with Israel. They also include Imams and thinkers and leaders like Mohammad Tawhidi (the Australian "Imam of Peace" and head of the Global Imams Council), Sheikh Abdullah bin Bayyah (professor of Islamic studies at the King Abdul

---

[8] As documented <u>here</u>, <u>here</u> and <u>here</u>.
[9] Research studies can be found from <u>GW</u>, <u>ADL</u>, <u>Pew</u> (and <u>here</u>), and others.

Aziz University in Saudi Arabia; chairman of the UAE Council for Fatwa; president of the Forum for Promoting Peace in Muslim Societies), and Sheikh Ahmed Al-Tayyeb (Grand Imam of Al-Azhar in Egypt, and president of Al-Azhar University), as well as prominent Arab-Israelis and Palestinians like Nuseir Yassin (better known as Nas Daily), Lucy Aharish, Yoseph Haddad, and this author's personal friends Mohammed Dajani, Khaled Abu Toameh, Ishmail Khaldi, and many others.

Two schools of Islam seem to vie today for the allegiance of believers: the extremist approaches to faith and national identity, as expressed in the pervasive culture of hatred in the Arab world and Muslim societies; and a more moderate understanding of the Quranic scripture and culture/tradition.[10]   This dispute must be resolved in any discussion of prospects for peace in the Middle East. To wit:

Allah is our objective; the Prophet is our leader; the Quran is our law; Jihad is our way; dying in the path of Allah is our highest hope. – Motto of the Muslim Brotherhood (including Hamas, the "Islamic Resistance Movement")

The true believers are those who show kindness to others and strive to spread peace. – Sheikh Ibn Taymiyyah (attributed)

We must work to cultivate a culture of peace and tolerance, and to reject any form of violence or hatred. – Sheikh Abdullah bin Bayyah (Marrakesh Declaration 2019)

Islam teaches us to respect all human beings, regardless of their faith. – Dr. Mohammed Al-Arefe

Islam is a religion of peace, tolerance, and brotherhood, and it calls for coexistence among all people. – Sheikh Ahmed el-Tayeb, Grand Imam of Al-Azhar (2018)

Wasatia's values are deeply grounded in peace, moderation, reconciliation, liberty, tolerance, empathy, mutual respect, soft dialogue, and dignity, in harmony with Quranic teaching. – Professor Mohammad S. Dajani Daoudi

---

[10] As reflected in the Wasatia movement led by Palestinian Muslim scholar Mohammad S. Dajani Daoudi

Part III: The Arab-Israel Conflict

Why is our context, as mentioned at the beginning of this section, "3500 years" and not around 130 years (since the beginning of the modern Zionist movement in 1896)? Or not about 80 years (since the establishment of the modern state of Israel in 1948)? And certainly not 60 years (of Israel's possession of the 'disputed territories of Judea and Samaria (the "west bank" of the Jordan River as many call it)?

The roots of the Arab–Israel conflict are often portrayed as modern, but the theological and historical dimensions are centuries old. The idea that Muslim sovereignty over Jerusalem is eternal means that Jewish sovereignty is seen not just as a political threat, but as theologically inconceivable, a religious impossibility. When Jews began returning to the land in significant numbers in the late 19th century – fleeing pogroms in Russia, economic hardship in Yemen, or persecution in North Africa – some Arab leaders welcomed the economic benefits. Most saw it as a dangerous breach of the historical order. And by the 1920s and 1930s, Arabs repeatedly resorted to violence. The 1929 Hebron massacre, in which 67 Jews were murdered and another 58 injured, is only one example of many, driven in part by the "fake news" of that era, rumors spread by the Grand Mufti of Jerusalem and others that Jews intended to seize the Al-Aqsa Mosque.

The timeline of what we now call the Arab-Israel conflict is simple. It did not start as opposition to what some call Israel's "occupation" of the territories in dispute in 1967, as many Palestinian and Arab leaders often claim (and as many European fellow travelers and their counterparts on American campuses parrot). Neither did it start as opposition to Israel's founding acceptance into the UN in 1948, as others like to pretend. Nor did it start as opposition to the international recognition of the legitimacy of the return of the people of Israel to their ancestral homeland, the Land of Israel, a century ago – i.e. in opposition to Great Britain's Balfour Declaration, the post-WWI San Remo Treaty, or the League of Nations' Mandate for Palestine given to Great Britain to advance the establishment of a national home for the Jewish people in the holy land.

The only objective starting point for what we today term the "Arab-Israel conflict" is the initial conquering and occupation of the eastern Mediterranean – the Land of Israel – by the forces of Islam coming from Arabia, led by Caliph Umar two years after the death of Mohammed, in 635 CE. That conquest, carried out against the existing occupiers of the holy land – the Christian Babylonian empire – was as much against the Jews as it was the Christians. As described in contemporaneous accounts and as related in Islamic sources, the invasion and capture of Jerusalem (Zion) was intended as, and interpreted as, a triumph of the new religion over both its predecessors on which it was based, as a miraculous territorial acquisition.

Thus, at its core, the "Arab-Israel" conflict began when Arabs occupied the Land of Israel in the early Islamic violent military campaign of empire expansion and colonialization of the mid-7th century. To be clear, the word "Arab" refers to the people of/from Arabia and in some contexts is used to include all Muslims, even non-Arabs. And "Israel" refers to the people of Israel (also known of course as Jews, even though 20% of Israeli citizens are Arabs, mostly Muslim), as well as the Land of Israel (that territory renamed "Palestine" by the original Roman conquerors), and its civilization… as well as the modern nation-state of Israel. So the notion of an "Arab-Israel conflict" is naturally a confusing amalgamation of all these constructs.

As mentioned above, the Arab/Muslim understanding of possession of conquered land is also a complex issue, but rather simple to summarize: Once Muslim/Arab rule was established over a region, the acquisition of the territory was (is) seen as irrevocable from both a religious and legal/political perspective. (This is of course as opposed to our modern notions, for instance under the UN Charter, of the "inadmissibility of acquisition of territory" by the use of offensive force.)

As noted by Islamic scholar Mohammed Haniff Hassan, *Dar Al-Islam* (Land of Islam) and *Dar Al-Harb* (Land of War) are concepts actually introduced not by Mohammed or his initial followers, the early Caliphs, but rather at the time of the Abbasid dynasty (750-1258CE) – i.e. after the capture and occupation of Jerusalem. *"Dar Al- Islam* refers to a land ruled by a Muslim ruler and the *Shari'ah* is held as the rule of the land. In contrast, a land is considered as *Dar Al-Harb* when it is ruled by non-Muslim or when the *Shari'ah* is not recognized as the rule of the land."[11]

Furthermore,

> The context that influenced those Muslim scholars was constant war between Muslims and non-Muslims (the Romans and the Persians). Muslim scholars felt that it was important to classify countries to ensure that laws pertaining to jihad were applied to the correct situation and place. It was a period where Muslims were dominant in the international political scene. The classification bore the psychological element of human beings in such a context – a sense of superiority above others. (ibid)

Thus, from very early years of the development of Arab/Muslim empire, the idea that none can rule areas where Arabs/Muslims were once dominant took on special importance – not only for the holy land but for much of North Africa and Europe as well. It can be argued that the "Arab-Israel conflict" originated as a "Muslim/Arab *vs* Everyone" conflict. And with the building of the Dome of Rock shrine on the site of the Israelites/Jews' Holy Temple in Jerusalem, also the site of the Roman Temple and a Byzantine Church, and then the building of the mosque nearby, the emphasis on the holy land was powerfully reinforced.

And yet, though Jerusalem and the holy land were respected, even revered, by the Sunni stream of Muslims, the myth of its centrality to Islam has been so exaggerated as to now be accepted as fact by most people, including some scholars. As many historians have noted, neither Jerusalem nor the region (let alone the term "Palestine") are mentioned in the Quran or early Suras. The lack of importance of the holy land to Muslims and Arabs is reflected in the fact that Mecca, not Jerusalem, was the central locus for prayer and pilgrimage across the Muslim and Arab world.

Similarly, and conclusively, no attempt was ever made to create an independent state or entity on the land, over the more than 1000

---

[11] https://rsis.edu.sg/rsis-publication/rsis/884-revisiting-dar-al-islam-land/

years it was held and ruled by succeeding Arab/Muslim empires. Not only is this true, the territory was ignored, and left to stagnate economically and politically, and there was no imperative expressed to visit or pray at the mosque on the Temple Mount, unlike the religious obligation to make the Haj to Mecca.

It is true that Arabs and Muslims did migrate to the holy land during certain periods – but primarily as traders or travelers, or as functionaries of the ruling regime or seeking employment; not as pilgrims nor as permanent settlers. Demonstrably, for almost a thousand years, Jerusalem remained a small and forgotten town, neglected by virtually every ruler since Saladin, with a population ranging between 5,000-20,000 or so, until even as late as 1874 according to the British Consul's report to Parliament.[12] Which brings us to the end of the 19th Century… and the modern influx of Jews as part of the modern Zionist movement.

Jewish migration to Israel over the past 2,000 years has been a recurring phenomenon driven by religious yearning, persecution, and periodic popular movements, culminating in modern Zionism. While most of the Jewish population lived outside the Land of Israel for much of this period, small-scale returns (*Aliya* in Hebrew, meaning the ascent to Jerusalem or pilgrimage) continued throughout the centuries, culminating in major waves during the late 19th and 20th centuries.

Following the Jewish–Roman Wars (66–136 CE), the Romans killed, expelled, or sold many Jews into slavery. Although Jewish life continued in the Galilee and other regions, the demolition of Judea began a long period of the Jewish diaspora, or "scattering". Despite persecution, a consistent Jewish presence remained, centered around holy cities like Jerusalem, Hebron, Safed, and Tiberias. Beginning in the Middle Ages, individual Jews and groups, motivated by religious devotion, made the journey back. Notably, Rabbi Nachmanides (the Ramban) settled in Jerusalem in the 13th century, and others arrived after the expulsions from Spain in 1492 and Naples in the 16th century.

The 18th and 19th centuries saw a significant influx of Kabbalists, Hasidic Jews, and their followers from Eastern Europe, who

---

[12] https://en.wikipedia.org/wiki/Demographic_history_of_Jerusalem

established or strengthened communities in the holy cities, and in the mid to late 19th century, a small but consistent stream of Yemenite Jews began migrating to the land.

Organized, large-scale immigration, known as the Zionist *aliyot*, or waves of *Aliya*, in the late 19th –mid-20th century, was triggered by increasing antisemitism in Europe and the rise of modern Zionism – the modern movement promoting the return of Jews to their ancestral homeland and the establishment there of an independent, sovereign entity, which expressed the millenia-old longing for a return in the context of contemporary nationalist liberation movements. These waves included:

- First Aliyah (1882–1903): Pogroms in the Russian Empire led approximately 35,000 Jews to what had then become known as "Palestine". Many settled in new agricultural communities, establishing some of the first modern Jewish settlements, including Rosh Pina and Zikhron Ya'akov.

- Second Aliyah (1904–1914): Primarily from Russia and Poland, this wave included politically-motivated socialists who were crucial in building the Jewish infrastructure for the burgeoning community, including Tel Aviv.

- Third, Fourth, and Fifth Aliyah (1919–1939): Tens of thousands of Jews arrived following World War I and throughout the British Mandate period, spurred by rising antisemitism in Europe, and Zionist commitment. This influx of immigrants helped build the economic, social, and political foundations for the future state.

With the emergence Zionism, at the end of the 19th Century, Arab Muslims from across the region came to the holy land seeking economic opportunity as the Jews developed agricultural and industrial infrastructure. As documented by Joan Peters and many others, Arabs migrated to the area of the Ottoman empire known as "Southern Syria" – i.e. "Palestine" or the Land of Israel on maps – from Egypt, Yemen, Syria, Iraq, Morocco and elsewhere, hired by the Jews in their ever-expanding efforts to build up institutions as well as a modern agricultural and business economy. The names of many of the leading families ("notables") and clans ("hamoula") still reflect these origins (e.g. Al-Masri, from the Arabic word for Egypt;

Dajani, from Arabia and Morocco; Husseini, from Arabia). Others have a longer history in the region, like the Nusseibeh family, who trace their ancestry to the original Muslim caretakers of the Church of the Sepulcher in Jerusalem. And still, they too were not indigenous to the land.

Although they came for work, most Arabs and Muslims over the past two centuries resented the increasing numbers of Jews in the holy land and Jerusalem (Jews again became the largest single community in Jerusalem in the mid-1800s). Similarly, they were bitter about the ascendancy of the Jews as business and farm owners. As above, resistance to the 'invasion' of the Jews (and of western powers as well – i.e. opposition to it all, not just Zionism), was a major religious and cultural theme in the region.

This was accompanied, interestingly, by a marked resistance to the very idea of a separate national identity, amid attempts to promote Muslim or Arab unity. As many scholars have argued, the new and western (Westphalian) idea of nation-states was very much seen as a foreign concept within the Arab or Muslim Umma. Thus, the establishment of new countries in the region – including Lebanon, Syria, Iraq, Transjordan, the Mandate for Palestine etc., as well as the UAE, Yemen and others – was often resisted as unnatural and even un-Islamic, in the same spirit in which they contested foreign invaders and Jewish immigrants and institutions.

In fact, we can note the repeated recent attempts to unify the people and territories of the Middle East by conquest, including Syria in Lebanon; Syrian and Iraqi threats to Jordan; Egyptian designs on Sudan and Libya; Saudi Arabia's conflicts with Yemen and domination of new entities like the UAE, Bahrain and the like. This, aside from the failed political attempts at unification like the short-lived "United Arab Republic" union between Syria and Egypt in 1958-1961, which Yemen briefly joined; the "Federation of Arab Republics" between Libya, Egypt and Syria from 1972-1977; and the "Arab Islamic Republic" created between Tunisia and Libya in 1974.

Moreover, even today we hear praise for and desires to emulate or reconstruct the eras of Arab or Muslim domination – from Iran (Persia), from Turkey (Ottoman), even in less aggressive terms from

Egyptian, Saudi Arabian and other countries' leaders.

Thus the reaction to the Zionist enterprise, combined as above with the rise of radical Islamism/Salafi ideologies, Hitler admirers, fierce and growing anti-Jewish animosity, and failed attempts at unity, created a perfect storm from the early 20th century, which was then exacerbated by the perceived 'humiliations' of the defeat of Arab armies in '48, '67 and since.

The United Nations voted to recognize the Jews' inherent rights as the indigenous people of the land in 1947, and for the sake of peace recommended that the land be partitioned into Jewish and Arab states. The Jews accepted, while the Arab leadership rejected it outright. Arab armies invaded in 1948, vowing to drive the Jews into the sea; they failed, but the war created hundreds of thousands of refugees on both sides – Jews from Arab lands, Arabs from the new State of Israel.

The Six-Day War of 1967 brought Jerusalem's Old City and other territories of the original Mandate areas under Israeli control. For Jews, it was a historic homecoming. For many Arabs and Muslims, it was another embarrassment – the loss of land they considered sacred and, as above, inviolate.

This conflict is not about borders or resources. It is about identity, history, and theology. You cannot negotiate away centuries of belief with a few diplomatic handshakes. Reconciliation will require confronting – and in some cases changing – the perspectives and sacred stories held by each side.

Without going into the details of each stage of the ongoing conflict, this meta-view provides a crucial and revealing perspective on the real sources of the conflict – and provides a window, then, into what potential solutions may look like.

Even as the leaders of Arab and Muslim societies convinced their populations that the Jews' return to their ancient homeland was a foreign and colonialist invasion, two wider social phenomena contributed to the escalation of the conflict. The first was/is a propensity to violence in Muslim and Arab culture;[13] the second was and is the industrial revolution and the impact of changing western social mores on these societies.

This work cannot review either of these trends in detail but must address them briefly.

On the first point, the Arabs' resort to violence did not start with the establishment of the state of Israel; nor is it limited to the Arab-Israel conflict. Far from it; there are numerous examples of violent hostility towards the Jewish community in the holy land and across the Arab and Muslim world well before that.

But perhaps as or even more important are the many examples of inter-Arab/Muslim conflicts, from Iran/Iraq to Egypt/Libya/Sudan, from Saudi/Yemen, Syria/Turkey to internal and tribal warfare across the region, over the past centuries. As extensively analyzed by scholars (Ibn Khaldun, Albert Hourani, Bernard Lewis, Ephraim Karsh, Fuad I. Khuri, Khaldoun al-Naqeeb, Mordechai Kedar and others) the primary loyalty to tribe/clan and militaristic ideology and values, honor culture and the like, are integral aspects of Arab and Muslim culture, religion and identity.

Violence in this culture – in the family, the neighborhood, the tribe/clan and nation, and between nations – as well as the resort to armed conflict (as a first, rather than last, resort) is similarly well-documented by leading researchers including Ṭāhā ʿAbd al-Raḥmān, Marco Demichelis, Nadia Maria El Cheikh, Thomas Sizgorich, Robert Gleave, Sami Miari, and Bashar Tarabieh.

In our context and with our focus returning to our conflict, eminent British scholar of Islamic history, Patricia Crone of Princeton's Institute of Advanced Study, reminds us of the broad

---

[13] This author does not shy away from statements of fact. The tendency towards aggression in Arab and Muslim society is well-documented by sociologists, historians and theologians including prominent Muslim and Arab scholars. We acknowledge the importance of efforts this century to return to a more peaceful interpretation of Islam and expressions of this in Arab culture, like those of the Wasatia movement and the political leaders of the Abraham Accords countries; these ongoing endeavors serve to support, not reject, the assertion made.

and violent meaning of *Jihad*:

> In classical [Islamic] law *jihad* is missionary warfare. It is directed against infidels, who need not be guilty of any act of hostility against Muslims (their very existence is a cause of war), and its aim is to incorporate the infidels in the abode of Islam, preferably as converts, but alternately as dhimmis [i.e., conquered tributaries], until the whole world has been subdued.[14]

The very existence as Jews or Christians is seen as an affront to Islamists and, from their perspective, as we've seen time and again not only in Israel but in New York, London, Paris, Sydney and elsewhere, the murder of Jews and Christians is not "senseless violence". As Egyptian-born scholar Raymond Ibrahim has written, *"The truth is that Islam engenders hatred for non-Muslims. It calls for intolerance, violence, and even the outright slaughter of non-Muslims simply because they are non-Muslims."*[15]

This is of course a very politically incorrect statement, and the largely secular West cannot comprehend the religious motivation of much of the Muslim world. Ibrahim asks, *"How are we to understand such violence if we refuse to listen to the perpetrators' own explanations?"*[16].

Ibrahim shares a January, 2024 online post by the Islamic State titled "And Kill Them Wherever You Find Them [Koran 9:5]" which includes the following explicitly detailed instructions:

Lions of Islam: Chase your prey whether Jewish, Christian or their allies, on the streets and roads of America, Europe, and the world. Break into their homes, kill them and steal their peace of mind by any means you can lay hands on. … detonate explosives, burn them with grenades and fiery agents, shoot them with bullets, cut their throats with sharp knives, and run them over with vehicles. … Come at them from every door, kill them by the worst of means, turn their gatherings and celebrations into bloody massacres, do not distinguish between a civilian kaffir [infidel], and a military one, for they are all kuffar and the ruling

---

[14] Patricia Crone, *God's Rule: Government and Islam* (New York: Columbia University Press,
2004), pp. 364-5
[15] *Defending the West* (2022)
[16] Raymond Ibrahim, *PJ Media* / RaymondIbrahim.com, 2013

against them is one…. Intentionally seek easy targets before hard ones, civilian targets before military ones, religious targets like synagogues and churches before others, for … our battle with them is a religious one and we kill them wherever we come upon them in response to Allah Almighty's command.[17]

One Pew poll, among many others, demonstrated that in 11 countries alone, at least 63 million and as many as 287 million Muslims supported ISIS at the time.[18] Similarly, 81% of respondents to an online Al Jazeera poll then said they support the Islamic State.[19] (Though not a scientifically rigorous poll, considering the popularity of Al Jazeera's Arabic platform in the region it serves as an important indication of widespread sentiment, with tens of thousands of respondents.)[20]

These facts seem to make a disturbing statement about Islam, and about Arab culture, suggesting that there is something inherent in them which encourages violence; and there are certainly trends in Arab or Muslim society and thought encouraging non-violence. Therefore, it is not actually a statement about Islam per se, but rather about the current state of cultural and theological norms in today's Arab and Muslim societies, which are not immutable. In essence, the theme of this book exhorts leaders to return to and focus on those trends and principles in traditional Islam which indeed point to moderation, tolerance, and non-violence.

Regarding the industrial revolution, others have reported on the significant disruption modern economics and migration patterns have had on the traditional family and society. Academics and

---

[17] https://www.raymondibrahim.com/03/04/2024/islamic-state-calls-for-beheading-and-burning-of-every-western-civilian

[18] https://www.americanthinker.com/blog/2015/11/pew_poll_between_63_million_and_287_million_isis_supporters_in_just_11_countries.html

[19] https://www.opendemocracy.net/en/north-africa-west-asia/aljazeera-poll-81-percent-support-for-islamic-state/

[20] In this context it is worth noting that – among other terror attacks over the years inspired if not planned by Iran, ISIS, Al Qaeda etc. – the most recent assault as of this writing, at Bondi Beach in Sydney, Australia in December '25, killing 15 Jews at a Chanukah celebration and injuring dozens more, was driven by Islamic State ideology, according to Australia's prime minister per the *New York Times*.

thinkers including Ali Mubarak and Rifa'a Rafi' al-Tahtawi, Timur Kuran, Olivier Roy and Mohamed Sadok Gassouma have outlined the challenges modernization and industrialization have presented to Arab/Muslim stability and security.

The interplay of both or all these issues, with their attendant complexity, outside the Arab-Israel conflict, can be demonstrated in the example of the Iran-Iraq war. Others include the conflicts between Yemen and Saudi Arabia, Afghanistan and Pakistan, Egypt and Sudan, and of course the internal deadly conflicts within Syria, Lebanon, Iraq and almost every other Arab and Muslim nation over the past 7 centuries.

The present work doesn't allow for a detailed exposition of how the dynamics of the Cold War and USSR/USA rivalry were expressed in this regional conflict, with the Soviet Union provoking (and providing much of the propaganda for) antisemitism and anti-Israel sentiment. Similarly, the non-aligned movement both sought a separate 'identity' and role, and to curry favor with oil-rich Arab leaders, with newly-minted Arab nations seeking to express their own independence by also attacking Israel and persecuting Jews. But these elements also have played a role – and continue to do so – in the hostility expressed by Arab and Muslim leaders towards Israel and the Zionist enterprise.

All the above dynamics added to growing frustration, anger and resentment due to the breakdown of hierarchical family and social roles. This, combined with the realization of progress made in western countries (including, eventually, Israel) which evaded their own societies, made many people looking for a scapegoat ripe for the sort of Hitlerian propaganda depicting the demonic Jews and Israelis as subhuman vermin blamed for everything from colonial exploitation to baby killings.

To a great extent, the popularity of Hitler in the Arab and Muslim world in general can be explained by this combination of economic, social, cultural and religious factors. In this vein, even a brief Internet search turns up thousands of examples of antisemitic and anti-Israel cartoons and caricatures reflecting the deep hostility of elites and publics towards Jews and the State of Israel today (notwithstanding reasonable criticism of the policies of any particular Israeli government). These themes include presenting the Jew/Israel (the Jew among the nations) as vermin, snake, octopus, rat, or as the Devil or evil incarnate; as Nazis, baby-killers, manipulators and controllers of the media and financial markets, even of the animal kingdom and the weather. This pervasive demonization and delegitimization of the Jews, Judaism, Israel and Zionism has been well-documented.

And finally, the additional perception/misperception of Zionism as colonialism as mentioned above continues to contribute greatly to the current and growing Muslim/Arab animosity towards Israel. As the ultimate component in this overview of the conflict, it is perhaps the most fundamental – and the most prejudicial – element of the Islamic/Arab antagonistic mindset towards Israel and the presence of the Jews in the holy land.

In this context, there is irony in the very real and historical colonialism of the area by the Arab/Muslim invaders of the seventh and eighth centuries. The conquering of foreign lands by imperial dynasties was hardly unusual over the millennia, and the argument here is not an attack on the Arab (and Seleucid, and Ottoman) Islamic forces who occupied and subjugated vast swaths of territory and various nations and peoples over the ensuring centuries. They were simply continuing a pattern set by many empires before them, from the Greeks and Romans to the Assyrians, Babylonians and eventually the British and French and other Europeans in the twentieth century.

Arabs/Muslims (and others) accusing Jews/Israelis of "colonialism" and "occupation" is absurd; but the allegations merely demonstrate both the complexity of the historical reality and the nefarious nature of their hypocrisy. And it demands a cogent analysis of why this is so.*

As Jerusalem is the focal point of this argument, our analysis will concentrate on the holy city as an illustration (and central element) of Islamic and Arab claims to the holy land (and their hostile rejection of the claims of the Jews), and in particular on the identification of the "Al Aqsa" mosque mentioned in the Quran with today's Al Aqsa on the Temple Mount in the Old City of Jerusalem. (Nothing in this depiction should be taken as diminishing the significance and holiness of Jerusalem and its Al Aqsa mosque for Muslims and Arabs; our aim is to clarify the historical record to serve our goals of understanding, acceptance, coexistence and peace.)

It is well known that Jerusalem is simply not mentioned in the Quran – not once, by any name – and was not 'claimed' by Islamic scholars or Arab philosophers for generations. When the Byzantine city was conquered by the armies of 'Umar, the Rashid caliph, in 635, it was referred to in Arabic as *Madinat Bayt al-Maqdis* "City of the Temple", a name restricted to the holy Temple Mount and reflecting the linguistic parallel with the Hebrew *Beit HaMikdash* ("House of the Temple"). The rest of the city was called *Ilyā*, reflecting the Roman name *Aelia*.

Furthermore, the Quran itself was already complete before the year 650 CE. The mosque at the southern end of the Temple Mount was not built until 705 CE, i.e. 55 years later; therefore, that mosque cannot possibly be the "Al Aqsa" mentioned in the Quran.

There is general agreement among many, though certainly not all nor even most, Muslim scholars and religious experts that the real "Al Aqsa" mosque ("the farthest mosque") mentioned in the Quran

---

* Those who reject all expressions of national identity may oppose the legitimacy of Israel and of the idea of a distinct "Palestinian" Arab people. But the current demonization of Jews as somehow foreign to Judea, ie. the people of Israel having no connection to the land of Israel, let alone the modern popular opposition to the presence of Israel in the disputed territories of Judea and Samaria, ie. the 'west bank' of the Jordan River, is patently ahistorical. This is not a political argument: One may oppose Israel's presence in the territories, or even Israel's very existence, without parroting the propogandist terminology of "colonialism" and "occupation".

is sited *in western Arabia.* As Osama Yamani has noted, early Islamic sources say that it was one of two mosques located near Ji'ranna, on the road between Mecca and Ta'af. The "farthest" mosque was indeed distant – in contemporary terms of religious pilgrimage and ritual activity, measured in days' journey by camel; but it wasn't connected to the ancient biblical city or then-backwater-outpost of Byzantium called Aelia Capitolina (renamed that by the Romans)/Jerusalem.

When Caliph 'Umar ibn al-Khaṭṭāb came personally to Jerusalem in 637/638 CE to accept its peaceful surrender, he did so at the insistence of the city's Christian leadership – not because the city or the Temple Mount yet held intrinsic Islamic sanctity. The site was neglected, and no mosque or dome existed there at the time; both were constructed decades later under the Umayyad caliphs 'Abd al-Malik ibn Marwān and al-Walīd I, as noted below, in the late 7th century.

'Umar instructed that a simple wooden prayer structure be erected, and Jews were allowed back into Jerusalem and to pray on the Temple Mount again, having been barred by the Byzantines. All this is recorded in early Muslim histories such as al-Ṭabarī's *Ta'rīkh* and al-Balādhurī's *Futūḥ al-Buldān*, both of which describe Jerusalem as a political and administrative prize rather than a sacred Muslim destination at that stage.

A common objection to this historical understanding invokes the Quranic reference to *al-Masjid al-Aqṣā* (Al-Aqsa Mosque) in Quran 17:1, widely assumed today of course to refer to that named mosque Jerusalem. Yet early Islamic sources do not make this identification. Classical commentators such as al-Ṭabarī and al-Zamakhsharī record multiple interpretations, including understandings of Al Aqṣa as a heavenly sanctuary or a distant place of worship, not a defined earthly structure in Jerusalem. As noted above, at the time of the revelation, no mosque existed on the Temple Mount, and Jerusalem itself was not yet a center of Islamic ritual life. And the later identification of Al Aqsa with Jerusalem reflects a subsequent theological development, crystallized only after the Umayyad construction of the Dome of the Rock (c. 691 CE) and the Al-Aqṣā complex (early 8th century). This reinforces the historical point:

Jerusalem's sanctification in Islam was gradual and retrospective, not foundational or contemporaneous with Islam's origins.

Political and religious rivalries led to the elevation of the Temple Mount and the dome and mosque there, and Jerusalem in general, to its status as a holy city. These enmities, and how they drove the Umayyads to name the mosque built on the Temple Mount "Al Aqsa", are well-documented.

Historians such as Alfred Guillaume maintain that it was this political rivalry between the Umayyads and the rival caliph Abd Allah ibn al-Zubayr which resulted in the sanctification of Jerusalem. In 682 CE, the Umayyads of Damascus were barred from making pilgrimage ("hajj") to Mecca, and consequently had to choose somewhere else to go. They chose Jerusalem, and the association of "Al-Aqsa" with Jerusalem developed over time due to various factors, including those political considerations. Umayyad Caliph Abd al-Malik (ruled 685–705 CE) played a significant role in solidifying the association of Jerusalem and the Temple Mount (Haram al-Sharif) with Islamic holy sites, including the mosque now known as Al-Aqsa; thus the religious status of Jerusalem was elevated in rivalry with Mecca during a period of civil strife within the early Muslim community.

Abd al-Malik commissioned the construction of the Dome of the Rock in Jerusalem around 691 CE, as above, and is also credited with initiating the construction or significant expansion of what became known as the Al-Aqsa Mosque. The earliest source indicating al-Walid's work on the mosque is the Aphrodito Papyri, which contains letters discussing the dispatch of Egyptian laborers and craftsmen to help with the building of what was referred to then as the "Mosque of Jerusalem" – not yet named nor claimed as the "Farthest Mosque" or Al-Aqsa mentioned in the Quran.

Oleg Grabar, a leading scholar of Islam, also affirms that the term "Al Aqsa" refers to a mosque in the village called Ji'ranna, which is in the Hejaz area of Arabia. He relies on contemporary sources such as Al Azraqi and Al Waqidi, Muslim travelers in the time of Mohammed, who mention "*Al-masjid al-aqṣā*" , and "*Al-masjid al-Adna*" in their writing.

Bevan has shown that among early traditionalists there are many who do not accept the identification of the masjid al-aqsa, and among them are to be found such great names as al-Bukhari and Tabari. Both Ibn Ishaq and al-Ya'qubi precede their accounts with expressions which indicate that these are stories which are not necessarily accepted as dogma. It was suggested by J. Horovitz that in the early period of Islam there is little justification for assuming that the Quranic expression in any way referred to Jerusalem. While Horovitz thought that it referred to a place in heaven, A. Guillaume's careful analysis of the earliest texts (al-Waqidi and al-Azraqi, both in the later second century A.H.) has convincingly shown that the Quranic reference to the masjid al-aqsa applies specifically to al-Ji'ranah, near Mekkah, where there were two sanctuaries (masjid al-adnai and masjid al-aqsa), and where Mohammed sojourned in dha al-qa'dah of the eighth year after the Hijrah.[21]

Similarly, those not familiar with the attitude of traditional Islam to Jerusalem are often under the impression that the Prophet Mohammed visited the holy city. Mohammed's trip to Al Aqsa was a dream-journey according to virtually all scholars including traditional Muslims, both Sunni and Shia.

Of course, in almost every religious tradition, dreams carry a sacred importance – and not least prophetic and revelatory miraculous experiences. Recognizing that what's being described is a vision/dream doesn't take away from its significance. But most people distinguish between dreams, with all their significance and spiritual power and the messages they carry, and reality.

It appears that Mohammed never physically visited the earthly city of Jerusalem; this is a fact of history. That doesn't diminish the importance of the holiday celebrated as *Lailat al-Mi raj* ("Night of the Ascension" or "Night Journey", the Islamic holiday commemorating his miraculous journey from Mecca to *Ilyā*/Aelia/the Temple Mount (Jerusalem) and his ascension to heaven, where he met prophets, saw heaven and hell, and received the command for Muslims to perform five daily prayers or *Salat*). But it's an important factor in how the journey is perceived – and in

---

[21] Grabar, Oleg (1959). "The Umayyad Dome of the Rock in Jerusalem". Ars Orientalis. **3**: 33–62. ISSN 0571-1371.

the implications of misunderstanding for our centuries-old conflict.

The story can be compared to the prophet Ezekiel's visions/dreams of the Lord's Chariot (*Merkava* in Hebrew) in the Hebrew Bible – a haunting revelation central to our understanding of the mystical foundations of higher spirituality, valued as an allegory or illustration but not necessarily to be taken literally.

Some take these things on faith (as the word implies); others explicitly see them as metaphors conveying valuable lessons; many, both.

Perhaps even more critical for our discussion, even those who suggest there *was* an actual physical journey can recognize it was almost certainly *not* to the city of *Ilyā*/Aelia (Jerusalem), as explained above – not least as there was no mosque there in Mohammed's life.

We can acknowledge that Muslim believers consider it a truism that "Al Aqsa" mosque is on the Temple Mount in Jerusalem, while also recognizing that this is most probably a mistaken understanding of history, geography, and theology. And this is the significant element to focus on: not whether Mohammed visited Al Aqsa physically on a flying horse or metaphorically in a dream vision, but that the Al Aqsa in question is conclusively *not* in today's Jerusalem.

What is historically true, verifiably by authoritative sources, is that Arab Muslim conquerors built a shrine on the Temple Mount, over the ruins of the Byzantine Church built there (which was built on the ruins of the Roman temple, which was built on the site of the Jewish Temple which the Romans purposefully destroyed). They called it the Dome of the Rock (i.e. it was and is not a mosque); they then built a mosque, called at first the "Mosque of Jerusalem" and eventually named "Al Aqsa", on the southern edge of the Mount compound; and in the first two decades of the 21st Century, the entire plaza began to be referred to by Arab and Muslim politicians and activists (and agitators), and thus by the international media, as the "Al Aqsa compound".

The occupation of *Ilyā*/Aelia (Jerusalem) by the Arab Muslim forces after Mohammed's death, and promotion of the idea that the Al Aqsa there is *that* Al Aqsa of the dream journey mentioned in the Quran, are intricately connected. These themes have considerably contributed to the enormous ideological battle between Islam and Christianity and Judaism, and between the Arab peoples and the nation of Israel, over the past 1300 years or more. And these refrains are similar to the attempt by the Romans to erase the connection of the people of Israel with the Land of Israel by renaming it "Palestina" 2000 years ago.

Serious Muslim scholars recognize these issues, and agree that accuracy is important; they promote an approach to this land which recognizes and advocates Muslim/Arab connection and promotes Arab identity without exaggeration or fabrication, or reference to eternal "ownership" of Jerusalem or the holy land. Our intention in this discussion is not to dismiss the Muslim/Arab reverence for Jerusalem; rather, our aim is to provide a historically and theologically rigorous perspective which can allow for other interpretations and, eventually, contribute to a basis for compromise.[*]

Thus, the two essential suppositions of this part of the Arab-Israel conflict are (1) that Jerusalem is the location of the "Al Aqsa" mentioned in the Quran and is therefore holy to Muslims, and (2) that Muslim/Arab rule over Jerusalem and the holy land, since its conquest 1300 years ago, is a necessary and permanent Islamic Waqf, a Muslim religious, principled, theological right or responsibility, as described previously. Following from these two claims, the Jews' presence, let alone sovereignty, is a religious insult and injury to Muslims everywhere and to Arabs' pride, fueling the hostility to both Jews and their nation-state.

From here, it is almost natural then for Arab and Muslim

---

[*] It must be noted that many scholars – including Professor Dajani – would take issue with the assessment offered here. It is perhaps an indication of the nature of our challenge that almost all contemporary academics and writers who identify as Palestinian or Arab disagree with this historical analysis, and promote the 'narrative' of the Islamic/Arab nature of Jerusalem and the association of the "Al Aqsa" of the Quran with the mosque built on Jerusalem's Temple Mount, whereas almost all western scholars concur with this presentation of the history of Jerusalem and Al Aqsa. Fortunately, Dajani and some (too few) others are willing to set aside this disagreement regarding history in favor of our shared goals of peace and coexistence. We must acknowledge, and respect, their courage.

thinkers and leaders to present the Jews as interlopers, foreign intruders alien to the region which Arabs and Muslims consider "theirs". When Jews claim the Land of Israel as an extension of their ancient connection to Jerusalem/Zion, many reject that association as "colonialist" rather than indigenous. They see and portray Jews as "settlers" rather than refugees returning to their ancestral homeland from an involuntary Diaspora.

Most Arabs and Muslims today (though not all), and most of their leaders, parrot the extremist propaganda of the current Iranian mullahs and the previous secular nationalist Arab leaders declaring Israel as an illegitimate state, and Jews as European colonialist implants in the Levant. Instead, the invention of a native "Palestinian" Arab people was introduced to posit a more acceptable recipient of the mantle of the indigenous people of the area.

Paradoxically, these opinions are in direct contrast to actual representations of traditional, normative Islamic thought and factual history, as explicated in prevailing and accepted sources, considered authoritative by Muslims for centuries.

The Quran and traditional Islamic sources not only explicitly recognize the connection between the land of Israel and the people of Israel, but express God's/Allah's gift of the promised land to the Jews and the blessings He promises to them. A few quotes from the Quran and other Islamic sources will suffice to demonstrate this acceptance and even embrace of the earlier and traditional association between the children of Israel and the land of Israel, between the Jews and Judea, in customary Islamic thought.

Surat Bani Isra'il (The Children of Israel), also known as Surat al-Isra', is one of those sources. Khaleel Mohammed, a scholar of Islamic law at San Diego State University, notes that Ibn Kathir, the leading Muslim medieval commentator on the Quran (1310-1373), considered this Sura to have established compellingly that the land of Israel is promised to the Jews. *"And We said to the Children of Israel after Pharaoh, 'Reside in the land, but when the promise of the Hereafter comes to pass, We will bring you all together.'"* – Surah Al-Isra 17:104

Khaleel Mohammed refers also to Sura 5 verse 21 of the Quran asserting that Israel belongs to the Jews, insisting it has been interpreted from the outset as "the final word" from God on this issue: "*And [remember] when Moses said to his people, 'O my people! ...Enter the Holy Land which Allah has written/ destined for you [to enter]. And do not turn back....*" – Surah Al-Ma'idah 5:21. Mohammed stresses that Ibn Kathir interpreted this verse explicitly: "'*...which God has written [destined] for you' i.e. that which God has promised to you by the words of your father Israel that it is the inheritance of those among you who believe.*"

Imam Abdul Hadi Palazzi, head of the Italian Muslim Assembly, quotes the Quran to support Judaism's special connection to the Temple Mount, noting that "*the most authoritative Islamic sources affirm the Temples.*" Jerusalem is sacred to Muslims precisely due to its earlier holiness to Jews, and the fact that it was where the prophets of the Bible and the kings of Israel, including King David and King Solomon, honored also in Islam, lived. According to Palazzi, the Quran "*expressly recognizes that Jerusalem plays the same role for Jews that Mecca has for Muslims*".

Regarding what the Quran says about the State of Israel, Palazzi states:

> The Quran cannot deal with the State of Israel as we know it today, since that State only came into existence in 1948, i.e. many centuries after the Quran itself was revealed. However, the Quran specifies that the Land of Israel is the homeland of the Jewish people, that God Himself gave that Land to them as heritage and ordered them to live therein. It also announces that – before the end of time – the Jewish people will come from many different countries to retake possession of that heritage of theirs. Whoever denies this actually denies the Quran itself. If he is not a scholar, and in good faith believes what other people say about this issue, he is an ignorant Muslim. If, on the contrary, he is informed about what the Quran and openly opposes it, he ceases to be a Muslim.[22]

Imam Mohammed Al-Hussaini in Britain also insists that traditional medieval Islamic commentators interpreted the Quran as explicitly stating that the Land of Israel was given to the Jewish people as a perpetual covenant by Allah. Hussaini cites Mohammed

---

[22] "Land of Israel is the homeland of the Jewish people – Imam Palazzi", *Weekly Blitz*, 5 (42), 13 October 2010

ibn Jarir al-Tabari, that this is *"a narrative from God... concerning the saying of Moses... to his community from among the children of Israel... ordering them to enter the holy land."* Hussaini contends that this promise to the Jews is eternal, and asserts: *"It was never the case during the early period of Islam... that there was any kind of sacerdotal attachment to Jerusalem as a territorial claim."*

These references are but the tip of the proverbial iceberg. Though multiple Islamic sources (primary – i.e. from the Quran and its commentaries – and secondary – from medieval and contemporary religious leaders and scholars) will be quoted at length below, relating to the specific elements of this book's arguments, the point here is simple: If the world's desire is to reach genuine accord in the Middle East, we have to distinguish between Islam as a faith/religion and *Islamism* as a political ideology.

The former, the religious tradition called Islam, is diverse and spiritual and promotes many of the values we associate with the Western world, including peace and tolerance as well as specifically an embrace of Jews as the people of Israel, including their connection with their ancestral homeland. The latter, the authoritarian dogma called Islamism, seeks to implement a specific interpretation of Islam in modern national societies and political programs – an ideology which is violent, rejectionist, intolerant and exclusionist. This latter is promoted today by Iran, ISIS, the Muslim Brotherhood and their satrapies Hamas, Hezb'Allah, Palestinian Islamic Jihad, the Houthis and others, as well as being supported by multiple regimes like those of Qatar, Turkey, Iraq, Afghanistan etc. and frequently Russia, China and other dictatorships... and too often by fellow-travelers in the free world.

It is to the former which this work looks for salvation, and on which real peace will one day be based.

As a general principle, from an Islamic standpoint, there is no opposition to sulh *or* salaam *with Israel.* – Sheikh Abdel-Rahman Hassan Hamed (Times of Israel)

Israel has been extending its hand in peace to Arabs and Muslims for a long time... Therefore, peace with the Israelis is an obligatory religious duty. – Syrian Sheikh Abdallah Al-Tamimi in a sermon (as translated by MEMRI); Al-Tamimi also condemns terrorist attacks, including

October 7, calling them "deplorable" and "Haram", according to MEMRI. (<u>Memri</u>, 21 August '24)

Inconclusion, the Arab-Israel conflict can be summed up in one word: rejection. This understanding is embedded in the wording: "Arab-Israel conflict". The basis for this clash is and always has been, for well over a century, the opposition by most Arab/Muslim leaders to any legitimacy given to the return and re-establishment of sovereignty in the land of Israel by the people of Israel. This hostility has been accompanied by violent antipathy towards the modern nation-state of the Jewish people – and to Jews who are not Israeli citizens – and is expressed repeatedly in war and horrific terror. (We can acknowledge that Israel's defensive military operations resulting in injury, loss of life and property damage, have contributed to the animosity, but they are not the first cause nor the primary reason for the continuation of the conflict, by any measure.)

Recognizing that our conflict is, in fact, provoked by a hateful, rejectionist ideology, which came out of a politicization of traditional Islam becoming what we now call Islamist doctrine, offers us an equally simple path to resolving the situation.

On the practical level, many people are familiar with the famous line attributed to Golda Meir, an early Jewish pioneer and prime minister of Israel in the early 1970s: *"If the Arabs put down their weapons today, there would be no more war. If the Jews put down their weapons today, there would be no more Israel."*

On the philosophical level, peace can only be achieved by a radical transformation of Islamic thought and Arab culture back to the more traditional, normative understanding of Islam as a "religion of peace"– i.e. a reformation of Islamic belief.

I hasten to add – as a Jew, an Israeli, an American, and a promoter of democracy and freedom – that this is not of course up to me or other outsiders. Moreover, it smacks of tremendous chutzpah – the Yiddish/Hebrew word best if imperfectly translated as nerve, or audacity – to recommend what amounts to a societal, civilizational, philosophical revolution in another culture/religion's way of life.

And yet too many of us – across the western and free world, let alone in Arab or Muslim society – hesitate to call for such a return to traditional Muslim values, for fear of the sort of backlash and persecution which is almost always the retort (in our modern cancel-culture of political correctness).

Nonetheless that is, by any objective analysis, what is desperately necessary today. And so perhaps an unknown writer, offering suggestions based on both personal experience and in-depth research, relying on ancient and modern scholars and religious thinkers to bolster the argument, is best-placed to issue such a call.

As Professor Mohammed Dajani explains, *"In the United States, there is a popular saying: 'Guns don't kill people; people kill people.' Similarly, the Quran and other holy books do not teach hatred and violence; radical followers teach that."*

There are many Muslim and Arab voices, including religious and political leaders, promoting these ideas. My aim here is to codify, and amplify, these voices, and not least to attempt to help the decision-makers of today (and tomorrow) in the West not only to become more familiar with these courageous individuals and the movements and ideas they champion, but to embrace these concepts and incorporate them into the policies they pursue regarding the Arab-Israel conflict.

Once – following the global catastrophe which was called WWII – such an objective perspective calling for changes in the ideologies of the racist, hateful, violent and intolerant regimes in Japan and Germany was not only not controversial, it was the shared perspective of all Allied leaders.

This approach to building the foundations of world peace included demands (demands, not gentle suggestions) for sweeping changes in the way the political, cultural, educational, religious and community leadership in Germany and Japan indoctrinated their populations and educated their youth. That it is seen as radical, or condescending, or politically incorrect today says more about the decline of our western society than it does about any supposed change in the reasonableness of the stance.

Standard approaches to resolving conflict, in the scholarly as well as the practitioner communities, revolve around a number of tactics, including avoidance, acceptance, gradual social reform, nonviolent confrontation, and violent confrontation. By contrast, the focus here is – and the emphasis of the parties and the international community should be – on a combination of reform and the elements from my first book: humility, acceptance, gratitude, forgiveness and a sense of purpose. Purpose, in this context, is based primarily on acceptance and forgiveness, and these together form the basis of the social reform.

The heart of this book and this approach to bringing real peace to the promised land rests then on two principles.[23]

The first is a factual understanding of the foundations of international support for the return of the people of Israel to its ancestral homeland and the legitimacy of the founding of and acceptance of Israel as a member of the community of nations.

The second is a factual understanding of Islamist Jihadist/Salafi political/religious ideology as the chief source of the conflict.

If either of these principles is rejected out of hand, clearly the reader may wish to move on to other works of interest. Yet I hope that, having come this far, even though you may not be comfortable with the expression of these two principles, you might consider venturing further with us. And nothing written here suggests that the holy land or Jerusalem is not held dear also by Arabs and Muslims (and Christians), or that there is no legitimacy for an expression of Palestinian national or ethnic identity.

But there is so much misinformation and propaganda today in mainstream and social media, and in general public discourse, let alone by and among politicians across the free world, that most people's understanding of the underlying causes of the conflict is wildly inaccurate. (As a quote often attributed to Mark Twain has it, "If you don't read the newspaper, you are *uninformed*; if you *do* read the newspaper, you are *misinformed*.")

Those who believe – and it seems to be a matter of faith – that Israel was born in sin as a European colonial enterprise, a settler movement which invaded "Palestine" and stole the land from its inhabitants through ongoing ethnic cleansing and even genocide,

---

[23] Both these principles are stated here baldly; clearly there are multiple and nuanced features of each, and this abridgment doesn't minimize these; and they are dealt with later in this work.

setting up an apartheid Jewish-supremacy state, may wish to check your biases at the door (or at the book-cover).[24]

As Daniel Patrick Moynihan was fond of saying, "Everyone is entitled to his own opinion, but not to his own facts" – and the genocide, apartheid and other canards are as outrageously erroneous as they are noxious.

Criticism of Israel's policies, and its defensive military operations in particular, is healthy and often warranted. We Israelis are famed for our hyper-critical political debates and critiques of our governments' policies. Natan Sharansky, a former Soviet dissident and Israeli leader, used to quip that if you don't criticize the policies of the Israeli government… you have no future in Israeli politics. This is of course criticism of a whole different nature than the delegitimization and demonization of Israel per se.

When evaluated objectively, the establishment of Israel as the

---

[24] In this context, one wonders if the reader's biases similarly extend to the 100+ newly-established states founded since 1945, few of whose historical or tribal connection to an ancestral homeland match that of the Jews' to the land of Israel and most of which were founded precisely as European colonialist outposts, whether in Africa, Asia, South America or the Middle East.

Similarly, the same can be said, or even more persuasively, about the supposed Arab/Muslim claim to the holy land (or anywhere outside of the Arabian Peninsula), considering that it was their military conquest and occupation which led to any connection with other lands – not any indigenous link.

This is true for all the recently-established modern Arab nation-states with perhaps the exception of Egypt, though it too was very much the result of European colonialist efforts. (And on the other hand, there are quite a few national groups deserving of independence which have not – yet – been granted sovereignty over their ancestral homelands – from Aborigines in Australia to Canada's First Nation(s), from the Basques and Catalonians to the Scotts, let alone the Tibetans and Kurds.)

Israelis have often marveled at how the terminology such as that listed here is used to delegitimize and demonize the Jewish State, while real ethnic cleansing, apartheid, colonialism, etc. and even genocide is carried out across the globe with nary a condemnation from the UN or the Human Rights Council or on campuses or in the media – from Iran, Syria, Sudan and Afghanistan to Burma, North Korea, China, Russia, Turkey and Venezuela, let alone Saudi Arabia, Yemen, Kuwait, Qatar, and most other regimes in our region here in the Middle East. But we digress.

nation-state of the indigenous people of Israel in its ancestral homeland – ratified by the international community both in the League of Nations and the UN – and its functioning multi-cultural and free society, stand in stark contrast to the propagandistic accusations repeated above. The same may be said for the morality of its defensive military operations when compared with all others (modern and over the course of history) in terms of innocents injured, killed or made homeless.

As someone who presumably picked up this book out of interest in peace in our region, you may wish to acknowledge that the complexity (and durability) of the issues might suggest a need for more nuanced discussion and policies, would we wish to truly work towards real peace.

And that – *real* peace – is the goal of this book.

Chapter Two: The Five Elements of Peace

How Humility, Acceptance, Gratitude, Forgiveness, and Purpose Can Transform Conflict – What they are, how they relate to each other, why they apply to international conflict)

When I hiked the Israel National Trail, it was not for adventure or sport. It was a lifeline. My life had collapsed. My marriage was over. My sense of self was in pieces. On that 1000-kilometer walk from Eilat to the Lebanese border, I learned lessons that rebuilt me from the ground up.

A framework for meeting personal challenges with the five elements introduced above emerged from that journey – humility, acceptance, gratitude, forgiveness, and purpose. This formula enabled me to move on with my life, and so I wrote my first book to help others face their own hardships. Not least thanks to those lessons learned on the Trail, within the context of exploring my own purpose in life, I spent a great deal of time over the past few years thinking how I personally can do something about the Arab-Israeli conflict.

Considering who I am, it's not so surprising that my mind turned in that direction. I am a Jew living in Israel, so the conflict has daily and existential ramifications for my life. And my academic and professional background gives me an inside perspective on the conflict, from my master's in international relations and work in the prime minister's office to the decade I spent helping foreign journalists report accurately from the region.

And so these ideas, though based on my experience on the trek, are as much a result of academic research and intellectual debate over the past few decades as they are of the personal growth and healing processes of more recent years.

Seeking possible scenarios for resolving our conflict, it was clear to me from writing the first book that the answers all correspond in one way or another to those five elements. These steps can apply not only to individuals, but to nations as well. I initially hesitated to call them steps, as a "5-step plan" seems a bit cliché. Nevertheless, they are steps, in as much as you cannot pass over steps 1-4 to reach

5. You must go through all the steps, and in order. There are no shortcuts.

These tools, or steps, are not vague spiritual slogans. They are hard, practical tools. In my life, they were the difference between despair and recovery. In relations between nations, they can mean the difference between endless war and amity. Many of them, as will be demonstrated, have been integral elements of reconciliation and peace between former adversaries – in recent history and across the planet.

1. Humility

The desert taught me lessons I didn't go looking for. Out there on the Israel Trail, with no one to hear my footsteps but the wind, I discovered how small I truly was. The hot, dry riverbeds stretched endlessly before me, stripped bare of distraction – no trees, no birdsong, not even the hum of an insect. It was humbling in a way I had never experienced.

I had spent my life thinking of myself as a man of impact: working in politics and business, influencing decisions, guiding teams, mediating disputes. Even in my marriage, I believed my skills in communication, negotiation, and problem-solving could fix what was broken.

Yet here I was confronted by a vast silence that didn't care if I walked or stopped, succeeded or failed. My existence in the desert literally had no meaning, left no ripple in the sand. That realization – that I was not the center of my own universe – could have been crushing. Instead, it freed me. As the Bible says: *For dust you are, and to dust you shall return.* (Genesis 3:19). My smallness was not insignificance; it was perspective.

Humility, I realized, is not self-abasement but the clarity to see ourselves in proportion. It is the first step toward peace – in a marriage, between neighbors, or between nations. Without it, leaders stride into the Middle East conflict convinced that their brilliance, power, or charisma will succeed where others failed. From Count Bernadotte to Presidents Clinton and Obama and Trump, many have carried this hubris into negotiations. But this conflict is older and deeper than any one personality. Humility is the soil in which real dialogue can take root.

Humility came when I realized I could not control everything – the weather, my aching legs, the rocky terrain. I had to adjust. In national terms, humility means leaders recognizing they don't hold all the answers, that their side's perspective may not be the only truth.

As one example from history, after the Second World War, Charles de Gaulle led France's postwar recovery by restoring national pride but also accepting that France was no longer the dominant global power. His humility toward geopolitical reality allowed France to focus on rebuilding rather than chasing a lost empire.

In the Middle East, humility has been rare. Israeli leaders have expressed premature expectations of "a new Middle East" and sometimes spoken as if power alone could guarantee peace. Arab leaders have often insisted that time is on their side and boasted of their ability to destroy Israel, and many have refused to admit that Jewish self-determination is legitimate. Without humility, both sides fall into the trap of believing they can win everything.

2. Acceptance

From humility, acceptance grows. As darkness fell one evening early in the trek, I began to panic, as I describe in Chapter Four below. Instead, I told myself: *You are here. This is real. No one is coming to save you. Accept it, then choose your next step.* That night I also accepted my divorce. I had fought it with every tool I had, convinced it could be reversed. But some realities do not yield to willpower.

Acceptance didn't mean approval; it meant facing the truth without denial.

In the same way, peace between Arabs and Israelis will never begin until both sides accept the reality of the other's existence and permanence.

For Jews, that means recognizing that Palestinian national identity, though shaped in the last century, is now a fact. For

Palestinians and much of the Arab and Muslim world, it means acknowledging the unbroken connection of the Jewish people to this land and the legitimacy of Israel's place among nations – and the absolute right to live in peace. As Jordan's King Hussein is said to have stated: *"Peace requires no surrender of one's principles, but a recognition of the other's humanity and presence."*

Acceptance is not surrender. It is clarity. Out in the wilderness, I had to accept when a day's goal was beyond reach. Refusing to face that reality would only have left me injured in the desert.

In diplomacy, acceptance means facing uncomfortable facts. For Palestinians, it means accepting that Israel is not temporary but is here to stay, and by right. For Israelis, it means accepting that millions of Palestinians are not going to disappear, and that their lives and dignity matter in any peace plan. For all, it means accepting the unfair, unjust realities of our situation, from every perspective.

History shows what acceptance can do. After centuries of war, France and Germany accepted each other's existence. The 1963 Élysée Treaty marked not just a political agreement but a cultural shift. Schoolchildren learned each other's language; joint history books were written. Acceptance created the space for reconciliation.

In our region, peace will remain impossible until both peoples accept each other's right to exist – not just on paper, but in the collective mind.

3. Gratitude

Acceptance paves the way for gratitude. On the Trail, gratitude came easily: the relief of finding shade, the taste of cool water, the laughter of friends waiting at day's end. In life, it meant treasuring the family and friends who stood by me, even in hardship. Gratitude is not naïve optimism; it is the discipline of seeing what remains whole and good amid what is broken.

In Jewish tradition, the morning begins with the *Modeh Ani* prayer: *"I thank You, living and enduring King, for returning my soul within me with compassion."* In Islam, gratitude (*shukr*) is a central act of worship: *"If you are grateful, I will surely increase you [in favor]"* (Quran

14:7). Imagine if political leaders approached negotiations not from a place of grievance alone, but also from an awareness of what they have – peace treaties already signed, security where it exists, economic partnerships that thrive despite politics. Gratitude can open doors that bitterness keeps shut.

Trudging along even the most uninspiring landscape, gratitude changed my mental state. Instead of fixating on what I had lost in life, I began to notice the simple joys – a cool breeze after hours in the sun, a hot meal shared with strangers.

For nations, gratitude reframes priorities. Israel has much to be grateful for: a thriving economy, democratic freedoms rare in the region, cultural revival, and more security compared to past decades (even given the harsh failures related to the Oct. 7th massacre). Palestinians, despite real hardships, have an educated young population, better prospects for freedom, travel, economic growth and prosperity than many other Arab societies, and international sympathy few causes enjoy.

Gratitude does not erase grievances. But it shifts the tone from constant demand to constructive engagement. Leaders who cultivate gratitude in their people open the door to compromise; leaders who stoke resentment close it.

4. Forgiveness

Even if everything I've suggested until this point is true, humility, acceptance, and gratitude are incomplete without forgiveness. For months after my divorce, forgiveness was an afterthought. Only when I forgave – my wife, God, and myself – did the tightness in my chest ease. In the Middle East, forgiveness is almost absent from political vocabulary. The rhetoric is of rights, justice, and history, but rarely of release.

And yet, both Judaism and Islam honor forgiveness. The Talmud teaches: *"Whoever forgives others, all his sins are forgiven"* (Talmud, Rosh Hashanah 17a). The Quran (42:40) relates: *"The recompense of an evil deed is an evil one like it; but whoever forgives and makes reconciliation, his reward is with Allah."* Mohammed said: *"The strong person is not he who can wrestle, but he who controls himself at the time of anger"*

(Hadith: Bukhari 6114, Muslim 2609).

Forgiveness here does not mean forgetting past wrongs or erasing legitimate claims. It means choosing not to let the past dictate the future.

History offers examples: Of course France and Germany after two world wars; South Africa after apartheid; Rwanda after genocide; US after the Civil War. None of these societies forgot their traumas, but they understood that reconciliation required forgiving enough to move forward. In our region, Israelis have to forgive centuries of Arab hostility and rejection; Arabs and Palestinians have to forgive Israel's insistence on its existence and its defensive military actions. Without this, even the best diplomatic plan will fail.

Forgiveness on the Trail meant letting go of the anger I carried toward my former wife, whose choice to break up our marriage and family nearly destroyed my life. Without forgiveness, I would have dragged that weight for 1000 kilometers and beyond – for the rest of my life.

In politics, forgiveness does not mean forgetting history or denying injustice. It means choosing not to live in permanent retaliation. Nelson Mandela is reported to have said, *"Resentment is like drinking poison and then hoping it will kill your enemies."* Post-apartheid South Africa's Truth and Reconciliation Commission was built on this idea. It did not eliminate all wounds, but it created a foundation for coexistence.

In the Middle East, all people have wounds – wars, terrorism, massacres, displacement. The refusal to forgive keeps the conflict alive. Forgiveness is not weakness; it is a strategic decision to stop the violence.

5. Purpose

Finally, these four elements must point toward purpose. Viktor Frankl wrote that *"Life is never made unbearable by circumstances, but only by lack of meaning and purpose."* In the last week of my trek, I rededicated myself to my family, my work, my community, and my country. A sense of purpose transformed my journey across Israel from a long walk into a turning point.

For Israel, purpose has long meant building a society rooted in the moral vision of the prophets while surviving in a hostile environment. For too many in the Muslim and Arab world, purpose has been distorted by the twin goals of annihilating Israel and asserting dominance.

The carnage of October 7th '23, and the celebrations it sparked in some quarters, showed how entrenched this destructive drive remains. But there are Arab and Muslim leaders – in the UAE, Bahrain, Morocco, Sudan, Egypt, Jordan, Palestinian areas and beyond – who are working to replace it with goals of education, cooperation and coexistence, drawn from their own traditions. As the Arab proverb says: *"A tree begins with a seed; peace begins with a word."*

Purpose is the thread that can bind humility, acceptance, gratitude, and forgiveness into something lasting. Without it, these virtues are temporary moods. With it, they become a shared vision of a future in which both peoples can thrive.

Purpose gives direction to recovery. On the Trail, my purpose was simple: keep walking; get to the end of that day's hike; finish the trek. Afterwards, it became: Live fully. Love again. Use my experiences to help others.

For nations, purpose means defining the future in positive terms. For Israel, it means ensuring a secure, thriving Jewish homeland that contributes to the world. For Palestinians, it could mean building a democratic, prosperous society alongside Israel.

Without purpose, political movements drift toward aggression. Hamas' charter speaks not of building a better life for its people, but of exterminating Israel. That is not a purpose – it is a death wish.

This is the work ahead: to replace the zero-sum purposes of the past with a common project of building – in the spirit of the Quran's call to *"cooperate in righteousness and piety"* (5:2) and the prophet Micah's dream that *"they shall sit every man under his vine and under his fig tree, and none shall make them afraid"* (Micah 4:4).

Only then will peace in the Middle East move from being a hope or a slogan to becoming, at last, a reality.

In Summary

Peace is not built only in negotiation rooms. It begins in how people think, speak, and teach their children. Our five elements – humility, acceptance, gratitude, forgiveness, and purpose – are the mental and moral tools for that transformation, and our coming chapters delve deeply into both the *why* and the *how* they can and should be applied to the Arab-Israel conflict.

I learned them on a personal journey across the holy land; I believe they can also guide a collective journey toward peace in the promised land, and beyond.

A journey of a thousand miles begins with a single step. – Lao Tzu

Chapter Three: Humility

Where we review the arrogance of so many, and note the importance and contribution of humility in various other situations and conflict-resolution experiences

> *"Everybody loves to talk about calmness and peace, whether in a family, national, or international context, but without inner peace how can we make real peace? World peace through hatred and force is impossible."*
> – Attributed to Dalai Lama XIV

One of the first lessons I learned while hiking through the desert, all alone, all day, was the importance of perspective regarding my place in the vast expanse of our universe.

Recognizing that I was alone; that no one really cared where I was or what I was doing; that whether I stopped or sped up, fell or ate or drank didn't matter to anybody was a bit disturbing. And acknowledging that what I did (or did not do) had absolutely no effect on anyone, or on my surroundings, or on the universe, was a new experience for me.

Until this time, I was an active participant in my personal and professional life, making an impact on others around me, on my country and community and family, on the businesses and organizations with which I was affiliated. Objectively, I had both influence and some measure of control over many aspects of my life. Over the course of the period between when my wife announced she wanted a divorce until the ceremony made it final – almost two years – I had tried all the tools at my disposal to understand and ameliorate the situation. My efforts to 'resolve the conflict' were as much a reflection of my belief in my ability to bring about change in others as it was of my objective evaluation of our situation. I really thought I had the capacity to fix it. After all, my natural and learned skills and talents – in communications, negotiation, therapy, sensitivity and problem-solving – put me in a unique position to successfully navigate the tensions and issues and work things out between us.

I was not unusually arrogant; pretty average for a 21st-century liberal American/Israeli man, relatively aware of my own weaknesses. Sensitive to others and willing to acknowledge my own failings. Not afraid of my emotions (or of expressing them). But I was not overly modest either; humility wasn't something I had really thought about over the preceding 50 years.

Walking hour after hour through hot dry riverbeds, often without any distractions (no birds or animals or even bugs let alone no trees or even shrubs), my mind began to assimilate a new understanding of my place in the universe; namely that I was not only not the center – even of my own universe – but I was basically irrelevant, insignificant… almost non-existent.

Although this could have been disconcerting – and at first was, in a way – in the end this new feeling was incredibly liberating and beneficial, in that it enabled me to develop a different outlook on my situation. Yes, I was divorced, alone and hurting; but in the wider scheme of things, to use a fitting cliché, given all the pain and suffering in the world and my warm and loving family and friends supporting me – and the privilege to be on the trek itself – my anguish was not only bearable, but enlightening. Adopting this sense of proportion enabled me to be more focused, more open, more accepting and eventually more successful than I was when I thought I was in control and had all the answers.

Applied to our situation and this discussion, the concept is simple: After over a thousand years of animosity and over a hundred years of warfare, we aren't going to resolve this conflict in an instant… and one individual, however talented and compelling their personality, will not be able to solve things with a speech or discussion, flash of inspiration or application of pressure.

Not that there's anything so profound about this observation; but it seems to have escaped many of those who have attempted to help the parties come to terms over the years (as well as the parties themselves sometimes). These include Count Bernadette a hundred years ago through presidents Obama and Trump in more recent memory – and countless others from the West and from the region. "I'm smarter" or "I make deals happen" or "I have the trust of both sides" or "I'm more powerful" (or similar sentiments) have motivated too many interlocuters over the years. A little modesty is necessary to enable real dialogue and understanding to emerge between the various sides to this conflict.

As described in the introduction, our conflict is multifaceted, multifarious and enduring – and that chapter literally just skimmed the surface of its complexity. To harbour the illusion that a single individual, or even a small group, over a short period of time, can succeed in bringing about transformational change after so many similar efforts have failed, is simply hubris.

A sense of perspective – some humility – can enable the parties involved, both facilitators and the Arabs and Israelis ourselves, to be more capable of real compassion and understanding of the 'other', and to be open to new approaches.

Unfortunately, humility is the rarest political quality in the Middle East. Leaders here are often rewarded for defiance, not for admitting limits. Pride is mistaken for strength. Concessions are treated as weakness. Yet without humbleness, no side will ever take the first real step toward peace.

As noted, I learned humility in the desert. There were days when the sun burned through every layer of clothing, and each hill felt endless. I had planned ambitious distances. But sometimes, by midday, I could see I wouldn't make it. My choice was simple: admit my limits and stop early, or push on and risk collapse.

Countries face the same choice. Deny reality, and you burn out. Face it, and you live to walk another day.

History is full of leaders who gained strength by admitting limits. Abraham Lincoln was mocked for his self-deprecating manner, yet his modesty helped him listen to opposing views. During the American Civil War, he filled his cabinet with rivals who challenged him. That humbleness helped preserve the Union.

After World War II, Japan's Emperor Hirohito accepted unconditional surrender. His radio address to the Japanese people acknowledged the unimaginable: *"We must endure the unendurable and bear the unbearable."* His humility saved millions of lives that would have been lost in continued war.

In 1972, U.S. President Richard Nixon – the anti-communist hardliner – went to China and met Mao Zedong. The trip acknowledged America's need to engage with a country it had shunned for decades. That act of diffidence reshaped global politics.

Humility as a value is cherished and promoted in both Judaism and Islam, and in Arab culture as well as Israeli.

Humility (*anavah*) occupies a central place in Jewish tradition, spanning the Hebrew Bible, rabbinic teachings, medieval philosophy, Hasidic thought, and modern Jewish thinkers. Far from being weakness or self-negation, such unpretentiousness is understood as clarity: seeing ourselves honestly in relation to God, to others, and to the responsibilities of life.

In the Torah (the first five books of the Hebrew Bible, the "Tanakh"), Moses is described as "exceedingly humble, more than any man on the face of the earth" (Numbers 12:3). Yet despite (or as our sages note, precisely due to) that modesty, he is both given the task of leading the people of Israel to freedom and the privilege of bringing God's word to humanity on Mt. Sinai some 3000 years ago.

The Tanakh continues to set the stage for humility as a divine ideal. The prophet Micah declares that what God requires of humanity is *"to do justice, love kindness, and walk humbly with your God"* (Micah 6:8). Proverbs teaches that *"with humility comes wisdom"* (11:2) and that *"the reward of humility is the fear of the Lord, riches, honor, and life"* (22:4). Humbleness in Scripture is thus linked to wisdom, blessing, guidance, and the capacity to walk closely with God.

The rabbinical sages intensified this focus. In the Mishna, almost 2000 years ago, Rabbi Levitas taught: *"Be very, very humble in spirit"* (*Pirkei Avot* 4:4). Maimonides (Rambam) in the Middle Ages emphasized humility as *"the finest of all character traits,"* urging that in this case one must lean not toward moderation but toward *exceeding* humility (*Hilchot De'ot* 2:3). For the rabbis, humility was not weakness but spiritual strength – the ground from which moral clarity and righteous action could grow.

Hasidic masters deepened the inner dimension of humility. Rabbi Nachman of Breslov explained that humility is not self-erasure but recognition that all talents and achievements are gifts from God. This view allowed a person to feel dignity without arrogance, gratitude without pride. And contemporary Jewish thinkers have reframed humility for the modern age. Rabbi Jonathan Sacks taught that humility means *"not thinking less of yourself, but thinking of yourself less"* — a reorientation toward service, community, and the larger whole. Rabbi Abraham Joshua Heschel saw humility as a theological posture: *"the awareness that we are not the masters of the universe, not even of our own destiny, but servants of God's will."*

Across eras, humility emerges as a thread binding Jewish ethics together. From biblical prophets to modern rabbis, it is presented not as passivity, but as strength: the ability to act justly, to lead responsibly, and to relate to God and others with honesty and reverence. In Judaism, humility is not simply a personal trait but a spiritual discipline, essential for wisdom, community, and covenantal life.

Not surprisingly, humility (*humilitas* in Latin, *tapeinophrosynē* in Greek) is one of the most central virtues in Christian thought, modeled above all by Jesus himself. The New Testament places humility at the heart of discipleship. Jesus teaches: *"Whoever exalts himself will be humbled, and whoever humbles himself will be exalted"* (Matthew 23:12). Paul writes: *"Do nothing out of selfish ambition or vain conceit. Rather, in humility value others above yourselves"* (Philippians 2:3). Jesus' life and death is itself framed as an act of divine humility: *"He humbled himself by becoming obedient to death — even death on a cross"* (Philippians 2:8).

The early church fathers saw humility as the antidote to pride, which they considered the root of sin. Augustine taught: *"It was pride that changed angels into devils; it is humility that makes men as angels."* Similarly, he wrote: *"If you would rise, begin by descending. You plan a tower that will pierce the clouds? Lay first the foundation of humility. The higher your structure is to be, the deeper must be its foundation."*

For Thomas Aquinas, humility was the foundation of the virtues, keeping us rightly ordered toward God. In the modern era, C.S. Lewis famously defined humility as forgetting yourself and turning your attention to God and your neighbors. Pope Francis often emphasized humility as essential for leadership: *"The world tells us to seek success, power, and money; God tells us to seek humility, service, and love."*

For Christianity, humility is both imitation of Jesus and preparation for grace. It enables service, love, and the overturning of pride, allowing believers to participate in Jesus' self-giving life.

Humility (*tawādu'*) is likewise central in Islamic spirituality, both in relation to God and to fellow human beings.

Palestinian Arab Muslim scholar Prof. Mohammad Dajani writes:

The Quran calls upon Muslims to believe in the intrinsic worth and beauty of all people and things, not to be proud and arrogant to think they are better than others. It mentions humility in many verses. It calls upon the believers to walk in humility and to respond to vulgar people with gentle and soft words, for God does not love wrongdoers.

- *"And the servants of the Most Merciful [the worshipers of God] are those who walk upon the earth in humility and calmness, and when the ignorant [foolish] address them [with nasty and bad words], they reply with mild words of gentleness."* (Quran, Surat al-Furqan 25:63)

- *"Call upon your Lord with humility and in private. Verily, He does not love transgressors."* (Quran, Surat al-A'raf 7:55)

- *"And turn not your face away from men with pride, nor walk in insolence through the earth. Verily, God likes not each arrogant boaster."* (Quran 31:18)

- *"Remember your Lord in yourselves with humility and in private without announcing it in the mornings and evenings, and do not be among the heedless."* (Quran, Surat al-A'raf 7:205)

- *"Lower to your parents the wing of humility out of mercy and say: My Lord, have mercy upon them as they brought me up when I was small."* (Quran, Surat al-Isra 17:24)

- *"Successful indeed are the believers who humble themselves in their prayers."* (Quran 23:02)

- *"Give happy tidings to the humble-hearted."* (Quran 22:34).

Those who show humility on earth are rewarded in the after-life: *"Indeed, they who have believed and done righteous deeds and humbled themselves to their Lord — those are the companions of Paradise; they will abide eternally therein."* (Quran 11:23).[25]

The Quran exhorts believers: *"And do not walk upon the earth arrogantly. Indeed, you will never tear the earth [apart], nor will you reach the*

---

[25] Mohammad Dajani, private correspondence

mountains in height" (17:37). Humility is thus both an inner posture before God and an outer behavior toward others.

The prophet Mohammad emphasized humility in both word and deed. He taught: *"Whoever humbles himself for the sake of Allah, Allah will raise him in status"* (Ṣaḥīḥ Muslim). He lived simply, mended his own clothes, and warned against pride: *"Allah has revealed to me that you must be humble, so that no one boasts over another and no one oppresses another"* (Ṣaḥīḥ Muslim). Similarly, he said *"Charity does not decrease wealth, no one forgives except that Allah increases him in honor, and no one humbles himself for the sake of Allah except that Allah raises him."* (Ṣaḥīḥ Muslim)

Classical Arab/Islamic Thinkers continued the theme. Imam al-Shafi'i (d. 820 CE) praised humility as the highest of virtues, saying, *"Humility is of the greatest of manners; it elevates the one who adorns himself with it."* Ali ibn Abi Talib (RA) writes, *"Humility is the product of noble character, and arrogance is the product of ignorance"*, while al-Ghazālī saw it as necessary for purifying the soul. Al-Hasan al-Basri (d. 728 CE) exhorts his followers: *"Do not sit with the arrogant, for their company humbles not the soul but corrupts it. Sit instead with the humble, for they bring peace to the heart."* Sufi teachers like Rumi taught that humility opens the heart to divine love: *"Be like a tree and let the dead leaves drop."*

Contemporary Muslim scholars continue this theme. Sheikh Hamza Yusuf has said: *"Humility is the hallmark of true knowledge; arrogance is the sign of ignorance."* Leaders across the Muslim world frequently describe humility as a prerequisite for wisdom and effective service. For Islam, humility is both a way of worship and a way of life – a recognition of human dependence on God, and a commitment to treat others with respect, fairness, and gentleness. A widely-quoted Arabic proverb puts it succinctly: *"Humility is a crown that never falls from the head of the one who wears it"* (source unknown).

Across all three traditions, then, humility is not weakness but strength: a way of grounding human dignity in relation to the divine and to others.

- Judaism frames humility as walking honestly before God and others, the foundation for wisdom and covenantal life.

- Christianity elevates humility as imitation of Jesus, the reversal of pride, and the opening to divine grace.

- Islam sees humility as submission to God (*islām*) and compassion toward people, a virtue that ennobles and protects from arrogance.

Today, however, such modesty is not valued in much of the political culture of the Middle East. Arab societies, shaped by tribal honor traditions, often see public concession as shameful. Israel's political culture, while more open to debate, also struggles with leaders who fear looking "soft" in front of voters. Self-effacement and unpretentiousness are not the keys to success in our region's societies. Nor, as noted, are they among the various leaders of the world – past or present – who always seem to be convinced that they are the ones to bring peace and salvation to our peoples.

Religious leaders can play a role here. As noted above, the Bible praises humility: *Before honor comes humility* (Proverbs 15:33), as does the Quran: *"Has the time not come for those who have believed that their hearts should become humbly submissive at the remembrance of Allah?"* (Surah Al-Hadid 57:16)

All Abrahamic traditions value it – but political actors, and the nations they lead, rarely practice it.

Humility matters for individuals, not just states. In the peacebuilding workshops in which I've participated, I've seen people arrive certain of their own righteousness. Over time, listening to the other side's personal losses, some soften. They may not change their political stance overnight, but humility allows them to see the other's humanity.

One Palestinian Arab participant once told me, "I thought every Israeli soldier was my enemy. Then I heard one talk about his brother killed in a bombing. Now I know pain is not only ours." That shift began with humility – an almost innocent openness – which encourages the willingness to listen. And that humbleness can and does encourage empathy, a sensitivity to the suffering of the other, whatever the cause.

Peace does not begin with grand treaties. It begins with the modesty to admit that our understanding is not complete, our solutions not perfect, our power not absolute.

For Israelis, this means recognizing Palestinian suffering and aspirations for self-governance. For Palestinians and other Arabs and Muslims, it means acknowledging Jewish suffering and legitimacy, and permanence in this land. For both, it means rejecting the fantasy of the disappearance of the other. It means recognizing the need to acknowledge that not all truth is on my side, nor is my/our place in this situation as central or pre-ordained as I previously believed. And it demands a new cultural milieu focused on tolerance and coexistence, infused with empathy for all humanity.

For Israelis, humility also means recognizing that military power, however essential, cannot solve every problem, and neither can technology and intelligence work. The 1973 Yom Kippur War was a wakeup call for Israel's highest military and political echelons, exposing too late their faulty conceptions based on hubris. The 1982 Lebanon War was meant to end cross-border terrorism. Instead, it dragged Israel into a costly, unpopular presence in southern Lebanon that lasted eighteen years. And, tragically, on October 7 '23 a terrible over-confidence in Israel's vaunted military intelligence and political leadership's analysis of the realities in Gaza was revealed, equaled only by the mistakes exactly 50 years prior, with Egypt.

For Arabs and especially those who identity as Palestinians, humility means acknowledging that Jewish sovereignty in the land of Israel is not a colonial accident but the return of an indigenous people. Egyptian President Anwar Sadat embodied this in 1977 when he stood before the Knesset in Jerusalem and said, *"I come to you today on solid ground… so that together we might shape a new life and to establish peace."* That modesty led to the Camp David Accords and a peace treaty that endures to this day.

Contrast that with leaders who refuse humility. In 2000, Yasser Arafat walked away from the Camp David summit without making a counter-offer, unwilling to acknowledge that compromise was necessary. The result was what I call "Arafat's War against Peace", what the Arab world called the Second *Intifada* – thousands dead, trust destroyed. The Muslim Brotherhood/Hamas and Fatah (PLO), like ISIS and Hezb'Allah and Al Qaeda and other Islamist groups, declare repeatedly their belief that time is on their side, that they will be victorious in annihilating Israel and the Jews – and that

God/Allah is on their side.

There is a direct link between an increased sense of perspective about our place in the universe, and our ability to reach true peace. Mahatma Gandhi said *"True humility means most strenuous and constant endeavor entirely directed to the service of humanity."*

Nelson Mandela is quoted as saying *"Great peacemakers are all people of integrity, of honesty, but mainly of humility."*

Israeli prime minister Menachem Begin, in his Nobel Lecture on Dec 10th '78, made that unequivocal connection between humbleness and peace, saying, *"I have come from the Land of Israel … and here I stand in humility and with pride … The ancient Jewish people gave the world the vision of eternal peace…"*

On the practical level, Harri Holkeri of Finland, a long-time peace negotiator and statesman, is said to have said, *"If you come to a negotiation table saying you have the final truth, that you know nothing but the truth and that is final, you will get nothing."*

For all Arabs and Israelis, all Muslims and Jews, humility also means understanding that we don't actually understand. Humbleness suggests modestly listening with empathy when the 'other' tells you of his/her pain and aspirations, not trumpeting your own. And it demands patience, as well as a strategic perspective, and (even with a belief in our own powers of healing and creating change) a recognition that we don't have all the answers, yet.

It will be helpful – in fact necessary – if Arab and Israeli leaders, as well as international participants in efforts to resolve the Arab-Israel conflict, adopt the approach US Secretary of State Antony Blinken promoted when he said, *"We will balance humility with confidence… the flip sides of… leadership.… Humility because we aren't perfect, we don't have all the answers.… But confidence because America at its best has a greater ability… to mobilize others for the common good."* This statement, almost lost amid the past few decades of American attempts at peace-making, was and is unique, and should be the basis for all future endeavors. (And we can note, too, its clear intention of a goal/purpose, to be addressed later.)

On the Trail, humility kept me alive. In international politics, it can do the same for nations.

Chapter Four: Acceptance

"It is what it is", how that attitude helped France and Germany end 800 years of warfare, and other stories

Acceptance is the natural extension of humility. Humility says, "I do not know everything, and I cannot do everything." Acceptance says, "This is the world as it is, and I will work with it."

"I am not the center of the universe" meets "I am not in control".

From the humility gained in the silence of the desert, and the encouragement it provided to view my life and its challenges in proportion to those of others and to the vastness of time and space, came a deep understanding not only of my relatively minor place in the universe but of the volatility of so many things in my life, and in all our lives.

Such an acceptance of reality didn't mean approval or celebration of those things which wounded me, but rather an extension of the modest understanding that I don't have power over everything to a recognition that stuff happens, and that a great deal of what happens is going to happen whether I like it or not.

On the Trail, acceptance came when I faced the facts of an imperfect body. A strained knee, a blister the size of a coin, a heatwave that turned every kilometer into punishment. I could not will the pain away. I could only decide what to do next.

Nations face the same reality. You cannot build policy on fantasies. You cannot base peace on conditions that will never be met. Yet in the Arab–Israel conflict, both sides have often refused to accept truths that are as solid as the rocks of the Negev.

I came to this conclusion while on the side of a steep and high Negev mountain, panicking as darkness fell. I considered calling the rescue services. Instead, I took three deep breaths – thank you, Thomas Crum – and told myself: You're here, sitting on a boulder three times your size. No one is to blame (except perhaps yourself); it is what it is; no one is coming to save you. Accept this reality, calmly, so you can make the correct decision regarding your next step.

And so it was that night, when I thought about applying this lesson to my life's situation, lying in my tent in the cold: It is what it is, you are divorced, now what?

I accepted that this divorce was something I could not avoid, could not fix or change, could not reverse. It didn't matter what I thought of it, or the reasons or even the person behind it; it was a fact, like gravity (or – more appropriately – death, and of course taxes).

Such an acknowledgement of reality may be the most fundamental, transformative element not only in our meeting personal challenges, but in our efforts to bring peace to the Middle East. If our leaders are humble enough to recognize they cannot make the world in their own image nor correct every wrong perceived or done to them, and accept the reality of the situation we now face, in all its complexity, we may have the beginnings of a process leading to real peace between Arabs and Israelis, and between Muslims and Jews (and Christians for that matter).

As we'll explore below, this means engendering a sea change in the way the region's leaders and people view many things – from history and geography to religious and spiritual mandates and philosophies, and in terms of cultural norms and civilizational values. So much harm has been done over centuries, so much suffering has been caused and experienced by so many – and so much propaganda has entered public discourse and affected the emotional and psychological makeup of the participants in our conflict – that this sort of acceptance seems an impossible challenge.

How can Jews/Israelis "accept" an invented claim of "Palestinian" [26] nationhood when it was not only created less than

---

[26] The term "Palestinian" identifying a member of a distinct ethnic/national Arab people within the wider Arab nation (Umma) is in quotation marks here to note that such a designation is both recent and contrived; this author uses the term with and without quotation marks interchangeably, and this usage expresses or implies neither denial of a current Arab national identity called "Palestinian" nor anything in the way of policy prescriptions regarding whether or where a Palestinian Arab state might be established.

100 years ago, but was done so expressly for the declared purpose of denying the connection of the people of Israel to their ancestral homeland? And how can Israelis accept the hand of peace from the representatives of those who have murdered and maimed their people over centuries of animosity and violence?

How can Arabs/Muslims "accept" the historical reality of the Jews' connection to their ancient and modern homeland when their leaders have educated them for decades that such a connection is deceitful, and that the Jews are colonialist racist settlers and occupiers? How can Palestinians accept the hand of peace from those who have injured and killed so many of their people over the past decades in their defensive military operations?

Without prejudice to the justice of any party's claims, the recognition that the 'other' exists – and is here to stay – is an essential element of any reconciliation in our region. Acceptance not of the others' assertions but of the others' very existence, and **right** to exist, is crucial. This may sound like a platitude – of *course* each accepts the others' existence, and right to exist they are right here in front of me! On the other hand, it may seem unnecessary: I don't have any need for you to recognize my existence; I know who I am, I know I live – your recognition of that is irrelevant to me.

And yet neither of these contentions ring true in our

It is merely a recognition of historical fact: that in the first 50 years of the 20th century, the term "Palestinian" denoted a *Jew* living in the Mandate of Palestine, and only was converted to refer to *Arab* residents of the area well after Israel was established. Hence the "Palestine Post", now the Jerusalem Post; the "Palestine Symphony Orchestra", today the Israeli Philharmonic; the "Bank of Palestine", today Israel's Bank Leumi; sports teams of Jews from the Mandate competing in international tournaments representing the Mandate of "Palestine"; the Mandate's stamps and official documents equating and listing "Palestine" as " ארץ ישראל" or "א"י" ("Eretz Yisrael", the "Land of Israel" in Hebrew, and abbreviated), etc.

The denial of a distinct "Palestinian" Arab national identity by Arab and Muslim leaders earlier in the last century has been well-documented. The acceptance of the fact that many Arabs self-identify today as "Palestinian", and that many others around the world recognize the idea of a "Palestinian" ethnic and national identity, is a key element of our approach to real peace; hence this footnote in this chapter on acceptance, purposefully.

circumstances. Many Arabs and Muslims – and most Palestinians, and unfortunately many others in the world – deny the existence of a Jewish/Israel national identity originating with the biblical Israelites and connecting today's people of Israel with their religious and cultural traditions and their land. That dismissal – aside from theological traditions maintaining that God rejected the people of Israel in favor of (first) the Christians and (later) the Muslims – is the basis not only for the hostility rampant in Arab and Muslim (and Palestinian) society towards Jews and Israel, but for a denial of the legitimacy of the founding of the Jewish State and for the obsessive calls for the elimination of the modern nation-state of Israel.

Many Arabs and Muslims do not accept the very existence – meaning the reasonable presence in our times – of the Jews as a people, or Judaism as a legitimate religion, or the Jews' state, Israel, as a recognized country in the family of nations. Similarly, many or most do not accept the right of Jews/Israelis to defend themselves when attacked – whether in medieval times or in the 21st century – partially based on the denial of their legitimacy and partially on the related status attributed to Jews as second-class citizens, or Dhimmis, in Islamic thought and practice. Combined, these two forms of rejection have galvanized the violent animosity towards Jews and Israel over the centuries, and inhibits progress towards resolution of the conflict.

Thus, acknowledgment by Arabs and Muslims of the reality of Israel and the continuity and survival of the people of Israel/the Jews is not a cliché and is indeed necessary; it is a fundamental aspect of reconciliation. This is true for the leadership and the people of every Muslim and Arab community, and especially for those who self-identify as "Palestinian".

The peace agreements between Israel and Egypt led by Anwar Sadat and Menachem Begin, and with Jordan signed by King Hussein and PM Rabin, and the more recent Abraham Accords between Israel and the UAE, Bahrain, Morocco and Sudan, have brought these concepts more clearly into focus. They began the process of introducing this acceptance of Israel into the public sphere. Yet there is still a long way to go, as evidenced by Pew and other polls as well as the social unrest continuing across the Arab and Muslim world.

For instance, 90-98% of Arab publics are reported to hold unfavorable views of Jews consistently in Pew surveys[27]; similarly 70-90% of adults in most Arab countries endorse antisemitic stereotypes according to ADL polling.[28] The Arab Barometer polls report less than 20% of Arab adults express any support for ties with Israel, including following the Abraham Accords.[29] According to Pew, Palestinian society is unfailingly ranked as the most antisemitic, anti-Jewish, anti-Zionist and anti-Israel of any Arab or Muslim nation.

The Abraham Accords reflected, and in turn encouraged, a genuine moderating of animosity towards Israel and Jews, at least in those four countries. But following the October 7th '23 attacks – and the support for them expressed among Arabs and Muslims – and Israel's war against Hamas in Gaza, that slight moderation was reversed to its previous "normal" and in many cases the animosity became even more disturbing.[30] Eric Mandel provides further numbers:

> Palestinians almost universally support Hamas terrorism. Reuters has reported that a poll by the Palestinian Center for Policy Survey and Research found: *"Almost three in four Palestinians believe the Oct. 7 attack by Hamas on Israel was correct."* Another poll by the Arab World for Research and Development found: *"98% of Palestinians said the Oct. 7 slaughter made them feel 'prouder of their identity as Palestinians.'"*[31]

Regarding Israel and the Jewish world, the situation is reversed: Israelis and Jews have recognized for decades, formally and informally, at all levels of society, the existence of a "Palestinian" people. There are some – not a majority or even a sizable minority, but enough (and vocal enough) to require addressing – who deny the authenticity of a Palestinian people. But there is no widespread rejection of the legitimacy of either the Muslim religion or the

---

[27] Pew Global Attitudes Project (2003–2019) –
https://www.pewresearch.org/global/
[28] https://www.adl.org/adl-global-100-index-antisemitism
[29] https://www.arabbarometer.org/2025/01/14619
[30] GWU Program on Extremism – "Rise of Online Antisemitism in Arabic: Six Months Post October 7" (Jan 2025)
[31] Eric Mandel, "How Many Palestinians Are Innocent" Jan 31 '24

concept of an Arab people among Israelis or Jews, nor of the validity of a "Palestinian" Arab identity.

Indeed, there are a small number of outspoken Israelis, Jews, and supporters of Israel who disparage the creation of a Palestinian Arab nationality. As described in an earlier footnote, the historical facts are clear, that this discrete Palestinian Arab identity is a relatively recent invention. Yet the historical facts are only part of the story, and the "narrative" of a Palestinian national, political character separate from the wider Arab nation is now also a fact, and even after recent decades of Arab terror attacks and violent hostility, including most recently, over 65% of Israelis consistently indicate an acceptance of a unique "Palestinian" identity.[32] (Whether this is irreversible is a different question, the answer to which hinges critically on the issues raised here.)

There are a number of reasons many Israelis and Jews accept that the Palestinians have a legitimate claim to a separate national identity from the wider Arab 'nation'. First, when Israelis and Jews argue for their own national identity – distinct from or just part of the idea of Judaism as a religion or faith community – they often stress the importance of self-identification. A people or group have the right and privilege to define themselves as they wish.

And yet it goes deeper, of course. After initially rejecting it, the wider Arab leadership and society have adopted the Palestinian's arrogation to themselves of this distinct ethnic or national label; so have the majority of countries in the world, and international organizations, reflecting a rather unique consensus in the international community. Israelis are cognizant of this. Moreover, Israelis have lived with and alongside Palestinian Arabs for decades now, and have come themselves to adopt the nomenclature almost as a matter of course. (In fact, some Arab Israelis now describe themselves as "Palestinian-Israelis".)

From the very beginning of the state, and even before its establishment, leading Israeli figures acknowledged that the conflict was not simply territorial, but one between two peoples. David Ben-Gurion, testifying before the British Peel Commission in 1937,

---

[32] See multiple results from the "Palestinian Israeli Pulse Index" at https://www.pcpsr.org/en/node/680

already framed it this way: *"There is a conflict between two national movements. Between the Jewish people that is returning to its homeland and building it, and the Palestinian Arab people that regards the country as its homeland."*[33] Even Golda Meir, who famously denied the existence of a separate Palestinian identity in 1969, later clarified in an interview with *The Sunday Times* in 1972: *"Today they call themselves Palestinians. They can call themselves whatever they want. They already have a state, Jordan, but we do not deny that those living here are Palestinians."*[34]

This recognition became explicit with the "Oslo process". Israeli prime minister Yitzhak Rabin declared at the 1993 Oslo signing ceremony, as noted in our introduction: *"We who have fought against you, the Palestinians, we say to you today: enough of blood and tears. Enough."*[35] A year later in the Knesset he made it even clearer: *"The Palestinian people is also entitled to self-expression, to its national existence."*[36] His successor Shimon Peres, speaking that 1993 day in Washington, told the Palestinian delegation: *"We are reaching out to the Palestinian people, to recognize their right to live in dignity, in freedom, in their own land."*[37] And years later, as president, he said simply: *"There is a Palestinian people, and they are our neighbors. We must find the way to live side by side."*[38]

What is striking, however, is that even conservative and right-wing leaders – often portrayed as hardline – have also recognized a Palestinian identity. Menachem Begin, in his inaugural Knesset address in 1977, put it thus: *"We extend our hand to our Palestinian neighbors, the Arab inhabitants of Eretz Israel, to live with them in full equality of rights, in mutual respect, as human beings and as nations."*[39] Yitzhak Shamir, at the 1991 Madrid Peace Conference, stated plainly: *"We have come here to negotiate with our Palestinian neighbors, because peace must be between peoples who live on the same land."*[40] Ariel Sharon, known for

---

[33] David Ben-Gurion, testimony to the British Peel Commission, 1937.
[34] Golda Meir, interview, *The Sunday Times*, 16 June 1972.
[35] Yitzhak Rabin, speech at Oslo Accords signing, Washington, 13 Sept 1993.
[36] Yitzhak Rabin, Knesset speech, Oct 1994.
[37] Shimon Peres, remarks at Oslo Accords signing, Washington, 13 Sept 1993.
[38] Shimon Peres, interview, *Haaretz*, 2009.
[39] Menachem Begin, Knesset inaugural speech, June 1977.
[40] Yitzhak Shamir, Madrid Peace Conference opening statement, Oct 1991.

his hardline approach, in his 2003 Herzliya Conference speech, said: *"We understand that the Palestinians have aspirations and a national identity that must find expression."*[41]

More recently, Benjamin Netanyahu, in his 2009 Bar-Ilan University speech, declared: *"In this small land of ours, two peoples live freely, side by side, each with its own flag, anthem, government. Each recognizes that the other has a right to exist."*[42] At the UN in 2011 he reaffirmed: *"We recognize that the Palestinians are our neighbors, and we do not want to rule over them. They too should live in a state of their own."*[43]

Presidents from across the political map have voiced the same idea – not only Peres, as above. Reuven Rivlin, a lifelong conservative from the Likud party, told Palestinian representatives in 2015: *"There are two peoples living here, the Jewish people and the Palestinian people. We are not doomed to live together – we are destined to live together."*[44] His successor, Isaac Herzog, former leader of the left-wing Labor party, reiterated at the UN in 2022: *"The conflict between us and the Palestinians is a conflict between two peoples, each with a deep historical connection to this land."*[45]

Beyond the politicians, leading Jewish intellectuals like Amos Oz, Abba Eban, and Yossi Beilin consistently emphasized that denying Palestinian identity was both unrealistic and morally untenable. As Oz put it, with real empathy, in 1982: *"The Palestinian people exist, and their pain and longing for a homeland are as real as ours."*[46] Similarly, Abba Eban told the UN in 1970: *"The Palestinian Arabs are a community with a sense of national identity, and this identity cannot be denied."*[47] And Yossi Beilin, one of the architects of the Oslo Accords and a leading Israeli liberal, was equally clear: *"The Palestinians are a people, and peace must be based on recognition of their nationhood alongside ours."*[48]

---

[41] Ariel Sharon, Herzliya Conference speech, Dec 2003.

[42] Benjamin Netanyahu, Bar-Ilan University speech, 14 June 2009.

[43] Benjamin Netanyahu, address to the UN General Assembly, 23 Sept 2011.

[44] Reuven Rivlin, remarks at meeting with Palestinian leaders, Jan 2015.

[45] Isaac Herzog, address to the UN General Assembly, Sept 2022.

[46] Amos Oz, interview, *Der Spiegel*, 1982.

[47] Abba Eban, UN General Assembly debate, 1970.

[48] Yossi Beilin, public statement, 1990s, cited in Oslo negotiations records.

Taken together, these statements demonstrate that acknowledgment of a Palestinian Arab identity has cut across Israel's political spectrum for decades. From pragmatic right-wing leaders like Begin, Shamir, Sharon, and Netanyahu, to Labor stalwarts like Rabin and Peres, to presidents serving as symbols of unity, the message has been consistent: Israelis have recognized that Palestinians constitute a people with legitimate claims to self-expression. The real debates have been over borders, security, and the form and location of statehood – not regarding the acceptance of the basic legitimacy of Palestinian identity itself.

The Arab and Muslim world, as demonstrated, are nowhere near such acceptance of either Jews as a people or Israel as that people's nation-state. This is not an anti-Arab or anti-Muslim statement; nor is it anti-Palestinian; it is a statement of objective reality. And following October 7th, Israelis' confidence in prospects for peace with their neighbors has plummeted – not least as the extent of anti-Israel, anti-Jew sentiment in the Arab world has been absorbed into the awareness of Israeli society. Recognition of the problem is necessary to the evolution of the solution, and if one of the foundations of the Arab-Israel conflict is Arab/Muslim/Palestinian hatred of Jews and rejection of Israel's legitimacy, then no resolution is conceivable without addressing that reality.

It is the thesis of this book that real peace requires real effort – on the part of all parties, but in particular on the part of the Palestinians and other Arabs and Muslims (their leadership and societies). If we focus more on the demands made on Arabs and Muslims, so be it: Truth requires truthfulness, not obfuscation.

Such acknowledgment of each side's right to exist, and acceptance of the assertion of their identity, does not require accession to or agreement with or approval of the claims of the other. In fact, as Einat Wilf and Adi Schwartz put it in their book *The War of Return*, the western world has actually *obstructed* the path to peace by indulging the Palestinians in their dream of "return".

But the acceptance of the other is a basic requirement of any form of peace, personal or national. It will require a great deal of humility as well as, critically, forgiveness – which we'll get to in chapter six. But first, let's explore how this acceptance can be encouraged and hopefully accepted – and even embraced – by Arabs and Muslims throughout the region, based on Islamic sources and inspiration from Arab leaders.

There are those who argue, especially Daniel Pipes of the Middle East Forum, that a decisive defeat of the Palestinians is a necessary component of bringing about the sort of acceptance, and societal/ideological reform, discussed here, just as the transformation of Nazi Germany and Imperial Japan required a total surrender and internal reform of their political and cultural milieu.[49] It may well be that a decisive military victory, over the Islamist regime in Iran, for instance, is indispensable for peace to be possible with the Muslim world. Our approach does not reject that assertion; rather, we seek additional or complementary – or alternative, if possible – means to foster such a paradigm shift.

We are fortunate, therefore, that there are quite a few voices and sources in the Arab and Muslim world promoting this acceptance. They are cited here, perhaps more than necessary to make the point, to illustrate the widespread nature today of this acceptance, though it remains tied to specific agreements and certain countries and particular individual leaders (emphasis mine throughout).

Anwar Sadat, former President of Egypt, said in Israel's Knesset (parliament) in 1977, "*We have lived together, and we will live together. The peace we seek with Israel is not a peace of surrender, but a peace of **mutual respect**. Let us put an end to wars, let us reshape life on the solid foundation of equity and truth. And it is a **fact that Israel exists in the region** and it is a **fact that there is a Palestinian people** who must have their own homeland.*"[50]

King Abdullah II of Jordan, in an address at Al-Hussein Mosque in 2014, said, "*We must work toward a future where Muslims, Christians, and Jews **live side by side** in mutual respect.*" And in an interview with Haaretz, 21 September 2010, he also said, "*Peace is not made with friends, but with former enemies.*"

More recently, Sheikh Mohammed bin Rashid Al Maktoum, Vice President of the UAE, said in a Cabinet statement in 2019, before the signing of the Abraham Accords in 2020, "*Our message to the world*

---

[49] Daniel Pipes, *Israel Victory – How Zionists Win Acceptance and Palestinians Get Liberated*

[50] President Sadat's <u>Speech</u> to the Knesset, 20 November 1977.

*is a message of peace, tolerance, and **coexistence**.*"

Mohammed bin Zayed Al Nahyan, Crown Prince of Abu Dhabi, said in an official statement in 2020, "*The UAE's decision to normalize **relations with Israel** was made in full sovereignty for the sake of peace.*"

Oman's Sultan Qaboos said in 2018, "***Israel is a state** present in the region, and we all understand this fact.*"[51] Similarly, at the Munich Security Conference in 2019, Oman's Minister Responsible for Foreign Affairs, Yusuf bin Alawi, said, "*Israel is a state in the region, and we all know this. **Perhaps it is time to treat it accordingly**.*"

Similarly, the entire royal family of Saudi Arabia sponsored and supported the Arab Peace Initiative or 2002, including then-King Fahd bin Abdulaziz, and the de facto ruler and the driving force behind the Initiative, Crown Prince Abdullah bin Abdulaziz (who later became King Abdullah). In its official Beirut Declaration, the Initiative refers explicitly to a "**peace agreement with Israel**" and commits to "establish **normal relations with Israel** in the context of this comprehensive peace".

The royal family has continued to support the Initiative; more recently, Saudi Crown Prince Mohammed bin Salman (MBS) recognized Israel's legitimacy in a 2018 interview with *The Atlantic* magazine when he said, "*I believe that each people, anywhere, has a right to live in their peaceful nation. I believe the Palestinians and the **Israelis have the right to have their own land**.*" In the same interview, he referred to "***normal relations***" as well.

Dr. Khaleel Mohammed (an Islamic scholar at San Diego State University) openly acknowledges the Jewish connection to Israel from an Islamic theological perspective. In an interview in FrontPage Magazine in 2004, he is quoted as saying, "*The Quran recognizes the **land of Israel as the heritage of the Jews**.... My position is that **the Quran affirms the Jewish claim** to the land.*"

Dr. M. Zuhdi Jasser (Founder of the American Islamic Forum for Democracy), has said, "*Israel has a **right to exist** as a homeland for the **Jewish people***", in a panel discussion at the Hudson Institute in 2011; similarly, in an article in the *Wall St. Journal* in 2012, he writes,

---

[51] Omani Foreign Minister Yusuf bin Alawi quoting Sultan Qaboos in an official press briefing, 2018 (widely reported in Reuters/AP).

*"We must confront the ideas that deny the **legitimacy of Israel**."*

Mahmoud Abbas, President of the Palestinian Authority, has given voice to this acceptance, numerous times. For instance, in his address to the UN General Assembly in 2011, he stated clearly, *"We are committed to the two-state solution, the State of Palestine living **side by side with the State of Israel** in peace and security."* (Unfortunately, in many of his speeches in Arabic, he rejects such acceptance of Israel.)

Even Palestine Liberation Organization (PLO) Chairman Yasser Arafat wrote in 1993: *"The PLO **recognizes the right of the State of Israel** to exist in peace and security."*[52] This was the first formal Palestinian acknowledgment of Israel's legitimacy. (Of course, Arafat played with that acceptance – he said it, then denied it in Arabic, then tried re-selling it – which demonstrates not only how important acceptance is but how resistant he and the Palestinian leadership were to the notion of true acceptance.)

These quotes reflect the evolving attitudes toward Israel among various leaders, emphasizing recognition and peace, normalization and coexistence. Many more can be found, though they are not reported as extensively in western or Arab/Muslim media outlets as the more outlandish anti-Israel and antisemitic sentiments of some leaders are. They all imply or explicitly state acceptance of Israel's legitimacy.

There are other precedents in Palestinian society as well, from earlier years. As'ad Shukeiri, an Imam and Muslim scholar near Ako (Acre, north of Haifa) in the early 20th century (who was the father of PLO founder Ahmad Shukeiri), rejected the values of the Palestinian Arab national movement and actively opposed the anti-Zionists. He met regularly with Jewish/Zionist leaders and played a role in virtually all pro-Zionist Arab groups from the beginning of the British Mandate, publicly rejecting Mohammad Amin al-Husseini's use of Islam to attack the Jews and Zionism.

Moreover, as Mohammad Dajani writes, acceptance is a value intrinsic to the Islamic faith:

---

[52] Letters of Recognition exchanged between Yasser Arafat (PLO) and Yitzhak Rabin (Israel). 9 Sept 1993.

The Quran calls upon people to be realistic, to accept the world as it is, and as God has created it, not as they would like it to be. Not all people would adhere to the same faith, and so they have to show acceptance of other faiths and other races. The Quran says: "*Say, 'You have your religion and I have mine.'*" (Quran, 109:6). It affirms "*There shall be no compulsion in religion.*" (Quran, 2:256); "*Had your Lord pleased, all the people on earth would have believed in Him, without exception. So, will you compel people to become believers?*" (Quran, 10:99).

There is no reason to reject others because they are different or because they hold different views or ideologies. No one should judge others since God on Judgement Day would judge among us in the in which we differed. "*On the Day of Resurrection, God will judge between you regarding your differences.*" (Quran, 22:69). "*O you who believe! Stand out firmly for Allah and be just witnesses and let not the enmity and hatred of others make you avoid justice. Be just: that is nearer to righteousness, and fear God. Verily, God is Well-Acquainted with what you do*" (Quran, 5:8).

The Quran instructs Muslims to respect others and treat them with gentleness and kindness: "*He does not forbid you to deal kindly and justly with anyone who has not fought you on account of your faith or driven you out of your homes: God loves the just.*" (Quran, 60:8). "*Good and evil deeds are not equal. Repel evil with what is better; then, you will see that **one who was once your enemy has become your dearest friend**.*" (Quran, 41:34).

People get discouraged in times of adversity, but in this verse, we are given the message of hope by accepting God's will. "*And had God so willed, He would have made you all a single community, but He did not so will, so that He might try you by what He has given you.*" (Quran, 5:48). "*But perhaps you hate a thing, and it is right for you, and maybe you love a thing, and it is terrible for you. And **God Knows, while you know not**.*" (Quran, 2: 216).[53]

This concept of acceptance of the other is not only theological or philosophical, or even ideological. There are historical

---

[53] Mohammad Dajani, private correspondence

precedents for traditional enemies and rivals to accept the legitimacy of the other for additional reasons.

The most famous modern example is economic, from postwar Europe. For centuries, Germany and France fought over Alsace-Lorraine and economic issues, as well as ideology. Millions died. After 1945, leaders accepted that the borders would never again be settled by war. The Élysée Treaty of 1963 turned enemies into partners. Today, you can drive from Strasbourg to Stuttgart without stopping at a border. This shift in attitude and the acceptance of the change was not ideological; non-acceptance just became too costly.

Another case is South Korea. The Korean War never ended with a peace treaty, only an armistice in 1953. South Koreans live with the reality that the North remains hostile and heavily armed. They do not like it, but they accept it – and they have built one of the world's strongest economies under that shadow. Again – war is too costly.

Acceptance does not mean being keen on reality. It means facing it. And there are many paths to such accommodation: decisive military defeat, in the case of Germany; the passage of time, perhaps, for South Korea; a societal understanding (also after military defeat) in Japan of a need for reappraisal and rehabilitation.

Postwar Europe and South Korea are of course not the only examples of national reconciliation based on acceptance. In Northern Ireland, in 1998, the Good Friday Agreement worked because the parties accepted each other's legitimacy. Irish nationalists accepted Northern Ireland would remain part of the UK until a majority voted otherwise. Unionists accepted the principle of shared governance.

Closer to our subject matter, in 1979, after four wars in fewer decades Egypt and Israel accepted they could not destroy the other without unacceptable cost. Anwar Sadat and Menachem Begin signed a peace treaty that gave Sinai to Egypt and ended the state of war between them (as noted in the quotations above). Egypt, as one of the leaders of the Arab world, was widely criticized at the time, yet gained not only tangible benefits of peace but eventual vindication, first from Jordan and then via the Abraham Accords.

In 1994, King Hussein accepted that his country's and people's interest lay in stability and cooperation, not in fueling the Arab rejectionist front and the ongoing conflict. The treaty between Jordan and Israel brought water-sharing, security coordination, and open borders.

The Abraham Accords of course are the most recent expression of genuine acceptance of Israel, and of the Jews' connection to their ancestral homeland. The joint declarations and treaties between the UAE, Bahrain and Israel, signed on September 15, 2020, are formal instruments of the UAE–Israel and Bahrain–Israel normalization agreements, and are explicit government-to-government recognition and establishment of diplomatic relations. These are primary legal/political documents, showing states recognizing Israel and agreeing to full relations.[54]

As noted earlier, UAE officials (including the UAE Foreign Minister) gave formal remarks at the Washington signing ceremony celebrating the move as a step toward peace, cooperation, and normalization. Similarly, the Kingdom of Bahrain issued an official joint communique with the U.S. and Israel establishing diplomatic relations – a government-level recognition.[55]

But unlike the sort of 'cold peace' based on governmental interests and state-to-state relations which comprise the peace treaties between Israel and Jordan and Egypt, the Abraham Accords were promoted – and accepted – on a much more basic societal and cultural level in the four countries participating, especially the UAE and Bahrain.

As the Abraham Accords are expanded to include other Muslim nations – not only Kazakhstan recently but Syria, Saudi Arabia, Oman and others (including many African nations) – the path towards real acceptance becomes ever smoother. And there is an entire generation of younger Arabs and Muslims who are ready to accept Israel's legitimacy, or at least nearer to that point, than ever before. Social media has played and continues to play an important role in the opening of minds and cultures to such an

---

[54] https://2017-2021.state.gov/the-abraham-accords/
[55] https://bh.usembassy.gov/joint-statement-of-the-united-states-the-kingdom-of-bahrainand-the-state-of-israel/

acknowledgement; a number of "influencers" leading the way have already been mentioned, such as Nuseir Yassin ("Nas Daily"). Another is Mustapha Ezzarghani, a Moroccan Muslim Arab, and author of *Arab Identity Syndrome*, who says explicitly that Jews are indigenous to the region and that "peace starts with accepting reality". [56]

For Palestinians and all Arabs and Muslims, acceptance means acknowledging that Israel is not going away. The dream of "from the river to the sea" is not a liberation slogan. It is a genocidal call for the erasure of a nation that will fight to its last breath to exist. Moreover, real acceptance means recognizing the legitimacy of Israel's establishment, not merely its existence.

For Israelis, acceptance means acknowledging that millions of Palestinians are not just "Arabs living in disputed territory." They are today a people with their own national identity, whether the political implications are supported or not. And real acceptance means an embrace of the neighbor, the former terrorist entity and sworn enemy, however painful.

Too often, both sides substitute denial for acceptance. Palestinians teach generations that Israel is temporary, a colonial project like French Algeria, that Judaism is "only a religion" (i.e. Jews are not a people), and that Jews/Israelis have no historical, legal, political or moral connection to or rights in the Land of Israel/"Palestine". Some Israelis occasionally speak as if the Palestinians will eventually "move on" without self-determination, and as noted, a minority of Israelis repudiate the existence of a distinct Arab "Palestinian" national/ethnic identity. Both are delusions.

There are many religious and cultural elements encouraging acceptance. Judaism recognizes that God accepts all of us, as it says in Genesis 1:27, *"God created humankind in his image"*; in fact one of the basic precepts of Judaism is a focus on *love* of all humanity, based on various interpretations of Leviticus 19:34, *"…you shall love [the stranger] as yourself"*. Islam teaches, as above, that your likes or hates

---

[56]

https://www.facebook.com/share/v/18R41KCYFP/?mibextid=wwXIf r are not relevant: *"Allah knows, while you know not"* (Quran 2:216).

Both traditions tell us reality is not always what we want, but it is still the reality we must live in.

Unfortunately, acceptance in the Middle East is resisted by identity politics, religious absolutism, and nationalist myths. In a zero-sum mindset, accepting the other side's legitimacy feels like surrender. But without it, peace is just a pause between wars.

This is the situation Israel has found itself in time and again, whether when facing Egypt and Syria in its early years, or Hezb'Allah and Hamas and Iran these past few decades. This is why almost all Israelis and many western leaders outside Israel as well as many Arab and Muslim leaders (whether they express it publicly or not) understand that destroying Hamas (and Hezb'Allah) is imperative to achieving peace. That they must be destroyed as a fighting force and they must be disarmed. And that allowing their ideology of rejection, denial and elimination/genocide to continue guarantees prevents any chance for true peace in our neighborhood and perhaps the world.

When I crossed the Judean Desert on foot, I couldn't change the mountains. I could only change my route. Leaders here must learn the same lesson. We cannot move each other's history, or erase it. But we can choose paths that avoid unnecessary cliffs.

Acceptance is not giving up. It is the starting line for realistic peace. Those who refuse it will keep walking in circles, wearing down their people's strength until there is nothing left to fight for.

Chapter Five: Gratitude

How appreciating what we have enables us to cease demanding what we cannot have

Gratitude is not the first word people think of when discussing the Arab–Israel conflict. Yet it might be the most underestimated force for change. Gratitude shifts the focus from what we lack to what we already have. It softens the heart and sharpens the mind. It does not deny injustice or loss – but it refuses to let them define us.

I learned gratitude on the Trail. After days of dust, a single orange offered by a stranger felt like a feast. A shaded patch of rock in the Negev was a palace. When you live with less, every kindness becomes a treasure. The support of friends and family was a lifeline – literally.

Nations are no different. When leaders foster gratefulness, they nurture resilience. When they feed grievance, they breed despair and aggression.

Psychologists have studied the link between gratitude and well-being. Research demonstrates the transformative power of gratitude, and shows grateful people are less depressed, less anxious, and more optimistic. In politics, optimism is not just a personal trait – it is a national resource.

Consider postwar West Germany. Defeated, occupied, and divided, it had every reason to dwell on humiliation. Instead, leaders like Konrad Adenauer focused on appreciation for the Marshall Plan aid and the chance to rebuild. That gratitude translated into policies that created the "Wirtschaftswunder" – the economic miracle of the 1950s and 60s.

Israel's early years were built on gratitude for survival. Jews expelled from Arab lands arrived with nothing but the clothes on their backs. Holocaust survivors came with even less. Yet they were grateful to be free in their own land. That gratitude fueled an extraordinary effort – draining swamps, planting forests, building cities, defending borders.

Israel's Declaration of Independence reflects this spirit. It calls the establishment of the state "the realization of the age-old dream – the redemption of Israel." Gratitude here was not passive. It drove action.

Over time, Israel's thankfulness has sometimes faded under the pressures of security threats, political division, and the pursuit of more – more technology, more growth, more comfort. The challenge is to keep that early gratitude alive even in success.

For Palestinian Arabs, gratitude is harder to find in public discourse, but it exists. In the first decades after the 1967 war, many Palestinians were thankful for various elements of Israel's contribution to their well-being (even while resenting Israel's control over many aspects of their lives), including Israel's implementation of a more stable rule of law and promoting greater democracy in decision-making, outlawing honor killings, encouraging economic growth, upgrading public health institutions and practices, establishment of universities and the promotion of the well-being of women. In the years after Oslo, there was cautious optimism, and some Palestinians expressed gratitude for self-rule in areas under the Palestinian Authority, for their first elected institutions, for international aid.

But too often, Palestinian leadership has replaced gratitude with grievance as their society's organizing principle – especially as the promise of the Oslo Accords receded. Their schoolbooks and media focus on loss and victimhood, with little or no acknowledgment of what is available now – education, cultural heritage, even opportunities for cooperation. The result is a population that is encouraged to feel perpetually cheated, even when progress is possible.

Both Judaism and Islam place gratitude at the center of spiritual life. There are clear and prominent roots in both Judaism and Islam for appreciation of the blessings in life. The first words a Jew traditionally speaks at the start of the day are *Modeh Ani* – "*I am thankful.*" The Quran reminds believers, "*If you are grateful, I will surely increase you [in favor]*" (Quran 14:7).

These are not abstract rituals. They are daily training in focusing on blessings before grievances. Applied nationally, this mindset could transform politics.

A few further examples exemplify this principle on the national level, where gratitude has changed history. After World War II, Japan, like Europe, repeatedly expressed appreciation for American investment in rebuilding, and this helped Japan and Europe forge lasting alliances with their former enemies. More recently, in post-apartheid South Africa, Nelson Mandela expressed thanks to his former jailers for facilitating a peaceful transition. That set a tone for reconciliation. Similarly, Ireland after the Good Friday Agreement, which as a document expresses gratefulness in various ways, was transformed: Communities once locked in hatred began to express appreciation for peace itself – the simple fact that children could walk to school without fear of bombs.

Gratitude can be a strategic asset in the Middle East, and takes many forms. Israeli leaders openly acknowledge the benefits of cooperation with Arab neighbors, from security and economic/business advantages to environmental and health advances. So do the Muslim and Arab leaders promoting the Abraham Accords.

Palestinian leaders could teach children to value cultural heritage, education, and opportunities instead of only mourning loss, and encourage appreciation for the various blessings afforded in the modern era – not least the fact that they are among the most educated and prosperous Arab/Muslim societies outside the oil-rich gulf states, as well as the recipients of more aid per capita than any other group on the planet or in history. (Given the acceptance of their national aspirations described in the previous chapter, Palestinians could certainly be grateful for the ubiquitous recognition of their national ambitions – including by Israel.)

Both peoples can and should of course acknowledge and express their appreciation for the shared blessings of stability, security, and prosperity when they occur. Voicing that gratitude now for those aspects already achieved will make an important contribution to peace.

Gratitude will not erase legitimate claims or end all disputes. But it changes the tone. It moves negotiations from "How do I get more?" to "How can we build on what we already have?"

On the Trail, gratitude made the hard days bearable. In politics, it can make the impossible seem worth attempting. Without it, we risk becoming nations that can no longer see the gifts already in our hands.

Desmond Tutu said, *"Like humility, generosity comes from seeing that everything we have and everything we accomplish comes from God's grace and God's love for us ... Certainly it is from experiencing this generosity of God and the generosity of those in our life that we learn gratitude and to be generous to others."*

Within the context of classic conflict-resolution theory, notions of gratitude are not prominent. Most approaches to international relations – realist, idealist, liberalist, constructivist, etc. – are academically robust and analytical, with little room for emotion. The idea that a party should appreciate its blessings would seem to be more appropriate to a meditative desert retreat campfire than around a hardened negotiation table. And yet to enable the sort of transformation(s) suggested here, sentiments such as thankfulness and an awareness of the possibilities resulting from a change in our attitudes will play an important role – as it did in this author's transformative experience on the trek.

There are poignant and profound references to the significance of appreciating our good fortune and acknowledging the hand of providence in all the religious traditions of the Middle East, including in Judaism, Christianity and Islam (as well as in Druze, Bahai, Zoroastrian, Hindu, Buddhist and other creeds in the region).

At the core of Jewish life and thought lies the practice of gratitude, *hakarat hatov* – literally, "recognizing the good." This is not merely a polite gesture or a passing feeling; it is a spiritual discipline, a moral obligation, and, ultimately, a way of seeing the world. The Hebrew Bible, rabbinic teachings, and modern Jewish thinkers all emphasize that without gratitude, there can be no genuine faith, no ethical society, and no inner peace.

Already in the Torah we are commanded, *"When you have eaten and are satisfied, bless the LORD your God for the good land He has given you"* (Deuteronomy 8:10). A meal is never complete without an expression of thanks, for nourishment and for the land itself. The Book of Psalms, woven into the daily rhythm of Jewish prayer, begins and ends with thanksgiving: *"Give thanks to the LORD, for He is good; His steadfast love endures forever"* (Psalm 136:1). Gratitude is not an occasional response but the foundation of worship itself, and a reflection of an understanding of the goodness of God.

The sages of the Talmud extended this principle even further, insisting that gratitude must be expressed in all circumstances. In *Berakhot 54b*, we read: *"It is a mitzvah for a person to bless [offer thanks] for the bad just as one blesses for the good."* This is a **radical** affirmation: even hardship, suffering, and disappointment are occasions to recognize divine goodness. Another passage in *Berakhot 60b* teaches: *"A person is obligated to say: 'Everything that the Merciful One does, He does for the good.'"* Gratitude, then, is not contingent on circumstance but rather a way of framing life itself.

This discipline cultivates a deep joy. As *Pirkei Avot* (Ethics of the Fathers 4:1) teaches: *"Who is rich? One who rejoices in what he has."* Wealth, in Judaism, is not measured in possessions but in gratitude. This insight carries over into the smallest details of life. Rashi, the great medieval commentator, observes that Moses himself refrained from striking the Nile during the plagues because the river had once protected him as an infant. Even inanimate objects deserve gratitude – how much more so the people around us.

Later thinkers reinforced this centrality of thanksgiving. Rabbi Samson Raphael Hirsch wrote that *"Gratitude is the moral memory of mankind."* Without gratitude, society forgets its debts and its responsibilities. Rabbi Jonathan Sacks, even more recently, carried the same message into the modern world, in his description of the literal meaning of the word "Yehudi" ("Jew" in Hebrew) as having the same root as the word "modeh" ("thankful", as above): *"To be a Jew is to feel a sense of gratitude; to see life itself as a gift; to be able to live through suffering without being defined by it; to give hope the victory over fear. To be a Jew is to offer thanks."*

Gratitude is not only about the past; it is a crucial perspective, a way of looking at the world. The rabbis captured this ethos with striking clarity: *"Whoever enjoys anything of this world without a blessing, it is as though he has stolen from God; as it is said, 'The Earth is for the Lord and the fullness thereof' (Psalms 24:1)"* (Babylonian Talmud, Berakhot 35a). In another passage in the Talmud (Shemot Rabbah 9:4), the sages' message is even sharper: to live without gratitude is, in Jewish thought, to live without integrity.

From biblical verse to rabbinic insight, from medieval commentary to modern philosophy, the Jewish tradition returns again and again to this truth: gratitude is central to a life of holiness, humanity, and peace. To recognize the good — *hakarat hatov* — is to recognize the Source of all blessing, and to train our eyes to see the world itself as a gift.

In Islam, gratitude — *shukr* — stands at the very center of faith. To be Muslim, in its deepest sense, is to live in awareness of the gifts of God, and to respond with humility, thanks, and obedience. The Quran and the sayings of the Prophet Mohammad return again and again to this theme: gratitude is both the beginning and the end of the spiritual life.

As above, the Quran itself declares: *"If you are grateful, I will surely increase you [in favor]; but if you deny, indeed My punishment is severe"* (Quran 14:7). Gratitude is not simply a matter of courtesy; it is a covenantal response. Blessings multiply in the presence of gratitude, but they wither in the absence of it. Another verse ties gratitude directly to faith itself: *"So remember Me; I will remember you. And be grateful to Me, and do not deny Me"* (Quran 2:152). To forget gratitude is, in a sense, to forget God.

The Prophet Mohammad made this teaching concrete in his daily life. He is reported to have said: *"He who does not thank people does not thank God"* (Hadith, Abu Dawud). Gratitude extends beyond the divine-human relationship into the fabric of human society. A sincere "thank you" to a neighbor or friend is, in Islamic thought, an act of worship. Another hadith teaches: *"Look at those below you, and do not look at those above you, for that is more likely to prevent you from belittling the blessings of Allah upon you"* (Sahih Muslim). Gratitude is not about envy or comparison, but about recognizing abundance in one's own life.

Islamic spirituality emphasizes gratitude not only in comfort but also in difficulty, as Judaism does. The Prophet advised: *"Wondrous is the affair of the believer! All of his affair is good — and this is for no one except the believer. If something good happens to him, he is grateful, and that is good for him. If something harmful happens to him, he is patient, and that is good for him"* (Sahih Muslim). Gratitude and patience form a pair:

one for times of ease, the other for times of trial. Together, they constitute the believer's path to peace.

Classical Muslim scholars reinforced this principle. Imam Al-Ghazali, the great theologian and mystic of the 11th century, wrote that gratitude is composed of three elements: recognition of the gift, acknowledgment of the Giver, and right use of the blessing. To misuse what one has been given, he taught, is ingratitude in its deepest form. Ibn Taymiyyah, centuries later, emphasized that gratitude is itself an act of worship, no less important than prayer or fasting.

In modern times, Muslim thinkers continue to stress gratitude as the anchor of personal and communal life. Turkish scholar Said Nursi described ingratitude as "the source of misery" and gratitude as "the key to happiness." Contemporary voices echo this message, urging Muslims to see gratitude not as a passing feeling but as a daily discipline, a way of reorienting one's life toward God.

At its heart, Islam teaches that every breath, every drop of water, every moment of life is a divine gift. The Quran exhorts: *"And He gave you of all that you asked of Him. And if you should count the favors of Allah, you could not enumerate them"* (Quran 14:34). Gratitude is not an occasional response but a constant awareness, a way of inhabiting the world with humility and wonder.

As before, my friend Mohammad Dajani offers a concise explication:[57]

> When we are grateful for the various things we are offered in life, small and big, we will see the world from a rosy perspective. The state of being happy is created by ourselves. The Quran indicates a positive link between practicing gratitude and feeling good. The Believers are instructed to show appreciation for favors bestowed upon them. Those who are grateful will be rewarded. *"Anyone grateful does so to the profit of his soul…"* (Quran, Surat Luqman, 31:12); *"If anyone desires a reward in this life, We shall give it to him; and if any desires a reward in the Hereafter, We shall give it to him. And swiftly shall We reward those that (serve us with) gratitude."* (Quran, 3:145); *"Why*

---

[57] Mohammad Dajani, private correspondence

should God punish you if you have thanked Him and have believed in Him." (Quran, 4:147).

The Quran teaches that whining and dwelling upon adverse events won't do us any good. We need to remain optimistic and keep our faith in God. The simple act of regularly practicing gratitude will improve the well-being of a person and lead to a sense of happiness in their lives. Looking back at the tough days we endured in our life makes us realize the many blessings God had bestowed upon us. *"And it is He Who made the Night and the Day to follow each other: for such as have the will to celebrate His praises or to show their gratitude."* (Quran, 25:62).

As God bestowed upon the Prophet different mercies, He grants believers similar mercies should they express gratitude. For instance, when the Prophet was an orphan, God gave him shelter (Quran, 93:6); the Prophet was given guidance in times of people worshiping false deities. (Quran, 93:7). By expressing daily gratitude, we learn how to deal with worries. It makes us appreciate what we have rather than feeling sorry for what we do not have. Giving thanks for what God bestowed upon us will make a remarkable positive change in our life.

Thus, for Muslims, as for Jews, gratitude is not optional or secondary. It is the lens through which life itself must be viewed. To practice *shukr* is to live in alignment with God's mercy, to nurture peace in the heart, and to create harmony in the community. To be grateful is, quite simply, to be faithful – in both Abrahamic traditions.

Although our focus in the book is primarily Jewish and Muslim thought, Israeli and Arab culture, we recognize that there are important Arab Christian minorities in the region (and in Israel). And so a word about gratitude in Christianity is in order. Gratitude is not simply an emotion but a way of life in Christian thought, a continual turning of the heart toward God in thanksgiving. The very word "Eucharist," the central act of Christian worship, comes from the Greek *eucharistia*, meaning "thanksgiving." From the teachings of Jesus to the letters of Paul, from the Church Fathers to modern spiritual writers, gratitude is understood as the foundation of faith and the key to peace.

Jesus himself modeled a life of gratitude, based of course on his Jewish faith and practice. Before multiplying the loaves and fishes, he gave thanks. At the Last Supper, in the shadow of betrayal and death, he "took bread, gave thanks, and broke it" (Luke 22:19). Gratitude was not dependent on circumstances but was the very form of his relationship with God the Father. For Christians, this sets the pattern: even in suffering, thanksgiving is possible, because God's love is constant.

The Apostle Paul, writing to the earliest churches, emphasized gratitude as the hallmark of Christian life. *"Give thanks in all circumstances; for this is God's will for you"* (1 Thessalonians 5:18). Similarly, in his letter to the Philippians, Paul exhorts believers to approach God with prayer "with thanksgiving" (Philippians 4:6). Gratitude, in Paul's vision, is not merely a response to blessings but an orientation of trust and joy in every situation.

The early Church Fathers reinforced this teaching, and in fact linked gratitude and humility: one cannot give thanks without first acknowledging dependence on God. Through the centuries, Christian mystics and theologians expanded on this theme. For instance, John Chrysostom taught: *"A grateful man is not one who gives thanks only for blessings received, but who thanks God even for trials."* Christianity, like Judaism and Islam, demands that we be grateful for what we perceive as bad, as well as for the good.

St. Francis of Assisi often wrote of gratitude as an antidote to despair and consumerism, and is credited with a popular aphorism: *"The joy of the heart is born of gratitude."* He urged believers to cultivate daily thanksgiving as the source of peace and generosity. Meister Eckhart, the medieval German preacher, famously is said to have said: *"If the only prayer you ever say in your entire life is thank you, it will be enough."* This radical simplicity underscores gratitude as the essence of prayer.

Modern Christian leaders have continued this emphasis. Protestant voices such as theologian Henri Nouwen emphasized gratitude as a spiritual practice: *"Gratitude goes beyond the 'mine' and 'thine' and claims the truth that all of life is a pure gift."* In more recent times, writers like Dietrich Bonhoeffer echoed the same truth, reminding believers in the midst of war and imprisonment that *"In ordinary life we hardly realize that we receive a great deal more than we give, and that it is only with gratitude that life becomes rich"* (from *Letters and Papers from Prison*).

At its heart, Christianity teaches that creation, redemption, and every moment of existence are gifts of grace. To live with gratitude is to live in the presence of God's love. Gratitude is not only central to worship but to every act of daily life. For Christians, to give thanks is to recognize God as Creator, Redeemer, and Sustainer. Gratitude binds communities together, turns suffering into hope, and transforms ordinary moments into encounters with grace. To live a life of thanksgiving is, quite simply, to live the Gospel.

Beyond these religious and spiritual themes, gratitude for the blessings in our lives is also a central part of psychological healing in personal relationships. Psychologists and therapists have long observed that focusing on gratitude softens resentment, reduces anger, and opens space for trust. When individuals pause to recognize the good – in a partner, a friend, or even in a difficult family relationship – the dynamic changes. Gratitude reorients the heart away from grievance and toward appreciation, and this shift often becomes the foundation for forgiveness and reconciliation. Modern research in positive psychology confirms what the sages of old intuited: gratitude enhances well-being, strengthens relationships, and enables healing after wounds.

What is true in personal life can also be applied to the life of nations. As noted earlier, conflict between peoples is often fueled by an exclusive focus on injury, loss, and injustice. While the hurt is real, when it becomes the sole lens, reconciliation seems impossible. Gratitude, by contrast, does not erase suffering, but it invites recognition of what is shared: the gifts of land, culture, resilience, and even the possibility of peace.

In the context of the Arab–Israeli conflict, this means acknowledging not only one's own suffering but also the endurance, creativity, and humanity of the other side. Each people has blessings they cherish – history, language, faith, loyalty to the territory. To honor and give thanks for these, even in the other, creates the ground for dialogue.

History offers examples of this principle in action. In South Africa, during the Truth and Reconciliation process, gratitude became a surprising element of healing: victims gave thanks for the chance to tell their stories, while perpetrators expressed gratitude for the possibility of forgiveness and reintegration into society. Gratitude did not erase the horrors of apartheid, but it reframed the future as something more than bitterness and revenge.

Similarly, when President Anwar Sadat of Egypt stood before the Israeli Knesset in 1977, he spoke not only of grievances but also of shared destiny. His words carried the tone of gratitude for the opportunity to turn enemies into neighbors, to transform generations of war into a chance for peace.

Gratitude in this sense becomes a political as well as a personal discipline. Just as in a marriage or friendship, where gratitude can shift the emotional climate from suspicion to openness, so too between nations it can begin to transform enmity into coexistence. To practice gratitude is not to deny past wrongs or current challenges; rather, it is to insist that the story of our lives – and our peoples – is larger than wounds. Gratitude expands the horizon of possibility. In this way, what begins as a personal virtue becomes a principle for reconciliation, a step toward healing not just hearts, but histories.

As a part of faith-based cultures, these premises, based on religious and other sources, can play a significant part in moving towards reconciliation, as will be shown below. Along with the themes of acceptance and forgiveness, they will form a solid basis on which to shift public attitudes from animosity to amity.

Thinking further on a more concrete level, we can relatively quickly suggest a number of approaches or applications of these themes to our current situation.

The Arabs should celebrate their amazing good fortune in discovering a commodity the world needs so desperately that it fuels (literally) the economies of twenty-one Arab countries (Jordan being the notable exception). They should be grateful for the recognition given in the post-colonial world to their various community identities (though the artificial divisions among them set up by the colonial powers is not something to be thankful for, as it continues to foster more conflict than accord among them, unfortunately).

Arabs can certainly appreciate the (relative) supra-national identity they have developed and inculcated, making them one of the stronger groupings in the world. And they might even be grateful for the economic impact of the Zionist enterprise, which gave work to hundreds of thousands of Arabs from around the region (and which has impacted, in various social and political ways, Arab society in general and "Palestinian" Arab society in particular).

That may be going too far, I realize. If not in logic, then in rhetoric. Aside from a few saintly individuals (whom I've been privileged to know), most Arab leaders can't really afford to express such sentiments. Not yet at least.

Turning to the Israelis, I can list (as I had started one day on the trek) all we have to be grateful for. The miracle of the resurgence of a Jewish national identity, and the reestablishment of our dominion in our ancient land, the resurrection of Israel as the nation-state of the people of Israel – is that not enough to be grateful for? "Dayeinu!" - "That would be enough!" – we Jews say at our Passover Seder meal, recounting all the miracles of the Exodus. I remember saying this out loud and laughing at myself and to myself as I hiked in the sun. And the economic miracle which is Israel? And our ability to defend ourselves (and the esprit de corps which contributes to it), and the support we have most of the time from the western world, and the in-gathering of the exiles which accompanies our development and contributes to it, and more....

The Jewish people's daily and festival prayers, which include continuous motifs of gratefulness even at commemorations of national disaster, reflect this connection between acknowledgement of our relative powerlessness and deep thankfulness for the wonders of the universe and the miracles in our lives.

Combining our three initial elements – humility, acceptance and gratitude – into a framework for pursuing peaceful relations between the people of the Middle East has never been tried. As a starting point for negotiations, this will dramatically alter both the approach and the environment within which productive discussion can develop.

Israelis celebrating with humility and gratitude the miracle of the re-establishment of Jewish independence in the Land of Israel after 2,000 years of dispersal and powerlessness can and must accept the reality of both the historical complexities of Israel's founding as well as the existence of an Arab community self-identifying as the national grouping now recognized as "Palestinian".

Arabs expressing gratitude for that very acknowledgment by the world (and by Israel) of their claim to self-determination can and must humbly accept the reality of those same historical complexities and the justified existence of the nation-state of the Jewish people as indigenous to this area.

These two steps – based on the humbleness necessary for such acceptance of the other and for this sort of appreciation for the many gains and successes of recent years – can form the basis for real and mutual recognition and the foundation for potential progress in peace talks.

But "acceptance" must extend beyond mere acknowledgement of the facts on the ground, leading to a deeper assent and toleration of that reality. The Jews are here, returned to their ancient homeland: Get over it, acquiesce to this reality, acknowledge the truth of the claim, even applaud and embrace that return as early Arab leaders did as part and parcel of the new international standard of national liberation movements (as well as for their own narrow interests).

And, similarly: The Palestinian Arabs exist, and whether historically they were a distinct national identity or not is now irrelevant; their claim to independence has been supported by the international community more strongly (and with less justification) than that of the Kurds or Tibetans, Basques or Scots, but it is a reality and should be recognized and promoted by Israel, even championed in international fora, rather than opposed.

The thankfulness which that acceptance brings can and should be a part of Israeli and Arab cultures. What a wonder this Land is; what stamina and strength these peoples have; what depth and meaning their religious traditions and culture. We in this generation are witness to the incredible, and incredibly poetic and inspiring, miraculous re-emergence of Jews on the world stage as a nation – *Am Yisrael,* the People of Israel – beyond any religious or faith-based cultural construct. And we are witness also to the emergence of a Palestinian people who, within the wider Arab national association, was until recently one of the most advanced, modern, moderate, educated and forward-looking ethnicities in the region (outside the fanatic terrorists of Hamas, Islamic Jihad, Fatah etc.).

These two communities have so much to rejoice over; focusing on these elements, with the power of positive thinking, rather than the criticisms and grievances towards "the other" and the world, will create a positive dynamic missing from previous attempts. These themes should permeate the religious and cultural milieu of the region, Arab and Jew, Israeli and Palestinian and Jordanian and Saudi and Egyptian and further afield.

The Jews as a nation, and Israel as a country, have much of this sort of can-do positivity. I know enough Arabs to believe there are those among them, and their leaders, who could sign on to such an endeavor – but their way will admittedly be tougher, given the ingrained hostility towards Jews and Israel, Christians and the West which has been taught over the years in most Arab and Muslim societies, especially among those identifying as "Palestinian", and especially recently.

This is not an anti-Arab or anti-Muslim statement; there are many Arabs and Muslims who publicly recognize and criticize this. It is an important element of the reality we live in (acceptance!) and one which must be overcome if there's any hope for our joint future.

I recall my old friend Ibrahim[58] talking, for instance, about "honor killings" in Arab society, the practice where a family (father/uncle/brother) kills a woman for perceived or real infractions of the tribal code of honor – anything from adultery to mixed dancing to holding hands in public to Facebook flirting or even just looking at a boy inappropriately.[59]

---

[58] Not his real name

[59] This is not meant as a casual list; these examples, and more, are real, and tragic; all the more so for the casual way even more 'moderate' leaders ignore or even encourage the practice, all over the Arab and Muslim world.

Israel's civil administration took concrete steps to prevent and punish "honor killings" in territories Israel controlled, as mentioned briefly above – without any public debate or discussion, as this was as obvious to Israelis as Jews and moral human beings living within a western, liberal ethical mindset. Ibrahim referred to this as just one example of benefits which accrued to residents of those areas, like the establishment under Israeli rule of five universities where there were none under Jordanian, or British, or Ottoman Turkish rule before 1967.

Or, as he was wont to note as an example, Israel promoted such a free environment for public debate and media that even today, more than 30 years after the onset of the "Oslo" process, Palestinian society still boasts more daily, weekly and monthly publications, with more freedom, than any Arab society on the planet. And this is still true today, even though an increasingly autocratic regime took control over Palestinian society through the Palestinian Authority (which jails activists for criticizing the PA president on Facebook), and the Islamist terrorist group Hamas has ruled Gaza with an iron fist for twenty years.

When others recognize and express that sort of gratitude, what a difference that will make. This has nothing to do with Israel, in fact. Ibrahim often spoke of the incredible progress the Palestinians have made over the past few decades; without knowing it, he was saying the same thing. He celebrates the fact that Palestinians have been showered with unprecedented amounts of aid; his eyes light up when describing seeing the word "Palestine" on the placard at UN fora and observing Palestinian Authority envoys being received as ambassadors throughout the world; he glories in the institutions created over the past few decades bringing his society into the 20th, and now 21st centuries. And he continually shows appreciation, with great emotion, for the recognition given his people by the nations of the world these last few decades, leading to their now being on the cusp of some form of real independence. "What a miracle!" he always says – sounding like me, we always laugh.

It is certainly the sort of thing I often say. I began to playfully connect these ideas to our national predicament in the third week of my trek, in the northern Negev desert, in the midst of my somewhat melancholy but still upbeat ruminations on how grateful

I was for all the blessings in my life. Little did I know that eventually I would apply all five concepts to our conflict. But at that time, I was focused on gratitude.

What if – I asked myself – the Jewish and Arab nations can, in their humility and acceptance of the reality we live in, reach a similar level of appreciation for all the incredible good in our world? I dismissed the idea then (this was in 2014) as a pipe-dream, though one day hoped to return to the theme. As I trudged through a hot, flat riverbed and climbed up hills overlooking the Jordan valley, I pondered how this might look, and in that spirit I'll share here my musings at the time which didn't make it into that first book. Informally, they reflect the germination of the ideas which became this book.

And it occurs to me, also, that in modern times certain societies – civilizations even –have been inspired to generate profound changes in their cultural attitudes, namely post-war Germany and Japan. These cultures were "nurtured", to use a diplomatic but accurate expression, in their efforts to throw off a militaristic, chauvinistic, fascist and racist ideology and replace it with a liberal, democratic and tolerant belief system – one in keeping with their historical, political, cultural and religious sensibilities and norms (i.e. not 'imposed' from foreign cultures, even if encouraged by the Allies).

I realize I'm actually sitting here philosophizing about tides of history and the clash of civilizations we find ourselves in (again). So as I marvel at my own upbeat attitude to the heat today, let alone to the state of affairs I've found myself in lately, and as I admire my people's continued hopefulness even at the darkest of times, I reflect on the possibilities which present themselves. Maybe if the Jews and Arabs were to learn how to appreciate our many blessings, maybe if we inculcate in our societies the humility to know we're not the only or even the most important player in God's plan, and the acceptance of historical realities however unfair, we can reach a much deeper sense of appreciation, gratitude and optimism. And if such a sense permeated our societies, led by our political and religious leaders and cultural icons, perhaps there might be a chance for real peace in our region.

My thoughts returned at the end of the next Shabbat (Sabbath) to the economic, social and political miracle (yes – after thousands of years of militant, misogynist, hierarchical culture) which is modern Japan. And naturally then migrated to our situation here in the Middle East.

I recalled something said to me by a very good friend, a Palestinian Arab Muslim academic and activist who is one of the few truly moderate, tolerant and liberal public figures in the Arab world and whose name I can't mention here (one indication of how terribly wrong things are in their society today; there are quite a few moderates – just not in public life). He insisted that most Palestinian Arabs are indebted to Israel for the many positive aspects introduced during the thirty years Israel controlled the areas of Judea and Samaria/the "West Bank", from 1967 to 1997 – i.e. prior to the Palestinian Authority taking control over 'Area A' where 96% of Palestinians live, in 1997 as part of the Oslo Accords.

He referred to principles not otherwise prevalent then – or, for that matter, now, tragically – in Arab or Muslim societies, including in the PA: values such as freedom of speech, of assembly, of the press, of religion; women's rights, children's rights, and mostly the rule of law and the responsibility of the authorities to obey the law no less than civilians. A casual reader of this account may find this list perplexing: Isn't Israel constantly being condemned as the grossest violator of human rights on the planet? Yes. But that doesn't make it true.

This isn't the forum to address those falsehoods and the ongoing demonization and delegitimization of Israel and its leaders, and of Zionism. Suffice to say that this Muslim Arab activist probably knows more about human rights and freedom in the Middle East than anyone, and he has more to say about the topic than I ever could – and it is he who insists on recognizing the reality of Israel as the champion of human rights it is.

My friend's point, though, was not a defense of Israel in the court of public opinion. He was expressing gratitude to Israel, as a democracy, which brought the standards it views as natural and incontrovertible to its military and civilian administration of the disputed territories when it controlled the population there. This is not a political statement. A fiercely patriotic, loyal, nationalist Palestinian Arab who wants and works for the establishment of a

Palestinian state, my friend's comments were not and are not to be construed as a call for Israel to return to rule Palestinians' lives. But his point was subtle, and absolutely relevant to my contemplations late that Saturday night by my campfire.

Irrespective of one's opinion regarding an eventual resolution of the Arab-Israel conflict, this proud Palestinian insists on acknowledging the reality of Israel's contribution to the development of modern Palestinian society, and expresses appreciation to Israel for helping Palestinian society to become the most advanced, academic, professional, pro-women, ready-for-democracy of any Arab society. This, despite the regression to authoritarian rule by the Palestinian Authority and Hamas in those territories over the past three decades.

Israel doesn't need the gratitude of those who resent it. But if more Arab, Muslim and Palestinian leaders were to not only accept the reality of our history and present situation, from a sense of humility, but to express their heartfelt thanks for what they DO have today (as many Jews and Israelis do), we might be able to put the past behind us.

Which, naturally, brings us to our next subject: forgiveness.

Chapter Six: Forgiveness

So much death, destruction & disappointment: Without forgetting, forgiving in order to look forward

Forgiveness is often misunderstood in politics. Many think it means excusing wrongs or forgetting the past. It does not. Forgiveness is a decision to release the grip of resentment, even while remembering fully. It is a choice to stop letting the past dictate the future.

When I was wandering through the countryside, forgiveness was personal. I carried bitterness toward people who had hurt me – in ways I thought I would never forgive. But carrying that weight slowed me down. I learned that forgiveness wasn't for them. It was for me. It freed my mind and my energy.

Nations also carry heavy packs of resentment, both as a people and as the individuals that make up the country. Wars, betrayals, and massacres pile into the national memory. If a people cannot forgive, those wounds fester into the next generation. And the one after that.

History offers powerful examples of forgiveness unlocking peace. Many of our earlier cases offer further insight when we focus on the power of compassionate understanding and absolution. Post–World War II Europe immediately comes to mind; the French and German people had fought three major wars in seventy years. Yet in 1963, Charles de Gaulle and Konrad Adenauer signed the Élysée Treaty, sealing a friendship that still holds and which formed and forms the basis for the alliance of the European Union as well as NATO. This was possible only because both sides forgave enough to work together.

Similarly, we can return to Nelson Mandela and South Africa. Mandela spent twenty-seven years in prison under apartheid; yet upon his release, he spoke of the need for courage to forgive for the sake of peace. The Truth and Reconciliation Commission allowed perpetrators to confess and victims to speak, creating a path – however imperfect – to national healing. And in Rwanda, over 800,000 people were killed in one hundred days of this modern genocide. Yet within a decade, survivors and perpetrators in some villages were living side by side. Local reconciliation councils worked on the principle that justice and forgiveness had to coexist if the country was to survive. Similar processes are under way in South Sudan, the Democratic Republic of Congo, Vietnam and other areas of historical conflict.

Unfortunately, forgiveness in the Middle East is rare. Israelis remember the Holocaust, the pogroms in Arab countries, the suicide bombings and the rocket attacks, and of course the massacres of Jews across the holy land over the past century, from the bloodbath in Hebron in 1929 to the brutality in the Gaza border communities on October 7th '23, and the many murderous attacks before, in between and since. Palestinians remember the loss of homes and lives in 1948, the checkpoints and indignities of Israeli rule in the disputed territories, and of course the injuries and deaths resulting from Israel's defensive military operations including the wars in Gaza.

It must be said, and clearly: The responsibility for the results of the violent hostility towards Jews and Israel – i.e. all the terror attacks and wars against the Jews and Israel – must be laid at the feet of the leaders and groups who instigated or incited the bloodshed, from Haj Amin Husseini to Hamas and all their supporters. And yet, our humanity demands recognition of the real sorrow and suffering of the innocents affected in the Arab and Muslim (and Christian) world, who have lost homes and families in the process of Israel's justified campaigns of self-defense. And so, yes: Arabs and Muslims, and especially Palestinians, must forgive Israel for the injury, death and destruction caused by its actions, however necessary and warranted they have been.

Each side's pain is real. But when pain is weaponized, empathy and forgiveness become almost impossible.

Egypt's Anwar Sadat broke this pattern in 1977. By visiting Jerusalem and embracing peace, after accepting the reality of Israel's continued existence, he effectively forgave decades of war. Israel's Menachem Begin responded in kind. They did not forget the Yom Kippur War or the War of Attrition, the 6-Day War in '67 or the '56 Sinai war or the attack by Egypt at Israel's independence in '48. But they decided not to live in those memories. King Hussein and

Yitzhak Rabin similarly forgave decades of animosity when signing the historic peace treaty in 1996, and Rabin had indicated similar forgiveness earlier when signing the Oslo Accords in 1993.

Such forgiveness is woven into both Jewish and Islamic traditions. In Judaism, Yom Kippur, the Day of Atonement, centers on seeking and granting forgiveness. The Talmud teaches that sins between people are forgiven only when one asks for forgiveness and the other grants it. In Islam, the Quran says: *"But if you pardon, overlook, and forgive – then indeed, Allah is Forgiving and Merciful"* (Quran 64:14). Both faiths recognize that forgiveness is not weakness but moral courage. When forgiveness is withheld, grievances harden into ideology.

In the Balkans, resentments from the Ottoman period fueled 20th-century wars. In the Middle East, old grievances have been passed down like family heirlooms, each generation polishing them instead of letting them fade.

Without forgiveness, peace agreements are paper-thin. The words are signed, but the hearts remain at war. But forgiveness does not mean abandoning justice; it can live alongside accountability. South Africa's reconciliation process, Rwanda's local courts, and even Germany's reparations to Holocaust survivors show that justice and forgiveness can be partners.

For Israelis, forgiveness means letting go of the idea that every Palestinian is an enemy, and relinquishing the resentment of the continual Palestinian rejection of peace proposals throughout the years. It means being willing to believe that Arabs/Muslims can change. For Palestinians, forgiveness means acknowledging that Israel was forced against its will to take action. It means letting go of the belief that every Israeli is an occupier with no humanity. For both peoples, forgiveness means letting go of the grievances of generations past and present, to position us for a life of gratitude, happiness and meaning for generations to come.

The first step is deciding that the future is worth more than the right to keep hating. Forgiveness is a strategic choice, not a concession or sign of surrender.

I forgave because I wanted to keep moving forward. Nations must do the same. Forgiveness is not the end of the journey to peace

– but without it, the journey never really begins. In truth, this may well be the most crucial – and most challenging – element in our process.

In the healing process following my divorce, forgiveness was almost an after-thought; my initial focus was on acceptance, and most of my attention was on the gratitude I felt regarding various aspects of my life. But in fact, forgiving my wife for leaving me, God for allowing it to happen, and myself for my own mistakes, opened up new vistas of acceptance and gratitude, as well as allowing for the possibility of moving on.

After years, decades, centuries in fact of death and destruction, there is so much which both parties have to forgive the other for. In psychological and emotional terms – which can and will be translated into practical and political terms – few of the actors in the region have given thought, let alone expression, to the sentiment.

In the Arab-Israel conflict, forgiveness plays almost no part, neither in the oratory of political leaders nor in guidance from religious leaders, not in pronouncements by activists on the ground or thinkers in academia. Public discourse is flooded with the rhetoric of rights and interests, legitimacy (and de-legitimacy), persecution and oppression; the idea of peace is often given primacy of place, and yet real plans for peace are few and far between and, when presented, often rejected out of hand.

In international relations, just as in interpersonal relations, resentment, anger, disappointment, rejection and humiliation are a powerful mixture often used to continue a conflict – whether purposefully or naturally. Unfortunately (as well-documented by MEMRI, Palestinian Media Watch, NGO Monitor, Human Rights Watch, NED and others), Arab and Muslim leaders, media, educational frameworks, entertainment and other sectors have inculcated nothing less than a culture of hatred towards Jews and Israel (and towards Christians and the free world more generally). As Natan Sharansky noted in his seminal *The Case for Democracy*, dictators require an external enemy to justify their repression at home; for the Palestinian Arabs (and many others), the Jews and Israel have served that purpose for generations.

The cognitive dissonance inherent in an Arab leader teaching his youth that Jews stole their land and raped their women and murdered their fathers but then suggesting they should live at peace and sign a peace agreement with the murderers/rapists/thieves is self-evident. Similarly, a Jewish or Israeli leader advocating coexistence but who frequently disparages the Arabs and Palestinians as terrorists or impostors damages his own cause.

Peace – lasting peace (as Rabin called it, peace of the brave rather than peace of the grave) – can only be reached if each side of the conflict actively absolves the other of their guilt for suffering caused (or perceived). This of course doesn't mean all claims must be relinquished. But forgiveness, in Jewish, Muslim, Christian and many other major faith traditions, which may come from a number of sources or angles, in essence requires a rethinking of the basis of our claims and a re-examination of our perspectives.

Beginning with a genuine acceptance of the other, both Arabs and Israelis will have to acknowledge the humanity of the other while also appreciating the other's 'narrative' (whether historically accurate or not). Israelis will have to forgive the Arabs for their centuries of animosity, their murderous attacks and unadulterated hatred, and their delegitimization and demonization of Jews and Israelis and Israel in the past hundred years and more. Arabs will have to forgive Israel (and Jews) for insisting on their rights to return to their ancestral homeland, and for defending themselves with military operations which have included much injury and damage and displacement, especially for those Arabs who identify now as Palestinian.

"Just put it behind you" is a facile and unhelpful suggestion to a couple bringing up past injuries and the accompanying anger and resentment built up over the years. And yet it is almost a requirement for reconciliation. Just as in our reference to examples of acceptance above, we can look to Germany and France after WWII for inspiration, or the North and South in the United States following the Civil War, or more recently to the rebuilding of South Africa by both white and black Africans. History is replete with powerful examples of nations and societies beset with (educated in) hatred who have put their historical enmity aside to build a better future, in peace.

Perhaps the most important element of all, such forgiveness will enable both parties to relinquish their anger and fear and turn to a positive and forward-looking search for meaning and purpose, to be discussed in the next chapter. Thus, given the centrality of forgiveness in our line of reasoning, it is worth illuminating the magnitude of this theme in all our religious, cultural, and national traditions.

Let us begin with Islam and the Arab world. At the heart of Islamic belief lies the conviction that forgiveness is both a divine attribute and a human duty. The Quran presents God as al-Ghafūr, "the Most Forgiving," more than seventy times, and urges believers to embody this quality in their dealings with one another. *"The recompense of an injury is an injury equal thereto; but if a person forgives and makes reconciliation, his reward is with God"* (Quran 42:40). Forgiveness here is not weakness but strength, a conscious choice to rise above cycles of retaliation.

The Quran further instructs: *"Those who restrain anger and pardon people – God loves those who do good"* (Quran 3:134). Forgiveness is described as the mark of those most beloved by God, a quality linked with self-control and moral excellence. The Prophet Mohammad reinforced this teaching repeatedly. Among his most cited sayings is: *"The strong man is not the one who overcomes others in wrestling; the strong man is the one who controls himself when he is angry"* (Ṣaḥīḥ al-Bukhārī 6114).

The Prophet himself modeled forgiveness even in moments of power. After the conquest of Mecca, when he could have exacted vengeance on those who had persecuted him, he instead declared: *"No blame will there be upon you today. Go, for you are free"* (echoing Quran 12:92; Ibn Hishām, *Sīrah*, vol. 4). This moment is remembered in Islamic history as the embodiment of mercy triumphant over revenge.

Classical Muslim thinkers deepened this ethic. Imām al-Ghazālī taught that forgiveness frees the heart from the burden of enmity and benefits the forgiver even more than the forgiven (Iḥyā' 'Ulūm al-Dīn). Jalāl al-Dīn Rūmī, the Sufi poet, placed forgiveness at the core of spiritual growth, portraying those who harm us as harsh but necessary teachers on the path to God (Mathnawī). Alī ibn Abī

Ṭālib, the fourth caliph, is remembered for sayings that praise the nobility of forgiving even when one has the power to punish (Nahj al-Balāghah).

Modern Islamic scholars echo these voices. Grand Imam Ahmed al-Tayyeb of al-Azhar has repeatedly called for forgiveness and reconciliation across religious divides, arguing that peace in the region must be rooted in God's mercy that embraces all humanity (Al-Azhar Peace Conference, Cairo, 2017). In a strange and almost incomprehensible contrast to his support for terror and suicide bombings against Jews and Israelis (as well as Americans and some Arabs as well), Sheikh Yusuf al-Qaradawi has also written that Islam calls believers to forgive whenever possible, because forgiveness heals hearts and helps rebuild societies (Fiqh al-Jihād, 2009). One might hope this contradiction, and this sentiment, expressed by one of the founders of modern Islamist extremist Jihadist movements, can provide a foundation for the sort of transition we advocate. It would seem possible, as both classical and modern Muslim voices present forgiveness as not peripheral but central – a divine command and a social necessity.

This ethic has found expression in Arab political and cultural life. Sadat framed his groundbreaking peace initiative not only in terms of politics but also as a courageous step toward ending war and opening a new era of peace and forgiveness, in his Knesset address in 1977. His words reflected an Islamic sensibility that reconciliation requires letting go of past grievances.

Jordan's King Hussein embodied this principle in 1997 after the killing of seven Israeli schoolgirls by a Jordanian soldier. He personally traveled to Israel to offer condolences to the grieving families, bowing before them and asking for their forgiveness (as widely reported in contemporary press accounts, March 1997). This act of humility and contrition remains one of the most powerful gestures in Arab–Israeli relations (and one which I personally remember well, having played a small role in welcoming the King to my hometown of Beit Shemesh, where the girls were from).

In the Gulf, Sheikh Mohammed bin Rashid Al Maktoum of Dubai has written extensively on tolerance and forgiveness as foundations of stability and progress for his people (e.g. *Flashes of*

Thought, 2013). Likewise, Oman's late Sultan Qaboos repeatedly stressed reconciliation over retribution in his speeches, insisting that lasting peace in the region depends on a spirit of forbearance more than on force.

Even in Palestinian political discourse, forgiveness has emerged at moments of vision. Mahmoud Abbas, speaking in 2005 after Yasser Arafat's death, urged his people to move forward for the sake of their children's future, signaling that letting go of some grievances was essential for nation-building. Rare of late, such statements reflect an undercurrent within Arab leadership that forgiveness, however difficult, is indispensable for reconciliation.

Forgiveness, then, in Islam and Arab culture, is not an abstract virtue but a lived ethic. It appears in scripture, in the sayings of the Prophet, in the works of scholars and poets, and in the public acts of modern leaders. It represents strength rather than weakness, and it offers a way out of the seemingly endless cycles of violence and retaliation. Whether in the intimacy of personal life or on the stage of international politics, forgiveness stands as the bridge between memory and hope, between wounds and healing.

Once again, Prof. Mohammad Dajani offers additional perspective and important source references:[60]

> The Quran begins 113 of its 114 chapters with a pronouncement of God's limitless mercy and beneficence. 'Forgiveness'غفور /Forgiving" occurs 91 times in the Quran. One of God's names is "Al-Ghafur". The attribute of forgiveness is not only restricted to God forgiving humans for their sins but it also includes forgiveness that His creation should show towards fellow beings.

> The Prophet Mohammad forgave Wahshi, the criminal who murdered and mutilated his uncle Hamza. At that time, the following Quranic verse was revealed: *"O My Devotees, who have committed excesses against their own selves, do not despair of the mercy of God. Surely, God forgives all sins. Indeed He is the most Forgiving, the Merciful"* (Quran Az-Zumar Surah, 39:53).

> The Quran calls upon us to forgive those who have hurt us,

---

[60] Prof. Mohammad Dajani, private correspondence

following in the footsteps of God, who forgives us for our wickedness and sins.

"And the recompense of evil is punishment like it, but whoever forgives and amends, he shall have his reward from God; surely He does not love the unjust" (Quran 42:40).

"They should rather pardon and overlook. Would you not love God to forgive you? God is Ever-Forgiving, Most Merciful" (Quran, 24:22).

"Whoever is patient and forgives, verily, that is among the matters of steadfast determination." (Surah Ash-Shura 42:43).

"And We have not created the heavens and earth and that between them except in truth. And indeed, the Hour is coming; so forgive with gracious forgiveness" (Quran, Al-Hijr Surah 15:85).

Turning to Judaism and Israel, similarly, forgiveness has always been a core value, not as an optional kindness but as a religious duty that binds individuals to one another and to God. The Hebrew Bible sets the pattern: *"You shall not take vengeance or bear a grudge against your kinfolk. Love your neighbor as yourself: I am the Lord"* (Leviticus 19:18). This command links forgiveness directly to love, framing reconciliation as a divine imperative.

The Psalms, recited daily for centuries, celebrate God as the model of mercy: *"You, Lord, are good, and ready to forgive, and abundant in lovingkindness to all who call upon You"* (Psalm 86:5). Similarly, the prophet Micah paints forgiveness as God's defining act: *"Who is a God like You, who pardons iniquity and passes over transgression? He does not retain His anger forever, because He delights in mercy"* (Micah 7:18).

The rabbinic sages made forgiveness a crucial obligation. The holiest day in the year for Jews is Yom Kippur, the Day of Atonement. In the Mishna we read: *"For transgressions between a person and God, Yom Kippur atones; but for transgressions between one person and another, Yom Kippur does not atone until one appeases his fellow"* (Yoma 8:9). Forgiveness is thus inseparable from reconciliation with others. The Talmud recounts that Rabbi Eliezer taught: *"Let one always be easy to appease and difficult to anger, and when asked for forgiveness, let him forgive with a whole heart and willing spirit"* (Rosh Hashanah 17a).

Medieval Jewish philosophers reinforced this ethic. Maimonides codified that it is cruel to withhold forgiveness: *"When the one who wronged you asks for forgiveness, it is forbidden to be cruel and not forgive"* (Mishneh Torah, Hilchot Teshuvah 2:10). He saw forgiveness not only as kindness to others but as a way of imitating God's own merciful nature. The 16th-century Kabbalist Rabbi Isaac Luria even instituted the practice of reciting each night before bed: *"I hereby forgive anyone who has angered or offended me"*, seeing forgiveness as a daily spiritual cleansing.

Modern Jewish thinkers continued this emphasis. Rabbi Abraham Joshua Heschel described forgiveness as the way history is redeemed, arguing that man's sin is never the last word and that God's forgiveness is the key to human hope (*God in Search of Man*, 1955). Holocaust survivor and writer Elie Wiesel, though deeply scarred by loss, reflected that forgiveness is an act of memory – remembering an injury while choosing not to let it determine the future (*Open Heart*, 2012). For both, forgiveness is not denial of suffering but a refusal to be imprisoned by it.

In Israeli culture and politics, this tradition finds real, if often difficult, expression. David Ben-Gurion, Israel's founding prime minister, recognized the necessity of moving beyond endless conflict and spoke about the need for Israel not to "live by the sword forever", but to seek peace so that the nation could truly flourish. His words framed forgiveness as part of nation-building itself.

Menachem Begin, who had led the armed struggle against the British and fought against the Egyptians, later signed peace with Egypt in 1979 and described it as the opening of a new chapter of peace between former enemies, extending a hand in peace and forgiveness to overcome the hatred of the past. Yitzhak Rabin, who as defense minister had been responsible for forcefully protecting his people against waves of Palestinian terror, embodied this transformation when he shook arch-terrorist PLO Chairman Yasser Arafat's hand on the White House lawn in 1993, proclaiming as quoted earlier in the chapter on acceptance: *"We who have fought against you, the Palestinians… we say to you today in a loud and clear voice: Enough of blood and tears. Enough"* (Oslo I signing ceremony, White House, 13 September, 1993). It was a statement of forgiveness –

not erasing the past, but refusing to be chained to it.

Acts of personal reconciliation have also marked Israeli society. After the 1997 massacre in Jordan, when King Hussein visited the families of murdered Israeli schoolgirls to ask forgiveness as related above, many Israelis publicly reciprocated with words of gratitude and grace, acknowledging the King's humility, I among them. Similarly, bereaved families in the Parents Circle–Families Forum, made up of both Israelis affected by terror attacks and Palestinians affected by Israel's defensive military operations, have long maintained that forgiveness is the only way forward. One Israeli member explained that he chose to forgive because he refused to let hatred define his life (Parents Circle testimony, 2015).

Forgiveness in Judaism and Israeli culture is therefore not a marginal idea but a fundamental one – rooted in scripture, shaped by rabbinic law, practiced by mystics, and enacted in the lives of statesmen and ordinary citizens alike. It is difficult, especially amid conflict, but it is held up as the noblest path. To forgive, in the Jewish imagination, is to imitate God, to choose life over vengeance, and to open the door to peace.

As for Christianity and western culture, forgiveness is also a principal component, woven into their very foundations. At the heart of the Lord's Prayer, Jesus teaches his followers to say: "*Forgive us our debts, as we also have forgiven our debtors*" (Matthew 6:12). Here forgiveness is not optional; it is reciprocal and necessary.

Immediately after giving this prayer, Jesus explains: "*If you forgive others their trespasses, your heavenly Father will also forgive you; but if you do not forgive others, neither will your Father forgive your trespasses*" (Matthew 6:14–15). Forgiveness, then, is at the core of Christian discipleship – a condition of being forgiven oneself.

Jesus modeled this teaching in his own life. When confronted with betrayal and violence, he responded with mercy. On the cross, he prayed for his executioners: "*Father, forgive them, for they do not know what they are doing*" (Luke 23:34). These words have echoed through the centuries as the ultimate expression of forgiveness amid suffering. For Christians, forgiveness is not weakness, but the very strength of divine love.

The writers of the Christian Bible consistently returned to this theme. Paul exhorted the early churches: *"Be kind and compassionate to one another, forgiving each other, just as... God forgave you"* (Ephesians 4:32). Similarly, the Letter to the Colossians insists: *"Bear with each other and forgive one another... Forgive as the Lord forgave you"* (Colossians 3:13). Forgiveness was not only moral advice but the marker of a community shaped by Jesus.

The Church Fathers and later theologians carried this forward. Augustine taught that without forgiving, a person cannot be healed of the wounds of sin and resentment. Thomas Aquinas defined forgiveness as an act of charity, a form of love stronger than resentment (*Summa Theologica* II). Martin Luther, centuries later, made forgiveness central to his theology of grace, insisting that human beings stand before God as beggars, dependent entirely on divine forgiveness (Table Talk, 1532).

In modern Christianity, this has often taken the form of social witness. Dietrich Bonhoeffer, imprisoned by the Nazis, wrote from prison that to forgive is to share in the Christlike suffering required of Christians in a broken world (*Letters and Papers from Prison*, 1944). Pope John Paul II, after being shot in 1981, personally visited and forgave his would-be assassin, emphasizing in many addresses that forgiveness is the fundamental condition for reconciliation, not only in personal relations but also between nations. Pope Francis continued this theme in the context of international conflict resolution, frequently reminding the world that genuine peace is impossible without the hard work of forgiving those who have wronged us.

This Christian ethic of forgiveness has profoundly influenced Western political culture. Nelson Mandela, drawing on both Christian and African traditions, declared upon his release from prison: *"As I walked out the door toward freedom, I knew that if I did not leave my bitterness and hatred behind, I'd still be in prison"* (*Long Walk to Freedom*, 1994). Forgiveness became the foundation of South Africa's peaceful transition, embodied in Desmond Tutu's Truth and Reconciliation Commission, which insisted in his words that there is *"No Future Without Forgiveness"*.

In America, Abraham Lincoln, in his Second Inaugural Address during the Civil War, called for *"malice toward none, with charity for all"*

(1865), framing national reconciliation as a form of forgiveness. Similarly, Martin Luther King Jr. drew directly on the Sermon on the Mount when he said: "*Forgiveness is not an occasional act; it is a permanent attitude*" (*Strength to Love*, 1963). He urged forgiveness not to erase injustice but to break the cycle of hatred and open the way for beloved community.

Forgiveness has of course been invoked as the path to peace in the context of international conflict. As we've had reason to reference at almost every step, after World War II, Konrad Adenauer of West Germany and Charles de Gaulle of France set aside centuries of enmity in favor of reconciliation; forgiveness was certainly one of the bulwarks of their efforts, laying the groundwork for modern European unity.

Forgiveness in Christianity and Western culture, then, is not a marginal virtue but the heart of moral and political transformation. It is rooted in the words of Jesus, elaborated by theologians, and embodied by modern leaders who chose reconciliation over vengeance. From personal acts of mercy to international treaties, forgiveness is presented as the only power capable of breaking cycles of violence.

Thus, across Judaism, Christianity, and Islam, forgiveness stands not as an optional act of generosity but as a pivotal demand of faith. Though each tradition frames it in its own language and stories, the common theme is unmistakable: forgiveness is both a divine attribute and a human duty, the bridge between past wounds and future peace.

To conclude:

- In Judaism, forgiveness (*mechila*) is grounded in God's own mercy. The High Holy Days call Jews to repentance and forgiveness, both toward God and one another. The Talmud teaches: "*Whoever is merciful to others, Heaven will be merciful to him*" (Shabbat 151b). Israeli leaders, from Yitzhak Rabin's plea for reconciliation to Shimon Peres' vision of coexistence, often drew on this tradition in urging peace with former enemies.

- Christianity takes forgiveness seriously, placing forgiveness at the heart of discipleship. Jesus' words on the cross, "*Father, forgive them*", and the Lord's Prayer "*Forgive us our debts, as we also have forgiven our debtors*" set forgiveness as the condition for receiving grace. This ethic shaped not only personal morality but also great movements of reconciliation, including those referenced above: Lincoln's call for malice toward none, Martin Luther King Jr.'s vision of a beloved community, Mandela and Tutu's insistence that forgiveness is the key to the future.

- In Islam, too, forgiveness (*maghfirah, 'afw*) is inseparable from God's mercy. The Quran describes God as "*Most Merciful*" (Quran 39:53) and urges believers: "*Let them pardon and forgive*" (Quran 24:22). The Prophet Mohammad himself forgave his persecutors at the conquest of Mecca, declaring, "*No blame will there be upon you today*" (echoing Quran 12:92; Ibn Hishām). Muslim scholars and leaders, from Imam al-Ghazali to King Abdullah II of Jordan, have emphasized forgiveness as the path to healing wounded societies.

Thus, what unites these traditions is the conviction that forgiveness is not mere sentiment, but an act of moral courage and social necessity; not weakness but strength: the power to break the cycle of vengeance. To forgive is not to erase justice, but to create the conditions where justice and peace can coexist. This is why forgiveness is woven into public life as well as private piety. From South Africa's Truth and Reconciliation Commission to the Franco-German reconciliation after World War II, forgiveness has proven itself as the only power strong enough to overcome entrenched hatred.

For Israelis and Palestinian Arabs, and for the broader Arab–Israel conflict, this shared moral ground offers profound possibilities. As each side draws upon its deepest religious and cultural traditions, the demand for vengeance can give way to the possibility of forgiveness and reconciliation, and mutual blame transformed into shared healing. Forgiveness does not deny pain; it honors it by refusing to let it dictate the future. The Jewish, Christian, and Muslim traditions all affirm the same: to forgive is to choose life over death, peace over endless war.

As I realized on my trek across Israel, this idea — authentic, genuine, sincere forgiveness, which enabled me to heal from my devastating divorce – is a necessary element in any potential reconciliation between the Arabs and the Jews and Israelis, between the world of Islam and the world of Judaism. This empathetic, compassionate forgiveness may be the most pivotal element on which real peace in the region rests. Without this aspect, all the resentment and hostility built up over the years, and reinforced by repetition, and educational/cultural frameworks which focus on blaming the 'other', render futile all our efforts at compromise or trust-building gestures.

Earlier, we noted how all of our elements are intertwined. We can't deny that the appreciation for our national blessings will be difficult for Arabs and Jews, given the suffering experienced on both sides (without reference to culpability). But those who reach a humble acceptance of the imperfect reality we find ourselves in, and who work to be grateful for the many good and great gifts we've been given, can find the path to forgiveness… and peace.

If our goal is peace, it is indeed possible.

But is that our mutual goal?

Chapter Seven: Purpose

What are Arab societies and Israel looking to achieve, in the long run? What will real peace look like for the countries and their people?

Purpose is the element that binds all the others together. Without humility, we lose perspective. Without acceptance, we deny reality. Without gratitude, we sour. Without forgiveness, we remain chained to the past. But without purpose, even if we have all the others, we drift.

My sense of purpose on the Trail was simple at first: complete that day's climb, get to the end of the week, finish the trek. But as I walked, it deepened. It became about healing, proving to myself I could endure, and finding joy and love again. Literally finding my (new) path in life, a reason to live and give my life meaning. Purpose turned the journey from a long hike into a life-changing experience.

For nations, purpose is the compass that points toward the future. Without it, politics becomes reactive, driven only by greed or grievance or fear. Purpose sets a direction and a goal that makes effort and sacrifice worthwhile.

Throughout history, nations that recover from catastrophe usually do so because they embrace a shared purpose that transcends immediate survival. For instance, in the United States after the Civil War, Abraham Lincoln's vision of "a new birth of freedom" gave the country a higher purpose than simply reuniting the states. In postwar Japan, after 1945, Japan's leaders defined their purpose as rebuilding their economy and becoming a peaceful, technologically advanced nation. Within a generation, Japan had transformed from a defeated empire to a global leader in innovation. A less-well known illustration of the concept is Singapore: In 1965, newly independent and resource-poor, Singapore could have spiraled into poverty. Instead, Lee Kuan Yew set the national purpose as building a prosperous, corruption-free, world-class city-state. That clarity drove every policy decision.

Purpose can unite, but it can also destroy. When a nation defines its identity by the destruction of another, it locks itself in permanent hostility. Nazi Germany's purpose was the domination of "Aryan" power and the eradication of Jews. The Khmer Rouge in Cambodia defined their purpose as eliminating all foreign and capitalist influence. This sort of negative purpose is destructive – to its own people, and to all others. As noted, Sharansky argues that dictators *need* these sorts of internal/external enemies to warrant their suppression of their own people – as Iran and others do today – while democracies force leaders to focus on providing benefits to their people to promote their own reelection. Free societies encourage the promotion of constructive purpose.

In the Middle East, far too many Arab and Muslim leaders, organizations, and even states declare – as Hamas's founding charter and as Iran's leaders do clearly – the obliteration of Israel as its central mission. That is not a constructive purpose. It produces no plan for education, prosperity, or cultural flourishing, let alone for peace or regional development – only for endless war. It is illuminating, however, that such a goal actually has united many societies which otherwise would be at odds. As Eric Mandel put it succinctly in an article in early '26:

> Hamas is Sunni Arab and jihadist; Iran is Persian and Shi'ite. Theologically and historically, they should be bitter enemies. Yet they cooperate closely because they share a higher priority: the destruction of Israel. When interests converge, identity conflicts can be set aside.

> Egypt and Turkey offer another example of apparent contradiction. Both are Sunni powers that once competed for leadership of the Sunni world. Erdoğan's Turkey is deeply rooted in Muslim Brotherhood ideology, while Egypt's President Abdel Fattah al-Sisi views the Brotherhood as a mortal threat.[61]

In other words, Muslim (and Christian) Arab ideology, politics and even religious rivalries have been subordinated to this idea of a shared aim or purpose. One need only observe how Hamas (and, for that matter, Arafat and Abbas' Fatah, the leading party of the Palestinian Liberation Organization [PLO]) have used the funds at their disposal, including massive international aid monies, to build

---

[61] https://mepinanalysis.org/2026/02/why-americas-western-lens-fails-to-understand-middle-east-dynamics/

terrorist infrastructure (tunnels, explosives, missiles etc.) and support the families of terrorists through the Palestinian Authority's 'pay-to-slay' programs like their 'Prisoner's Fund' and 'Martyr's Fund', to recognize how extensive this purposeful and perverse allocation of resources is.

In contrast, Israel's founding purpose was clear: to be a secure homeland for the Jewish people. Over decades, that purpose expanded to include building a vibrant democracy, advancing science and technology, and contributing humanitarian aid abroad. This conscious goal has given Israel resilience in the face of constant threats.

Palestinians have shown moments of constructive purpose – building institutions under the Palestinian Authority, investing in education, developing cultural life. But too often, leadership has let the destructive purpose of "resistance" overshadow constructive goals. A vision that defines success only by Israel's disappearance leaves no space for building a better life for Palestinians themselves.

In February 1947, in a speech to the British Parliament, British Foreign Minister Ernest Bevin explained lucidly why Great Britain could no longer carry out the mandate with which it was entrusted by the League of Nations (to foment the creation of a national homeland for the Jewish people in Palestine), sending the issue back to the United Nations: *"His Majesty's Government have thus been faced with an irreconcilable conflict of principles… For the Jews the essential point of principle is the creation of a sovereign Jewish State. For the Arabs, the essential point of principle is to **resist to the last the establishment of Jewish sovereignty** in any part of Palestine"* (emphasis added). Needless to say, this "resistance" as a singular and overriding goal damages the Arab and Palestinian cause, as it has for well over a century.

Yet both Jewish and Islamic traditions link purpose to divine mission.

- The Hebrew Bible describes Israel as a *"light unto the nations"* (Isaiah 42:6) – a moral and ethical calling beyond survival.

- The Quran calls Muslims the *"best nation produced [as an example] for mankind"* (Quran 3:110), charged with enjoining what is right and forbidding what is wrong.

In both cases, the higher purpose is constructive, not destructive. It is about improving the world, not erasing the other.

For peace to take hold, both peoples need a shared layer of purpose. This does not mean identical national visions – Israel will remain a Jewish state, Palestinian Arabs will seek their own self-determination – but it means both must include stability, prosperity, and coexistence as part of their future.

When leaders focus on this kind of purpose, negotiations stop being just about dividing land. They become about building a shared future worth having. The 1994 Jordan–Israel peace treaty worked in part because both sides saw common interests and mutual purpose: water security, economic cooperation, and a stable border. The Abraham Accords, even more importantly, connected a principled acceptance of the natural place of the people of Israel in the region with the benefits of peace, focusing on the shared aims and values, history and religious traditions of all the parties – and not just shared interests.

When I lost sight of my purpose, walking with a 50-pound backpack became a grind. When I remembered it, every step made sense – even the painful ones. The same is true for nations. Purpose turns survival into progress, and conflict into a challenge worth overcoming. A purpose focused on building can unite. A purpose focused on destroying will always divide. Every nation must decide which path it will walk.

Nationally, as a people, within a cultural and religious tradition, having a sense of purpose provides meaning which transcends; in Judaism and for Israel, there is a keen and intentional, aspirational commitment to the future on two levels: covenant, and renewal.

In Jewish thought, purpose is not a philosophical afterthought but the foundation of life itself. The covenant between God and Israel defines existence: not survival for its own sake, but survival as mission. *"See, I have set before you this day life and good, death and evil … therefore choose life, that you and your offspring may live"* (Deuteronomy 30:15,19). Purpose is thus bound to choice, to aligning life with higher values.

The prophets crystallized this mission. Micah declared: *"What does the Lord require of you? To act justly, to love mercy, and to walk humbly with your God"* (Micah 6:8). Isaiah broadened the scope outward: *"I, the Lord, have called you in righteousness … and set you as a light unto the nations"* (Isaiah 42:6). Jewish purpose was thus never inward-looking. It demanded moral example.

The rabbinic tradition reinforced this sense of collective responsibility. Rabbi Tarfon's words in *Pirkei Avot* (2:16) endure: *"It is not your duty to finish the work, but neither are you free to desist from it."* Even if redemption is incomplete, every Jew is bound to contribute to it. Maimonides taught that each person must view themselves as if their single action could tilt the balance of the world toward salvation or ruin – a radical reminder that every deed has purpose.

Modern Jewish experience has both tested and affirmed this idea. The Holocaust created unspeakable suffering, yet Viktor Frankl, its survivor, transformed it into insight: *"Those who have a 'why' to live can bear almost any 'how'."* (*Man's Search for Meaning*). His words encapsulate the Jewish conviction that purpose anchors dignity even in despair.

The rebirth of Israel in 1948 carried this same ethos. As noted in the introductory review of the conflict, David Ben-Gurion insisted that the State of Israel will be judged by its moral character and human values. Golda Meir challenged the Arab nation with a similar charge, widely quoted as saying: *"Peace will come when the Arabs love their children more than they hate us."* Her words framed peace itself as a purpose that transcends grievance.

Yitzhak Rabin linked purpose with courage when he declared on the White House lawn in 1993 – worth quoting again – *"We who have fought against you, the Palestinians, we say to you today in a loud and clear voice: Enough of blood and tears. Enough."* Even Menachem Begin, the hardline conservative leader who signed the peace agreement with Egypt, said of Anwar Sadat's visit to Jerusalem: *"History will record your courage, for you came to us with an outstretched hand."*

Benjamin Netanyahu, often viewed as hawkish, nevertheless has reflected similar themes that Israel must not only defend itself, but must also be a beacon of progress, of freedom, of innovation. This reflects a continuity: for Jews and Israelis, purpose is covenantal, national, and moral, a compass pointing outward toward creation and contribution.

In Islam and the Arab world, purpose is also clear and unambiguous, focused on submission and community. God declares in the Quran: *"I did not create jinn and humans except to worship Me"* (Quran 51:56). Worship (*'ibadah*) encompasses prayer, charity, justice, and striving for good. Life is thus purposeful by design, aligned with divine will.

The Quran consistently ties worship to justice: *"We sent Our messengers with clear proofs and sent down with them the Book and the balance, so that the people may uphold justice"* (Quran 57:25). Mohammad himself taught: *"The best of people are those who are most beneficial to others"* (al-Mu'jam al-Awsaṭ 5937). Life's meaning is not found in selfishness but in service.

Classical scholars deepened this. Al-Ghazali emphasized *jihad al-nafs*, the inner struggle against arrogance and desire, as the true foundation of a purposeful life. Ibn Khaldun argued that civilizations rise or fall depending on whether they remain faithful to their founding purpose. A society without purpose decays.

Modern Arab leaders have drawn on this heritage. King Faisal of Saudi Arabia once said: *"Our mission is not only to defend our lands but to protect the values of Islam which give meaning to our lives."* Gamal Abdel Nasser framed Arab independence as a restoration of dignity, insisting that the most important thing is that the Arab people should regain their self-respect.

King Abdullah II of Jordan frequently speaks of collective purpose. Aside from his statement quoted above regarding a future where all peoples of the region live together in mutual respect, he said (in a speech at the UN General Assembly in 2012), *"The children of this region deserve a future free of conflict and full of opportunity."* And in an address to the European Parliament Address in 2007, he said, *"We seek a peace that honors the dignity of every human being."*

Anwar Sadat's 1977 visit to Jerusalem was perhaps the most dramatic embodiment of national purpose redefined, when he told the Knesset that he had come to establish a durable peace, out of a conviction that the Arab and Israeli/Jewish peoples deserve to live in security and dignity. His assassination four years later only underlined the courage of reframing Arab purpose from war to peace.

Cultural voices, too, have invoked purpose as endurance. Palestinian poet Mahmoud Darwish wrote: *"We suffer from an incurable disease called hope."* Despite conflict, he cast purpose as continuity and vision. More recently, Sheikh Abdullah bin Bayyah, a leading Muslim scholar, has said that the purpose of religion is to make the world a dwelling place of peace, mercy, and justice.

Mohammad Dajani writes:

Humans, in general, are looking to achieve the same goals, such as happiness, security, prosperity on earth, and to be admitted to paradise after death. This objective cannot be achieved when people conflict, but when they live in peace.

In Islam, the purpose of the meaning of life is rooted in faith in the belief in the Oneness of God as described in the messages taught by the prophets to the various nations of the world and reaffirmed in the Quran: To recognize the Oneness of God and to worship Him. *"I do with this bear witness that there is no god but God."*

According to Islam, there has been an important message which God has revealed through all prophets: *"Indeed, We have sent a messenger to every nation (saying), 'Worship God and avoid false gods...'."* (Quran, 16:36). Consequently, the humankind of different faiths has an equal chance to eternal life, as ordained by divine justice.[62]

Thus, in Islam and Arab culture, purpose is both divine and communal, a balance of submission to God and service to humanity, guiding societies through struggle toward dignity and peace.

Christianity, for its part, locates purpose in Jesus' message of love and redemption. Jesus declared: *"I have come that they may have life, and have it abundantly"* (John 10:10). Abundance here refers to meaning, not wealth. He taught: *"Whoever wants to be great among you must be your servant"* (Mark 10:43). Paul expanded this into communal life: *"We are co-workers in God's service; you are God's field, God's building"* (1 Corinthians 3:9).

The Western political imagination drew deeply on this theology.

---

[62] Prof. Mohammed Dajani, private correspondence

The Puritans envisioned America as a "city upon a hill", with a life of work and service at its core. Abraham Lincoln aside from framing America's purpose as mentioned above as "a new birth of freedom," in his second inaugural he called on the nation to heal: *"… let us strive to bind up the nation's wounds."*

In the 20th century, this tradition inspired many movements for justice and peace. Martin Luther King Jr. preached: *"Life's most persistent and urgent question is, 'What are you doing for others?'"* He called for the "beloved community," a vision of shared purpose grounded in Christian love and civic responsibility. John F. Kennedy echoed this civic ethic: *"Ask not what your country can do for you – ask what you can do for your country."*

Western leaders carried this forward into reconciliation. Konrad Adenauer of Germany insisted: *"The future belongs to those who build it with courage and purpose, not to those who cling to the bitterness of the past."* Nelson Mandela, as an African drawing heavily on Christian themes, declared: *"Courageous people do not fear forgiving, for the sake of peace."* Pope Francis, in a global register, insisted that our goal today must connote unity: *"A nation's greatness is measured by how it treats its most vulnerable, and our shared purpose is to build a common home."*

More recently, in his Dec '25 Christmas address, Pope Leo XIV quoted from the poem "Peace Upon You" by none other than the Israeli poet Yehudah Amichai (in Hebrew) – namely, Amichai's yearning for "peace without the noise of clashing swords. Let it be light above us, like lazy white foam." The pope said he wanted to "express God's will for peace and reconciliation" through the words of the renowned Jewish Israeli war veteran and peace activist.

Thus, Christianity and the West see purpose as service, redemption, and moral responsibility –the transformation of suffering into renewal and the creation of societies anchored in justice and love, and peace.

Placed together, these traditions converge. Judaism frames purpose as covenant and renewal – to be a light to the nations. Islam frames it as submission and service – to worship God by building just communities. Christianity frames it as love and redemption – to heal and serve.

Modern leaders across these traditions echo this in strikingly similar language. As noted, Ben-Gurion said Israel's true test would be its moral values. Sadat declared that peace itself was Egypt's new purpose. Lincoln spoke of binding wounds; King of a beloved community; Mandela of courage to forgive. All affirm Victor Frankl's insight: *"Ever more people today have the means to live, but no meaning to live for."* Without a "why," nations become lost; with it, they endure and transcend.

For Israel, for the Arab world, and for the West, the challenge is not only to survive, but to redefine purpose beyond grievance or domination. Purpose must mean building, creating, and reconciling. Humility lowers barriers; gratitude heals bitterness; forgiveness opens the future. Purpose directs these virtues toward a common horizon.

This shared purpose has, at rare but unforgettable moments, revealed itself in acts of mourning that became acts of reconciliation. When Anwar Sadat was assassinated in 1981, his funeral drew world leaders from across the divides of the Cold War and the Middle East. Three U.S. presidents – Carter, Ford, and Nixon – stood alongside Israel's Prime Minister Menachem Begin, Syria's Vice President, and Jordan's King Hussein. The ancient Jewish teaching, *"He who saves a single life saves an entire world"* (Mishna Sanhedrin 4(5), is echoed in Islamic tradition: *"Whoever saves one life, it is as if he had saved all of humanity"* (Quran 5:32). Sadat's vision was to save his people from endless cycles of war; in death, his funeral testified that his purpose transcended borders, compelling even adversaries to honor him. His life and death became a demonstration of Islam's insistence that purpose is bound to mercy, reconciliation, and the pursuit of justice.

Similarly, at Yitzhak Rabin's funeral in 1995, global leaders – Bill Clinton, King Hussein, Hosni Mubarak, Prince Charles and others – mourned along with tens of thousands of Israelis, myself included, who filled Mount Herzl in silence. King Hussein, once Rabin's battlefield enemy, eulogized him tenderly: *"You lived as a soldier; you died as a soldier for peace. We shall not rest until the mission you began is completed."* Rabin's personal purpose, rooted in the Jewish command to *"seek peace and pursue it"* (Psalm 34:15), outlived him and was taken up even by his former foes. His funeral became a Jewish moment of covenantal renewal, in which Israel's purpose was publicly affirmed as much more than survival – it was the sacred duty to transform conflict into peace.

From the perspective of the Christian West, both funerals bore unmistakable echoes of its own ideals of forgiveness and redemptive purpose. Bill Clinton's farewell to Rabin – *"Shalom, ḥaver"* ("Goodbye, friend") – captured the Christian-inflected hope that love and friendship can overcome hatred and division. Sadat's funeral, too, with American leaders present in solidarity, illustrated a Christian understanding of purpose as the building of bridges, the breaking down of walls of hostility (Ephesians 2:14), and the possibility of peace that transcends enmity.

Taken together, the funerals of Sadat and Rabin embody what Judaism, Islam, and Christianity teach about purpose: that it is not merely about power, survival, or prosperity, but about guiding nations toward justice, healing, and peace. Sadat and Rabin were slain by extremists within their own communities – yet their funerals gathered enemies into a single human congregation, however briefly. Their deaths revealed the power of purpose to outlive violence, to point beyond vengeance, and to gather Jews, Arabs, Muslims, Christians, and Westerners alike under the same sky of grief and hope.

Purpose, then, is not merely an abstraction. It is manifest when enemies bow their heads together, when prayers are spoken across divides, when the dead call the living to a higher loyalty. It is only when nations rediscover such a shared purpose – survival tied to service, justice, and renewal – that reconciliation becomes not just possible but inevitable. Purpose is the compass that points from war to peace, from fear to hope, from division to the possibility of a common future.

A sense of purpose; a shared goal; a focus for the national enterprise – these are standard fundamentals of the ethos and identity which bind like-minded people sharing a history in a particular place together. Goals are what give our life meaning, as Viktor Frankl taught us. In a very real way, as I finished walking the Israel Trail, I rededicated myself to some of the main purposes in my life – personal, communal, professional and national – and this was an important, and fitting, conclusion to the trek, the healing it engendered, and the beginning of my life-after-the-divorce. This sense of purpose on many levels enabled me to finally move from anger and pain to a forward-looking empathy and positivity, to regain my natural exuberance and optimism. The parallel to national healing and focus on goals is clear.

The Jewish people – the people of Israel – have returned to sovereignty in their ancient homeland, the land of Israel, and established their modern nation-state of Israel. A combination of humility, acceptance, gratitude and forgiveness has enabled a rededication to the shared values of the past millennia, to build an ethical and productive, mutually-supportive society. Through its success this society is bringing light and goodness and prosperity to humanity, while carrying the moral message of the prophets to the world – now in a modern nation-state. This deliberate commitment to making a difference, inherent in Jewish tradition over 3500 years, was augmented by the more recent dedication to creating a state for the Jews – i.e. Zionism – and then to helping to build or support and defend that newly re-established Jewish commonwealth since 1948.

This devotion to purpose permeates all aspects of Israeli society today, driving a diverse set of accomplishments from the world's leading public health system to the celebrated "startup nation" innovation in technology and medical and agricultural science and many others to boot – not least promoting regional and international cooperation efforts. All this, while under constant attack – military, diplomatic, media, academic and philosophical – from those who would deny legitimacy to Israel's founding and who wish to destroy it physically.

Frankl's understanding of purpose is presented as a basic aspect of human nature: that with goals and aims which rise above our own mundane needs we can imbue our lives with meaning and satisfaction. And people with reason to live are more likely to both survive and thrive.

So too with nations. As a people, we can carry out deeds and innovate new ideas, policies and products; relate and cooperate with others, both individuals or countries; and develop as a people both morally and physically. Anyone with any familiarity with Israel – the real Israel, in all its complexity, not that presented by the world's media – knows that the nation-state of the Jewish people, with all its creative energy, its reaching out to the nations around it and across the globe, and its continual and constant development and advancement, is a phenomenal example of just that. Moreover, the technology innovations invented in Israel are persistently shared with the world, not least among them life-saving medical tools and skills; and Israel is a leading first-responder to catastrophes – even in countries with which it has no diplomatic relations.

This idea of purpose, when relating to the Arab-Israel conflict, might seem the most obvious element of a solution, and yet it presents specific challenges. As mentioned above, many of the political, religious, educational and cultural leaders of the Arab and Muslim world have focused, over the past century and especially the last few decades, on one of two specific goals, which they relate to as expressions of the highest values of Muslim and Arab identity.

The first is the expansion and glorification of Islam as the revelatory endpoint of human development (and the primary component of Arab identity); the second is the annihilation of Israel and subjugation of the Jews (and Christians, and all non-Muslims). Both of these aims play a significant role in the rhetoric of a full return of Islam to supremacy, in the region and the world – and are echoed by non-Arab Muslim proponents in Iran, Turkey and elsewhere.

As noted in the prologue, the October 7th, '23 Hamas massacre carried out on the Shabbat celebration of Shmini Atzeret/Simhat Torah came as a wake-up call as this book was being written. It serves to magnify the points made here and the need for other voices in to be heard, listened to, amplified and encouraged.

In the days, months and years since that infamous day, Hamas' rhetoric of hatred, violence, rejection and extermination, repeating these two aims, was parroted not only by Salafi and Jihadist regimes like Iran and Hezb'Allah, ISIS and the Taliban, but by many mainstream affiliates of the Muslim Brotherhood and governments from Qatar and Yemen to Turkey and Iraq. (Some of these countries are considered to be 'allies' of the US and the West. And these themes have also been repeated by many of the Islamists' fellow-travelers on university campuses and in parliaments, media outlets and religious institutions around the world, to their shame.)

Why *should* the Arabs or Palestinians or Muslims in general *want* to end the conflict? To a great extent, it has *defined* them, it gave their leaders a focus, as Sharansky had taught me over the years, to deflect attention from the failings of their societies. The Islamist extremists have used this conflict to warp their ideological and religious world view such that continuing the conflict has become, for many, a foundational element of their belief system.

And yet, Muslims, Arabs and Palestinians should desire an end to their centuries-long war against the Jews and Israel for one simple reason: *for their own benefit*, not to mention in keeping with *their own values*, as quoted and articulated here. The details, and justifications, and sources in Islamic and Arab thought and word and deed, are far more numerous than those presented in this work; but they all come together to form a single conceptual framework: Resolving this conflict can and should be part of the central purpose of every Arab or Muslim leader, individual, and state. It is imperative, from their own perspective, not for Israel or the Jews or the West, for Muslim leaders to move away from the fanatics and promote the moderates.

Our future, and the peace of our region (and of the entire world in essence), depends on the result of the efforts of those taking the lead in seeking to inculcate a new set of goals for their people, based on traditional Muslim values and Arab culture.

The argument made here is that the twin goals of annihilating Israel and broadening the influence and power of Islam are incompatible with both resolving the bitter struggle over the land and promoting the human, social and economic development of the people of the region. These goals must be replaced with other objectives – whether directly tied to the benefit of their people or of a more general nature for all of humanity.

It is indeed a tall order: A radical transformation of a culture of hatred into one of love; of a culture of intolerance into one of tolerance; of a culture of violence and war into a culture of peace. This means a sweeping conversion from a Palestinian national enterprise focused on obliterating another nation/people to one focused on responsible state-building. And even more challenging is our call for the profound reformation of a religious identity based on the rejection of other religions to one based on the embrace of other faith communities.

And yet there are ample historical precedents for this sort of communal re-configuration.

Civilizations can reform their worldview – dramatically – when a set of powerful forces converge. History shows, again and again, that profound ideological transformation is possible when:

- moral leadership redefines the narrative;
- violence becomes clearly self-destructive;
- education and religious messaging change;
- forgiveness replaces grievance as the central ethic; and
- new national stories emphasize coexistence rather than domination.

What I am arguing for in this book – a reformation within Muslim and Arab society toward tolerance, coexistence, and peace – is not unprecedented, nor naïve, nor impossible. It fits into a universal historical pattern. It has been done before. Many times. Often by societies as or even more rigid, wounded, or violent than those in the Middle East today.

Human beings – at the personal, communal, and civilizational level – can choose new meanings and new moral horizons. And when they do, entire cultures shift. Here are several examples that illustrate this timeless capacity for transformation.

After the brutal conquest of Kalinga (ca. 261 BCE), the Mauryan Emperor Ashoka realized that empire-by-violence was destroying both soul and society. He renounced expansionism, embraced Buddhist ethics, and redirected state power toward compassion, welfare, and peace. A militaristic empire became a moral one – not perfectly, but unmistakably. Ashoka's reforms show that even an expansive imperial power can redefine its identity around non-violence, moral governance and coexistence.

Christianity itself began as a movement persecuted by Rome, later became the religion of empire, then fractured and re-shaped again during the Reformation – from persecution to conscience.

What had been a system enforcing uniformity with violence eventually became, in much of the Western world, the foundation for doctrines of conscience, human dignity, and religious freedom. A faith once used to justify coercion later became the wellspring of tolerance.

When the Second Temple was destroyed by Rome in 70 CE, and the people of Israel enslaved and expelled from their land over the next century, Judaism underwent one of the most radical ideological and civilizational paradigm shifts in history. A culture centered on sacrifice, priesthood, monarchy and pilgrimage became a nation rooted in prayer, charity, study, and ethical behavior. What should have been the end of Judaism and the Jewish people became instead its rebirth. A religion and culture of land and ritual re-emerged as a global civilization grounded in moral responsibility.

The earliest Muslim community itself underwent profound change. At first, in Mecca, the message emphasized patience, non-violence, and spiritual resilience under persecution. Then, in Medina, Prophet Muhammad restructured tribal society around law, accountability, and coexistence, replacing inherited vendettas with a unified community bound by ethics, responsibility, and mercy. This was not merely a geographic shift; it was an ideological revolution: tribal identities gave way to a moral vision of justice and restraint.

Similarly, the abolition of tribal vengeance in early Islam was a revolution of sorts itself. Pre-Islamic Arabia was dominated by cycles of blood-feud. Early Islam replaced that system with legal restitution, forgiveness, and limits on retaliation. As we've seen, the Quran repeatedly praises those who forgo vengeance, and prophetic practice turned forgiveness into moral power. An entire culture moved – rapidly – from honor-based revenge to a principled framework emphasizing mercy.

A thousand years later, the Ottoman Islamic Empire recognized that its old system was unsustainable. Through the Tanzimat reforms between 1839-1876 it introduced equal citizenship for Muslims and non-Muslims, modern legal codes, religious tolerance policies, and new administrative structures. Thus, a centuries-old Islamic empire attempted – imperfectly but sincerely – to reorganize itself around equality and coexistence. (Unfortunately, many earlier changes have been reversed in recent decades, through the efforts of the Muslim Brotherhood, ISIS and the other fanatical groups.)

Of course, we've referred numerous times to the civilizational shifts of both imperial Japan and Nazi Germany from militarist expansionism genocidal ideology to pacifist democracy, after their moral reckoning and reconciliation.   Likewise, our repeated reference to the conversion in Northern Ireland from sectarian war and violence to coexistence and social harmony, or to the creation of the European Union as a supernational peace project after centuries of perpetual warfare.

And in a more modern example from the Muslim and Arab world, after extremist attacks in Casablanca in the early years of the 21st Century (2003), Morocco undertook one of the most significant contemporary religious reforms in the Muslim world. The state reorganized the training of imams, reasserted a moderate Maliki–Ash'ari tradition, elevated women as spiritual guides (*murshidat*), and built a nationwide educational program promoting tolerance. A society dealing with extremism chose a path of moderation, reform, and coexistence.   (And there are additional Muslim societies nurturing similar transitions and promoting more moderate interpretations of Islam, from Uzbekistan, Azerbaijan and Kazakhstan to Malaysia, Indonesia and Bangladesh, among others.)

An illustration of the possibilities inherent in an Islamic and Arab trend towards moderation can be seen in a number of statements and actions made by leaders condemning Hamas and the Islamist ideology of ISIS, Al Qaeda and the Muslim Brotherhood etc. following the Hamas massacre and kidnapping of October 7th '25.

A few references should suffice to make the point:

- Professor Dr Salman al-Dayah, a former dean of the Faculty of Sharia and Law at the Hamas-affiliated Islamic University of Gaza and leading Gazan Islamic scholar, issued a fatwa (religious ruling) criticizing Hamas's attacks and follow-on conduct as inconsistent with Islamic Sharia law and principles of jihad.[63]

---

[63] https://www.bbc.com/news/articles/cj4vw1l8xvdo

- A group of UK Muslim leaders published a statement that "denounce[d] Hamas' killing and abduction of innocent people on the 7th of October 2023". The declaration continued, "We utterly condemn all acts of Antisemitism… on our streets here in Britain.… Mutual respect and dialogue between Muslim and Jewish communities at home and abroad, along with a shared commitment to peace, justice, and the safety of all communities are ever more important."[64]

- Mansour Abbas, an Arab-Israeli politician heading the United Arab List, called on Palestinian faction leaders to take a "moral, humanitarian stance reflective of the values of Islam" and release all hostages, stating it is forbidden to hurt the innocent.[65]

- In an unprecedented move at a July 2025 conference, the entire Arab League, led by Sunni Saudi Arabia, issued a joint statement condemning the October 7th attack and demanding Hamas disarm and leave Gaza.[66]

And most recently – on December 15, 2025 – Imam Mohammed Tawhidi, representing the Global Imams Council, condemned the Islamist murder of Jewish worshippers at Bondi Beach, Sydney as a "barbaric terrorist attack". Tawhidi branded the assault on Jewish families celebrating Chanukah as a "calculated antisemitic act of terror" and an "unforgivable crime that stains the conscience of humanity". Moreover, he insisted that Australian and Western authorities find and punish not only the perpetrators but also the "networks, ideologues, Imams, supporters and enablers behind them", and argues "terror must be crushed decisively".[67]

More important perhaps, for our purposes, Tawhidi distinguishes between Islam as a "divine religion from God" and Islamist extremist organizations that hijack the faith for political purposes. He maintains, for instance, that "the name 'Muslim

---

64 https://hyphenonline.com/2023/10/19/exclusive-uk-muslim-leaders-call-for-restraint-by-israel-and-condemn-hamas-attacks/

65 https://www.kan.org.il/content/kan-news/politic/561075/

66 https://edition.cnn.com/2025/07/30/middleeast/arab-league-hamas-gaza-israel-intl

67 https://x.com/Imamofpeace/status/2000397865022271496?s=20

Brotherhood' is almost blasphemous; they've hijacked the name of the religion and then they've hijacked the term 'brotherhood.'"[68] He views it as a duty for Muslims to stand against fanatics to protect their religion. As a Shia Muslim leading the GIC, an organization uniting Sunni and Shiite clerics from around the world – based in and supported by the Islamic Seminary of Najaf, Iraq – Imam Tawhidi expresses the kind of new/old Islamic theology and political ideology of which we can only hope to see more.

It is true that Tawhidi and his cohorts at the GIC do not (yet) command the sort of support needed to carry out a real transformation in Islamic thought and Arab culture. Established in 2014 by a coalition of Sunni and Shi'a clerics in Iraq to combat the onslaught of ISIS, the GIC has become ever more explicit in its call for a reformation of Islamic thought and its criticism of actions taken by Arab and Muslim governments and terror organizations. As one final illustration, it is worth quoting the published summary of their approach to the related issues of Islamist terror and ideology, peace and coexistence with Israel, and more:

> On December 4th '24, The Global Imams Council (GIC) signed a historic declaration in the precincts of the Canadian Parliament, hosted by senators and witnessed by key figures and MPs. The declaration reaffirms a commitment to the monotheistic principles of faith, compassion, and acceptance as revealed through the Prophet Abraham, peace be upon him. It embraces Abraham's ethos as a model of courage for confronting those who distort the Holy Quran to justify terrorism and violate the dignity and rights inherent in Islam. It emphasizes the Abrahamic ethos as vital to establishing freedom, justice, and peace. Furthermore, the declaration reaffirms the importance of the Abraham Accords in advancing peace, mutual understanding, and interfaith collaboration globally, particularly in the Middle East; and commits to working with governments and diverse communities to fully realize the promise of the Accords, striving for a future of prosperity free from terrorism and

---

[68] https://www.jpost.com/diaspora/antisemitism/article-868609

hatred.[69] [70]

These may be – we can only hope – an indication of the beginning of a possibly momentous paradigm shift.

Across continents and centuries, the story is the same: Civilizations transform when they decide that the old path leads only to ruin, and a new path – rooted in mercy, restraint, and purpose – offers life. Societies that once glorified war turned toward peace. Societies that defined themselves by vengeance turned toward forgiveness. Societies built on exclusivity turned toward coexistence.

All these transformations included ideological re-orientation led by religious, cultural and political leaders dedicated to coexistence and peace as part of their own societal value system.

This is the work that now confronts the Muslim/Arab world – not because their history is uniquely dark, but because every civilization eventually reaches a moment when it must choose its future. (As the final version of this book is being written, millions of Iranians are taking to the streets with calls for reform reflecting almost all our themes. Thousands are sacrificing their lives and freedoms to bring about radical change in their societies. Our message is not merely one of solidarity but a demand for tangible support from the free world – for their sake and for ours.)

The contention in this book is not that Arab or Muslim culture is innately flawed. Quite the opposite: we demonstrate here that all cultures have the capacity for renewal – and that the religious, ethical, and historical resources of Islam itself already contain the foundations of that renewal.

We are at a pivotal moment.

Just as others have done before, Arab and Muslim societies can redefine their worldview:

- from grievance to dignity;
- from rejection to coexistence;

---

[69] https://imams.org/ottawadeclaration/
[70] https://imams.org/wp-content/uploads/2024/12/GICs-Ottawa-Declaration-Signatories-Final.pdf (full text)

- from stories of victimhood to stories of shared purpose;
- from inherited hatred to deliberate peace.

History proves this is possible. The question – as always – is which path will be chosen.

At base, such a reformation must come from the people and leadership of the these nations and communities in the area and across the planet. An Israeli/American Jew will not effect such a momentous change.

The argument made here is compelling, if simple in its elegance: Without a re-orientation of the value system from destruction to creation, from animosity to acceptance, from confrontation to peace, there will ***never be a resolution to the Arab-Israel conflict*** or peace in the promised land (or elsewhere in the Middle East). In other words, this is not so much an appeal to or advice for the Arab and Muslim world as it is an observation of our reality: If there is to be peace, there must be an ideological change on the part of the aggressor. It cannot be stated more baldly.

Such a revolution is possible, and can and should be encouraged and supported by all those interested in promoting peace in the region, including and especially the leaders of the free world and prominent western cultural, media and academic figures.

There is no point – in fact it is counter-productive, and promotes further war and conflict – to pretend that 'negotiations' over ceasefires or territory are of any use or help. The world was witness in October '25 when Hamas regained control over some of the territory of the Gaza Strip in a ceasefire – and it turned its guns on the civilian population of Gaza immediately, murdering and beating and imprisoning scores of Gaza residents and rival clan leaders. As Jared Kushner, one of the US mediators in the ceasefire negotiations along with Steve Witkoff, said on CBS' "60 Minutes" program a few days later, "Hamas right now is doing exactly what you would expect a terrorist organization to do…". And they were doing it not to their declared enemy, but rather to their own people.

Only when the moderate and rational Arab and Muslim leaders actually lead their people on the path of peace will the more tangible aspects of conciliation be possible to pursue, from territorial agreements to issues of self-government, identity, economic relations and the like.

The thesis of this work is that a little humility and gratitude, and a great deal of acceptance and forgiveness, can lead to the emergence of national, religious and cultural goals compatible with peace. This entire book is dedicated to elaborating these ideas, providing sources and references for diplomats and policy-makers to incorporate these themes into their approaches to the region and their efforts to help bring the ongoing war to an end. After the element of forgiveness, the issue of and Arab/Muslim commitment to a new set of objectives which do not include the ambition to wipe out Israel and the Jews is vital for any change of peace.

Purpose is the element that gives meaning to struggle and direction to effort. In Arabic, purpose can be expressed as *ghāyah* (goal) or *maqṣid* (objective). Without it, even noble values drift without a destination. In the Arab–Israel conflict, purpose is what separates movements that build from those that only destroy.

The Quran affirms that human life is not aimless: *"Did you think We created you without purpose, and that you would not be returned to Us?"* – Quran 23:115

Imam al-Ghazali taught that purpose is found when one's actions serve both worldly benefit and the higher goals of God – justice, mercy, and the preservation of life.

History shows that nations recover from disaster when their purpose is constructive. As above, postwar Japan rebuilt around the purpose of peace and economic growth; similarly, Singapore, under Lee Kuan Yew, focused its national purpose on becoming a prosperous, corruption-free society. By contrast, movements defined by destructive purposes burn out or bring ruin. We know how Nazi Germany defined its purpose around the domination of one race and the eradication of others – ending in its own destruction – and how the Khmer Rouge's purpose of purging "foreign influence" in Cambodia left only devastation. The devastation wrought in Gaza by Hamas' continuing aggression and barbarity needs no elaboration.

Arab leaders who made peace with Israel often framed it in terms of a higher purpose. Anwar Sadat told the Knesset in 1977: *"I have chosen to set my sights on the great objective: a permanent peace based on justice."* King Hussein of Jordan, in 1994, said: *"Let us not risk the life of any child, Arab or Israeli. Let us work together to build a future in which they will live in peace."*

In both cases, the purpose was not merely ending war, but building something worth the peace.

For Israel, as noted in the beginning of this section, purpose began as returning to the people of Israel's ancestral homeland and re-establishing sovereignty there, and providing a safe homeland for the Jewish people. Over decades, it expanded to building a thriving democracy, a global technology hub, and a center for humanitarian outreach. Of course in times of conflict, survival becomes dominant, but Israel has proven that it remains focused on its goal to create a moral society reflecting Jewish and universal values, from its commitment to limiting civilian casualties in all its wars to the provision of aid, electricity, water etc. to the civilian population even in the midst of the recent war in Gaza, among many other examples.

For Palestinians, as we described also in brief in the opening of this section, purpose has often been framed around liberation and defiance, let alone annihilation and death. While self-determination is a legitimate and necessary purpose, when 'resistance' becomes an end in itself, it can crowd out the parallel purpose of building a functioning society. Palestinian-American scholar Ziad Asali once warned that if we define ourselves only by what we oppose, we will have nothing left when the opposition ends.

In 2024, Ahmed Fouad Alkhatib, a Palestinian-American and member of the Atlantic Council (who espouses "radical pragmatism" in his Realign for Palestine initiative), wrote on Twitter that Palestinians are

> victims of incompetent and unskillful leadership, empty slogans, short-sighted decisions, unrealistic expectations, and, most importantly, decades of delusions that are so difficult to challenge and dispel. The Palestinian people desperately need pragmatic and realistic leaders who courageously tell their people uncomfortable and inconvenient truths: there will be no "right of return" to the entirety of historic Palestine; custody over holy sites must

be shared; refugees must return to developed Palestinian territories or be given options to become citizens in their current countries; armed resistance is detrimental/futile and must be abandoned; and Jews have an undeniable connection to the land regardless of how that connection was expressed and how it negatively impacted the Palestinian people. Time is running out for Palestinian leaders to help their people make the most of the land and resources they have and to focus on **who they want to be as a people** within realistic constraints of today's shifting and evolving landscape. I am nevertheless hopeful that many Palestinians, particularly in Gaza, are finally realizing that Hamas's martyrdom is but an illusion and will not bring about a liberated Palestine, concluding that life and peace are the only path forward.[71]

As the crucial element in our five steps, we can go even deeper into just what is meant by, and what the power is, of "purpose".

Stephen Covey has written that purpose is the first principle of what he calls ethical power: "By purpose, I don't mean your objective or intention – something toward which you are always striving. Purpose is something bigger. It is the picture you have of yourself-the kind of person you want to be or the kind of life you want to lead" (Covey, *Seven Habits*).

Interestingly, John Calhoun's research with mice in 'paradise' starting in 1958 suggests that having purpose is part of our animal biology. Without a reason to live (no predators or disease, abundant food and shelter), hundreds of mice exhibited aggressive and other destructive behavior leading to social collapse and extinction. Not once but over two dozen times.

As noted above, both Islamic and Jewish traditions envision purposes that extend beyond survival.

- In the Quran: *"You are the best nation produced for mankind – enjoining what is right, forbidding what is wrong, and believing in Allah"* (Quran 3:110).

- In the Hebrew Bible, in a separate verse from the one quoted

---

[71] https://twitter.com/afalkhatib/status/1758744092224504054

above: *"I will make you a light unto the nations, that My salvation may reach to the ends of the earth"* (Isaiah 49:6).

These verses call both peoples to see themselves as contributors to the good of the wider world – not as obstacles to each other's existence. This creates a **strategic purpose for peace**.

Sheikh Abdullah bin Bayyah explains the wisdom of constructive purpose: *"The highest purpose is to preserve life, then to preserve dignity, then to build what will endure after us."*

Yet a shared layer of purpose does not require identical visions. Israel can remain a Jewish state, and Palestinians can pursue self-determination, while both include prosperity, stability, and coexistence in their national goals.

When the 1994 Israel–Jordan treaty was signed, water security and economic cooperation were explicitly written into the agreement as shared purposes – making the peace tangible and self-sustaining.

A clear destination while hiking changes how you walk. Each step becomes part of a greater whole. In politics, purpose turns temporary truces into lasting transformations. Without it, every gain will be temporary, and every setback will feel like the end. The choice facing both peoples is whether to root their purpose in creating something worthy of their children – or in defeating the other, even at the cost of their own future. And this is most apparent regarding the Arab and Muslim leadership.

One can imagine all sorts of fascinating possibilities, once the Arab/Muslim purpose is peace and prosperity rather than destruction and death. On the strategic plane, options can include concepts of a United States of the Middle East; or a federation between Israel, Jordan and a new "Palestine" in between; or confederations between an expanded Israel-with-Judea & Samaria and an Arab/Muslim entity including Syria, Lebanon and Jordan; or multi-ethnic states like Lebanon, Israel, Jordan and Egypt (with its 10% minority of Coptic Christians) turning into democracies, with even Iraq doing so, while Israel retains the territories and gives all resident Arabs citizenship. We already are seeing a potential transformation in Syria after the fall of the Assad regime and the conclusion of the vicious civil war there.

In this spirit, we can wander into a new imagined reality. Arab leaders, and Muslim leaders –and Palestinian Arab Muslim leaders in particular – turn from blame and the perpetuation of victimhood to explore a myriad of prospects leading to peace to our area.

Imagine the King of Jordan declaring the renaming of his country "Palestine" (given its history as the eastern 75% of the original Palestine Mandate and the majority of its population Palestinian), and inviting all Arabs identifying as "Palestinian" or descendants of refugees identifying as such, to take citizenship there, and reaching out in earnest translate the decades-old peace agreement into actual peaceful and harmonious relations between Arab and Jew in the region.

The myriad of alternatives available in our circumstances, were goodwill to prevail rather than hatred and rejection, is astounding. Over the past few decades, I and many others have written about democratic and liberal trends in Arab and Palestinian society and promoted a number of truly moderate Arab leaders from the disputed territories. And while walking through the sandy desert on my trek, I spent hours building castles in the sand with thoughts like these.

Unfortunately we are not there yet. Instead, we see the continuing and growing trends delegitimizing and demonizing Israel, as well as the Jewish people. This should concern any thinking and caring person in a free society. As this formula for conflict resolution was percolating, I was almost despondent in the realization that until the Arab and Muslim leadership changes – i.e. returns to their core ideology – there was little point exploring all these amazingly creative frameworks for regional peace. And it did not seem likely that it would happen

But we are at a different stage now. In fact, today we face a decisive moment, and we can focus on options and choices which are possible, specifically with those Arab Muslim moderates who are the real future of their societies and who personify the reasons for my optimism regarding resolving our conflict.

There are many people, who I *know* will embrace all the possibilities present in our situation – although some cannot be named, which itself indicates the extraordinary nature of the situation. There are others, most of whom are unfortunately not well known nor supported as they should be by the free world.

Models of genuine moderates across the Arab and Muslim spectrum include public figures such as Ali Rashid Al-Nuaimi (UAE, chairman of the Defense & Foreign Affairs Committee), Ahmad Mansour (Israel/Germany, psychologist and reform advocate), Tareq Oubrou (Morocco/France, Chief Imam of Bordeaux), Maajid Nawaz (UK/Pakistan heritage, former member of Hizb ut-Tahrir), Tarek Fatah (Pakistan/Canada), Hamza Kashgari (Saudi Arabia), and Sara Idan (Iraq, human rights activist).

There are Palestinian academics and intellectuals like Ahmed Fouad Alkhatib (Gaza-born, writer/commentator), Iyad al-Baghdadi (writer/activist), Hisham Younis (academic), Noor Dahri (Pakistani-Palestinian, counter-extremism scholar), and Ramy Najjar (Palestinian-American, pro-coexistence analyst). There are Palestinian activists and civil society leaders including Walid Salem (director of Jerusalem's Panorama Center), Bassem Eid (Jerusalem-based human-rights activist), Mosab Hassan Yousef (former Hamas insider and reform advocate), Samir Qumsiyeh (Bethlehem journalist), Walid Shoebat (ex-terrorist turned peace advocate), Rami Nasrallah (Jerusalem, founder of the International Peace and Cooperation Center), and Bassem Ayoub (peace activist).

More recently, many cultural voices and even social-media influencers have emerged, such as Loay Al-Shareef (Saudi Arabia/UAE, Jewish–Arab history communicator), Irshad Manji (Ugandan-born Muslim reformer), Jonathan Elkhoury (Lebanon/Israel, coexistence activist), and Muhammad Shehada (Gaza, writer and commentator), as well as those already mentioned like Nuseir Yassin (Arab-Israeli social media creator – "Nas Daily") and Lucy Aharish (Arab-Israeli TV journalist).

Alongside these courageous figures stands a wider constellation of thinkers, dissidents, scholars, and ex-Muslim reformers whose work, though often overlooked, reflects the same moral trajectory. Beyond the Arab world itself, thinkers such as Ayaan Hirsi Ali (Somalia/Netherlands), and non-Muslims like Raymond Ibrahim (US) have called for profound ideological reform within Islamic societies, advocating universal human rights and coexistence, though speaking from outside the traditional religious framework.

All of these reformers openly accept Israel's legitimacy and advocate a future built on coexistence, reform, and the rejection of hatred.

Their voices come from Cairo and Casablanca, Beirut and Berlin, London, Toronto, and Los Angeles – places where the cost of speaking plainly about political Islam or coexistence with Israel can be severe. Writers like Shadi Hamid, Ibn Warraq, Ali Rizvi, and Sarah Haider challenge inherited dogmas and press for a secular, humane reading of modern Muslim identity. Non-Muslim scholars such as Bernard Lewis, Daniel Pipes, Olivier Roy, Gilles Kepel, Brigitte Gabriel, Bat Ye'or and Nonnie Darwish have likewise illuminated patterns of religious extremism and offered frameworks for ideological renewal.

Though these critics speak from different traditions and with different emphases, they share a commitment to intellectual honesty, to the rejection of violence as a political tool, and to the conviction that Arab and Muslim societies are capable of profound moral evolution. Their work reinforces the message of the moderates within the region itself: that dignity, freedom, and peaceful coexistence are possible – and that embracing Israel's legitimacy need not contradict Arab identity, Muslim faith, or national pride. Together, these voices form an emerging moral chorus pointing toward a future freed from the hatreds of the past.

This isn't necessarily a new idea. As described earlier, there were Muslim and Arab leaders a hundred years ago calling for an embrace of the Jews and Zionism, with the goal to bring benefit to their own society and the region. But in our current context, it seems radical. And putting it in the framework of our five elements is unique. More than ten years ago, while trudging along a dry hill outside Tel Aviv towards the end of the trek, I recall saying to myself (a passage which didn't make it into my first book):

All this cogitating on my personal goals – family, personal, work, Jewish world, wine, Israel's legitimacy and more – leads me to thoughts of our national goals, and regional and international too. And putting it all in one package seems so basic, so simple – even if I'm the one always railing against simplistic approaches. And it appears so obvious, too. But as a student of the region and its history I know it hasn't been tried in any serious fashion. Humility; acceptance; gratitude; forgiveness; now a sense of purpose and goals (and all the possibilities inherent in openness and patience) – these could form the foundation of real peace! Really? I have to work this out.

In that last week of hiking, the realization came to me that the sum of these applications and the lessons I'd learned are not only relevant to our predicament; they are in fact a profound departure from everything attempted before. And this cannot be expressed in a brief op-ed, or forty-minute talk, or even a magazine article – though I did try. Certainly not if it were to include source texts and quotes as well as practical steps forward, let alone the context of the trek, with all the color and experiences of the hike itself lending weight and meaning to the concepts.

And this crucial element – having a sense of purpose and meaning, while recognizing all the amazing possibilities open to us – is what is missing from the Arab-Israel peace equation.

As I made my way around the bends of the Yarkon River outside Tel Aviv on the last, eighth week, I thought again, *"But why should the Arabs/Palestinians want to make peace with us?"* I began to realize – or to accept (as I think I'd known this for years) – that herein lies the true fallacy, the real pain, the stark explanation why we haven't yet been able to achieve peace here for generations – the politically incorrect crux of the issue.

The Arab leadership, and Palestinian in particular, seem to have no aim other than either to create another Arab state and to put an end to Israel. Or to create a new Caliphate. And after that? What then? We have not seen much in the way of strategic goals. The above are all tactical by nature; founding a Palestinian State, demolishing Israel, or even establishing a wider Muslim/Arab Caliphate, are merely mechanisms to be implemented to achieve some broader goal.

What is that goal, or purpose? There aren't many Arab or Muslim leaders talking about their future, aside from "restoring honor" or regaining lost territory (from Israel, or Spain, or France, or others) or achieving stability and security; again, a means to what end? A handful do call for a more moderate, conciliatory and tolerant form of Islam. But few articulate a vision for humanity like those of other major religions and societies.

Wilson spoke of "making the world safe for democracy"; Kant called for the creation of idealistic societies and an ideal international community; Marx saw the sharing of the means of production as the key to creating equal and equitable societies; Gandhi suggested non-violence not only as a means of conflict resolution but as a goal for a peaceful humanity; Buddha insisted on the discipline of meditation as a way to achieve an earth-bound Nirvana as well as a heavenly paradise. Jesus taught that love is the instrument through which we progress towards the goal of redemption.

The Torah, Judaism and Israel have always held the betterment of humanity as a principal goal; the mandated role of the Jewish people is to be a representation of the "light" of God to other peoples, which is nothing short of a commandment to make the world a better place, whether morally, spiritually, technologically, intellectually or otherwise.

For the record, Jews never saw themselves as 'better' than any others (despite what the antisemites throughout the ages have proclaimed), but rather as being given the task to bring the word of God to humanity – i.e. the moral code and understanding of the nature of the relationship between God and creation, and between people, with the resulting implications for our behavior towards each other.

These are the concepts which have motivated the Jewish nation, the people of Israel, over centuries to be so very innovative in philosophy, medicine, business, politics and otherwise; these are the foundations of the curious statistics which have Jews inordinately over-represented in the lists of Nobel Prize laureates let alone of business, political and cultural leaders wherever they have lived. They also form a substantial part of the basis for both Christianity and Islam, as well as for the fundamental values of western civilization and the free world. And none of these reflections suggest that Arabs or Muslims – and in particular their leaders – cannot or do not have the capacity to reach similar achievements.

Yet the absence of an overriding purpose in Arab and Muslim ideology is a historical and cultural fact, and the lack of such a desire has impeded development in the Arab world significantly; and crucially, this has impeded peace.

Islam by tradition *does* set a goal and purpose for its adherents: to worship God (Allah) alone and strive to be "best in deed" in preparation for the eternal afterlife. "Worship" (*ibadah*) in this context is comprehensive as described earlier, encompassing not only rituals like prayer and fasting, but every action, thought, and intention performed in obedience to God's commands and seeking His pleasure. Life is considered a test of faith and conduct, and success is measured by righteousness and moral character.

But over centuries of military and political expansion and conquest, mainstream Islamic thought and political leadership seems to have forgotten their religion's original purpose. They have become fixated on the tactical goals of power enhancement and spreading Islam (or, worse, attacking others) rather than the strategic purpose of providing meaning and tangible benefit to their followers. Their original purpose appears to have been lost.

Reports in recent decades have documented the dearth of progress in many Arab and Muslim societies, the absence of freedoms, the want of educational success and innovation. Arab and Muslim leaders themselves have spoken out on these issues – like Malaysia's PM Mahathir Mohamad at the Islamic Conference in '03[72] – as has the UN. But none have addressed the 'Why'. Few of influence have reached the obvious conclusion that this is a willful process which retards development, not an inevitable march of history, and that what is needed is a powerful, widespread campaign focused on a broader goal than just declaring statehood or overcoming a particular enemy. And there is no question this can only succeed if championed by genuine and recognized Muslim/Arab leaders, with the courage to steer their societies in a constructive direction.

The argument is compelling: If the Arabs and Muslims – their leadership – were to focus on any one of a number of over-arching

---

[72] Speech by Prime Minister Mahathir Mohamad of Malaysia to the Tenth Islamic Summit Conference in Putrajaya, Malaysia, October 16, 2003.
http://archive.adl.org/anti_semitism/malaysian.html#.V87Ig5h95hE

strategic goals, whether their own development (also a means to an end), the betterment of humanity (as sought by Mohammed), or world peace (not to be trite), or another of their own choosing but one which was positive, wide-ranging and far-reaching, then reconciliation with Israel and Jews becomes itself not a goal (about which Muslims and Arabs might argue) but a means to achieve that more comprehensive aim.

This may sound clichéd and pretentious. Where do I come off preaching to Muslims and Arabs how to restructure their entire ideology and society? Who Am I?

Who Am I indeed. If I am a thinker, I am also a do-er. And that's certainly one of the reasons I chose to write this book. We have quoted multiple Arab and Muslim sources to prove how peaceful Islam is and how innovative Arab culture was once. Of course I am happy to leave further explication of these themes to the experts, both Arab and Muslim and otherwise. But I am encouraged – have always been encouraged – by my Arab and Muslim friends who truly look for ways to better the world, and bring peace to our region. One of the themes I have heard from them, repeatedly over the past thirty plus years, is that they await the emergence of a truly moderate Arab/Muslim leader to bring the Islamic and Mediterranean world into the modern era, similar to what the post-Temple period did in the times of Rabbinic Judaism and what the Protestant Reformation did for Christianity, and what the French and American revolutions did for western political society.

My friend and mentor, former boss and hero of the Jewish (and Soviet) people, Natan Sharansky, along with his co-author Ron Dermer (who then became a long-time trusted advisor to PM Netanyahu), started that ball rolling when promoting the idea of increased freedom and democracy in the Arab and Muslim world, including through their book *The Case for Democracy – The Power of Freedom to Overcome Tyranny and Terror*. He and others far more impressive intellectually and influential than I argue compellingly for such a transformation in Arab and Muslim society, but it hasn't happened yet. I am hoping that perhaps I may have a different way of saying it, a new urgency and formulation, and a unique proposal for action which goes beyond simply encouraging greater respect for political and civil rights in the autocratic societies of the Middle East.

In another passage from over a decade ago which was excised from my earlier book, I describe my thinking that last week on the Trail:

What I'm talking about here is hard to say without sounding incredibly patronizing. But as I walk beside these groves, I allow myself to articulate the non-sayable (in polite society): The Arabs/Palestinians should be more like the Jews/Israelis! There is no judgment here; Jews are not 'better' than Arabs or Muslims or Palestinians. But objective reality is incontrovertible: because the Jews valued the establishment of our state more than almost anything, we were willing to compromise on territorial issues again and again (and still do so). Partially, this is due to our value system which respects, and encourages, compromise, in many ways. But it is also due to our understanding of the balance between the perfect and the good; between the desired goal and the attainable opportunity; between the justice of our cause and the reality on the ground. And most importantly, we saw the re-assertion of our sovereignty in our Land as itself only a step along our national path, as a means as well as a goal in itself.

This theory can offer an important contribution to our public discussions of prospects for peace in the region, a new approach with practical steps to finally resolving our conflict with the Arabs, after all these years, based on these five basic principles. And as painful as it is for me to articulate, it seems to me we must acknowledge the lacunae in the Arab and Muslim world, and that in Palestinian society in particular.

We all need a sense of purpose; we all need meaning in our life – which is what 'life' means, in a way. Eating, sleeping, eliminating, breathing – this is not life. Loving each other, having a family, building community, helping people, learning new things, making the world a better place: this is living. This is true not only for the nation-state of the Jewish people, but for Arabs and Muslims/Christians as well.

That's basically the point. Something so obvious but which has yet to be presented as the focal point of attempts to solve our conflict:

The Arabs, and in particular those who identify as Palestinian,[73] must have a goal beyond the destruction of Israel and even beyond the establishment of a Palestinian state.

What goal, what purpose, does the Arab/Muslim/ Palestinian leadership place before their people? Certainly the more fanatic jihadists have one, as mentioned above: the victory of Islam and its acceptance by humanity, by choice or by force, and for many of them, politically, the establishment of a global Caliphate to ensure compliance with (their version of) Sharia law the world over. As just one authoritative demonstration, among so many others, Raymond Ibrahim asserts that *"despite the propaganda of al-Qaeda and its sympathizers, radical Islam's war with the West is not finite and limited to political grievances – real or imagined – but is existential, transcending time and space and deeply rooted in faith"* (Washington Post, 2007).

Much can be said – has, in fact, by scholars of great renown, and with great eloquence and compelling logic – regarding whether this extremist Islamist strain of Islamic thought is mainstream or divergent, a continuation of Mohammed's traditions or a hijacking of his teachings.

Here is not the place for an exploration of this belligerent approach to Islam; but it is evident, and irrefutable, that this radical, terror-filled, violent and extreme version of Islam is popular, and pervasive, in many societies – not least in Israel's neighborhood (and growing more popular among Israel's 20% minority of Muslims as well).[74]

It is reflected in the culture of hatred fomented by the leadership of many Arab societies, not least the Palestinian Authority – expressed explicitly in their glorification of "martyrs" (as they term the terrorists who kill innocents indiscriminately, including Jews and

---

[73] I'll leave the wider Muslim world aside, though non-Arab Muslim leaders' contribution may be critical in this process

[74] Interested readers are directed to the excellent research of Bernard Lewis and Rafael Israeli, as well as of The Middle East Forum; MEMRI; IMRI; PMW and others; statistics regarding public opinion in Arab and Muslim societies can be found in PEW Research and BBC recent world opinion surveys.

non-Jews, Israelis and others), in their payments to the families of terrorists, in their terming terror "resistance", and in their use of terms like "evil", "dirty", "usurper", "Zionist enemy" and "colonialist" to describe the Jewish people and their state and "Naqba", or Catastrophe, the establishment of that state.

The extreme Islamist goals of the worldwide expansion of Islam and the annihilation of Israel cannot serve as a focus for a society wishing to live in peace with Israel or the Jewish people or with the rest of humanity.

As demonstrated in this work, we know there are Muslim scholars, Imams, religious leaders and community leaders who can articulate the values and goals Islam has for itself and humanity which would correspond with ideas accepted as universal standards of morality accepted by the overwhelming majority of humans on the planet today. They are in the minority, but they a critical element in any progress toward peace.

These goals and values may not be – would not be, perforce – exactly the same as those of other religions or cultures. We are not talking here of specifics regarding abortion or gay rights, gun control or women's rights or capital punishment, issues among many which reasonable and moral people may argue over for decades or even generations to come, as we have for generations, even centuries, already, across the free world. Yet once the Arabs redirect their energies from opposition to Israel and the West to the creation of their own moral societies (based on moderate Islamic modes of belief), peace is virtually inevitable, both within their communities and between them and the free world, including Israel.

Such a transition is bound to happen. After decades of familiarity and collaboration with Palestinian and other human rights activists promoting freedom and democracy in the Middle East, I remain confident this revolution will occur – both in terms of Arab/Muslim society and in terms of embrace of and peace with the Jews and Israel. The only question is whether it will come about in two years, or two decades… or two generations. That depends on the Arab and Muslim people themselves.

This is another of Sharansky's primary themes, for decades now, based on Andrei Amalrik, Andrei Sakharov and others. Dictatorial regimes cannot control their people forever; autocracies are bound to fail, as their people rise up against their repression. But more important for our purposes, democracies don't make war with other democracies; free societies compete economically, culturally, even ideologically with each other, but do not attack each other violently. They don't teach their children to hate, but rather to love and accept others. They teach their children that violence is not an acceptable method of conflict resolution.

Applying Frankl's aphorism about purpose giving life meaning, and all these other elements, to our reality and to the Arab and Muslim and Palestinian world, has real power.

It is, in fact, quite simple: When the Muslim world focuses on a positive, strategic purpose based on the Quran and Islamic sources, beyond the confines of their current political and military, ideological and religious struggles against Israel and the West, there will be peace.

Even such simple ideas may contain major, transcendental truths. Peace will come for us, for them, and for many others the world over, when Arabs and Muslims look beyond the conflict and beyond their resentment and blame of the other for their travails – all the "others", from the Jews and Israelis to Christians and Americans or Sunnis or Shiites or Greeks or Romans.

Not only does it sound simplistic; to say so will surely be considered condescending, arrogant even, full of chutzpah; or of what former President Obama would call audacity. It will be seen as patronizing, considering I am both a party to the conflict and an outsider (not an Arab, nor a Muslim, nor considered a "Palestinian", though I live in that land). The intention is not to absolve Israel of responsibility for contributing to the creation and perpetuation of the conflict. But it may be that being an 'outsider' is more helpful than harmful, as it is the wider perspective which seems to be missing in most analyses of our situation, let alone the courage to call a spade a spade.

Ours is an objectively tenable position, with a compelling and powerful argument behind it, which can be expressed bluntly: Peace will come when a transformation in the Muslim and Arab world allows for radical jihadist Islamist ideology to be replaced with the moderate interpretations of the Quran and Islamic thought which have been abandoned and rejected over the past few generations by too many political and religious leaders in the Arab world.

These trends of thought exist, though many in the West (and most unfortunately, in the Muslim world as well) are often unaware or unfamiliar with them. As demonstrated here, they are consistent with traditional Islamic philosophy and theology, and are wholly compatible with the elements I discovered on my quest for internal peace and have described here. As we have seen, humility, acceptance, gratitude, forgiveness, and a sense of meaning and purpose all are found within the canon of mainstream Islamic thought, humility most explicitly and as most popularly understood, with the "submission" to God the very word Islam signifies.

My friend Mohammed Dajani, head of the (relatively small, unfortunately) Wasatia movement in Palestinian society and professor at Al Quds University in Jerusalem, whom I quote in this work a number of times, is one of the primary advocates of such a re-evaluation, and of a richer understanding and interpretation, of Islamic sources, as mentioned above. On the website of Wasatia – which means "the middle way" in Arabic (akin to the English aphorism "golden mean" and the Rambam's "golden path" in Judaism) – a new/old purpose for Muslims and Palestinians is thus articulated:

> Al Wasatia is the first Islamic Palestinian movement that calls for a negotiated peace with Israel that would help to bring peaceful solutions to the acute religious, economic, social, and political crises plaguing Palestinian society. It advocates the establishment of an independent, tolerant, democratic, secular, non-militarized state that fosters economic prosperity and social justice and would adopt liberal values of [equality], tolerance, pluralism, freedom of expression, rule of law, and respect for civil and human rights. **Al Wasatia believes that all of these are values advocated in Islamic holy texts and traditions** (emphasis added).[75]

Similarly, Dajani is clear where he sees the priorities for the

---

[75] http://www.wasatiamovement.com/

Muslim world lie in setting goals for the future:

> Moderate Muslims cannot remain bystanders. We have to join forces in recognition that our religion has been hijacked by a small minority for political ends. We must raise our voices, no matter the risk, and stand up for what we believe. Only our voices can stem the allure of radical Islam. We must draw on our creativity and innovation to promote moderation in religion and politics, and strive to create a world of egalitarianism, democracy, and prosperity. This is the right path. [76]

Once the Arab and Muslim leadership focus, and inculcate in their people this emphasis, on the broader, existential goals beyond their own narrow interests, then economic development, education, civil and human rights, peaceful relations with neighbors, and peace itself, become supreme values.

True: This means an overhaul of Islamic and Arab thought, philosophy, politics and society. Yet it cannot be denied that without this, in the pursuit of narrow interests, however defined, we have seen and will continue to see a continued march of war, conflict, repression, hatred and violence. I – and others much greater than I – see no alternative. Whether those interests are the establishment of states (or regime-change in states) or the imposition of fundamentalist religious norms (which I define as "narrow" in spite of their goal of a world-wide Caliphate sometimes being global and utopian), the resulting policies and actions have been proven this past century to be vicious and oppressive, discriminatory and murderous.

It may well be that freedom of speech – which implies freedom of thought and belief – may be the most important place to start, as press freedoms, religious freedoms, freedom of movement, open public debate on issues, criticism of authority, women's rights, etc. all follow from the right to speak your mind. And freedom of expression leads inexorably to an open exchange of ideas, which leads to tolerance and acceptance of others' ideas – whether they be

---

[76] https://www.washingtoninstitute.org/policy-analysis/plea-moderate-islam

of a religious, political, social or other nature.

There are 13 countries on the planet today in which one can be executed for apostasy; they are all Muslim nations, as Egyptian dissident Houssein Aboubakr has noted. The Organization of the Islamic Conference has repeatedly proposed the "legislation" of UN regulations outlawing blasphemy, criminalizing the defamation of religion in an international treaty. In 2012, the UN Human Rights Council, led by stalwarts of rights including Iran, Saudi Arabia, Egypt, Lebanon, Kuwait and others, passed a resolution "combating defamation of religions".

In the face of such attempts, Muslim society – its leaders, academics and people – must have the ability to speak freely and explore the intricacies of their heritage, philosophy and belief system, in order to allow for the development of non-radical, non-Islamist trends to take root and achieve traction. Though this might seem outside the scope of a discussion of the Arab-Israel conflict, it is, in fact, central to any possibility of real change in Arab and Muslim society, including moves towards the acceptance and forgiveness necessary for our peace.

At this point, having delved deeply into all five concepts, we can see how they coalesce into a formidable methodology to settle the conflict.

Walking the Israel National Trail taught me a lesson that maps alone could never give: You cannot see the end from the beginning, but you can continue to stride ahead. Peace is the same. The five elements – Humility, Acceptance, Gratitude, Forgiveness, and Purpose – are not a magic key to instant resolution. They are the trail markers that keep you moving in the right direction.

Humility strips away the arrogance that blocks understanding. It is the leader who listens before speaking, the negotiator who can say, *"I might be wrong,"* the citizen who can admit the other's pain with empathy without diminishing their own.

Acceptance takes humility further. It is the recognition that both peoples are here to stay, and that no solution built on the other's disappearance will last. It allows policies to be grounded in reality instead of fantasy.

Gratitude changes the atmosphere. It softens bitterness by focusing on what can be valued – a working water system, a functioning school, a treaty that has held – and builds a culture that looks for opportunities instead of just grievances.

Forgiveness is the risk of releasing the hold of the past. It refuses to let yesterday's injury dictate tomorrow's choices. It is not forgetfulness, nor the abandonment of justice, but the breaking of chains that bind entire societies to cycles of retaliation.

Purpose is the compass that **aligns all the other elements**. Without a shared layer of constructive purpose, progress drifts. With it, each concession, each act of cooperation, becomes part of building something enduring for future generations.

If these five elements sound like moral ideals, that is because they are – but they are also strategic necessities. Every successful peace process in history has used them in some form. Sadat's humility, Hussein's forgiveness, the shared purpose of rebuilding Europe after World War II – these were not sentimental gestures; they were deliberate political choices.

The question is whether leaders and peoples here can choose the same.

If I were to chart the first concrete and realistic steps for this region, they would be modest but meaningful:

- **Humility**: Leaders from both sides acknowledging – in Arabic and Hebrew – the legitimacy of the other's historical association to the land.

- **Acceptance**: Public statements making clear that neither side seeks the elimination of the other's state or national identity.

- **Gratitude**: Joint media projects highlighting positive cooperation – in water, health, conservation, renewable energy and security – to shift public narratives.

- **Forgiveness**: Expanding grassroots encounters like the Parents Circle–Families Forum to reach more communities.

- **Purpose**: Launching shared projects – environmental restoration, trade initiatives – that visibly benefit both peoples.

None of these will solve the conflict overnight. But like the first steps on a long hike, they will make the destination possible.

We'll now move beyond the principles themselves to examine how they can be embedded into institutions, education, religious discourse, and grassroots movements. Because values alone are not enough – they must be anchored in systems that survive changes of leadership, political swings, and the shocks of violence.

The trail ahead will not be smooth. But as I learned step by step across this land, every hard climb brings a view you could not see before – and every view makes the journey worth it.

Chapter Eight: From Vision to Blueprint – Practical Steps for Real Peace

From history and humility through acceptance and gratitude, with forgiveness and a clear peaceful purpose, outlining the next steps to implement a (Real) Peace Plan

Principles are the soul of peace. But without a body – institutions, laws, education, and shared projects – they drift like prayers in the wind. Having explored the five elements that can transform mindsets – humility, acceptance, gratitude, forgiveness, and purpose – now we turn to the task of rooting them in the ground so they can grow and endure beyond speeches and handshakes.

I recall climbing up a steep hill on the Trail, overlooking the Kineret, the Sea of the Galilee. On a climb, with large rocks and boulders making the ascent treacherous, you have to look not only at where your boot is being placed, but at the next step, and the next. True in business, and in diplomacy, and in strategic planning for peace: we have to map out the initial steps, and the steps which will follow.

The Quran warns against words without deeds:

"O you who believe, why do you say what you do not do? Most hateful it is in the sight of Allah that you say what you do not do" (Quran 61:2–3). Jewish tradition echoes this with a blunt proverb from *Pirkei Avot*: *"It is not the study that is the main thing, but the doing."*

This is where the work begins: translating moral vision into practical systems.

Institutions matter. History offers proof that values alone do not survive without structures to protect them. South Africa's reconciliation was sustained by a Truth and Reconciliation Commission, not just by Nelson Mandela's personal grace. Postwar Europe's peace was built on the European Coal and Steel Community, which tied former enemies' economies together.

In the Arab–Israel context, this means creating frameworks where the five elements are not optional gestures, but operating principles built into education, religion, governance, media, and civil society. The goal of this chapter is to move from ideas to infrastructure: to show how humility, acceptance, gratitude, forgiveness, and purpose can be embedded in systems and daily life.

We will look at five main arenas:

1. Education

2. Religion and religious leadership

3. Governance and policy

4. Media and public discourse

5. Grassroots and daily life

Then we will turn to a longer-term horizon of what peace could look like here, and a phased roadmap for how to walk toward it.

Some of these ideas are new; others have been around for perhaps a century. Some were built in to various peace plans – from the UN Partition Plan of 1947 through the Rogers Plan and the Bush administration's RoadMap for Peace, through Tony Blair's Quartet recommendations and the first Trump administration's "Peace to Prosperity" plan in 2020, to the Abraham Accords and the second Trump administration's 2025 20-point Gaza peace plan.

The following plan incorporates many aspects of these past proposals within the framework of our five elements. This program is based on Arab and Islamic voices of moderation and liberal moderate Israeli and Jewish sentiments, and offers a unified theory of pragmatic steps to be taken to change the mindset(s) of the region and foment radical transformation. As a blueprint, this plan can be carried out by Muslim, Christian, Arab, Jewish, Israeli, American, European and other leaders at every level of society; in fact, it requires that sort of broad and deep commitment to action to be successful.

1.   Education as the First Foundation

If peace is to last longer than the lifespans of the leaders who sign it, it must be planted early – in the minds and hearts of children. Schools are not just places to learn facts; they are where societies pass on their understanding of the past, their vision of the future, and their attitude toward "the other."

<u>Islamic and Jewish Pedagogical Parallels</u>

Jewish tradition treats education as a sacred duty: "*You shall teach them diligently to your children… when you sit in your house, when you walk on the way, when you lie down, and when you rise up*" (Deuteronomy 6:7).

The Quran presents education as a divine command: "*Read in the name of your Lord who created – created man from a clinging substance. Read, and your Lord is the Most Generous – Who taught by the pen – taught man that which he knew not*" (Quran 96:1–5).

Both faiths frame knowledge as a trust from God. The Prophet Mohammed said: "*The best of you are those who learn… and teach*" (Bukhari). Rabbi Hillel taught: "*An ignorant person cannot be pious*" (*Pirkei Avot* 2:6). These parallels can be powerful when educators draw them explicitly, showing that respect for learning – and for other learners – is a shared value rooted in both traditions.

In both traditions, education is not only about knowledge, but about shaping moral character.

<u>Teaching Humility Through 'Dual Perspectives'</u>

Humility in education means acknowledging that one's own history is not the only history.

As Imam Ali ibn Abi Talib has taught, we should not look at who is speaking, but look at what is said. The Mishnah in Pirkei Avot says "*Look not at the bottle but rather at what is inside*". Similarly, as Rabbi Donniel Hartman argues, if we do not learn the other's story, we only understand half of our own.

This is the spirit behind 'dual-perspective' teaching, where Israeli and Palestinian students learn each other's historical experiences alongside their own. Pilot programs like "Learning Each Other's Historical Narrative" (PRIME – the Peace Research Institute in the Middle East) have shown that when students see the other side's perspective presented seriously – not as propaganda – they are less likely to dehumanize.

As some Palestinian educators themselves acknowledge, they cannot teach children to hate and then expect them to build a culture of peace.

If humility is to become a shared norm, both sides must stop teaching hatred as a civic virtue and instead introduce with empathy the idea that the other's pain and story are real, even when we disagree about their meaning.

Acceptance in Curriculum Design

Acceptance requires that students be taught that the other side's existence is legitimate, even when political disputes remain.

As Sheikh Abdullah bin Bayyah teaches, the first step is to accept the existence of the other; without that, there is no potential partner. *"We don't want a place where Muslims feel safe and others don't. We want a land where everyone feels safe"* (quoted by Sheikh Hamza Yusuf in the 2018 Templeton Prize address[77]).

In practical curricular terms, this can mean:

- Palestinian textbooks acknowledging the State of Israel on maps, and referring to Israelis as a real, enduring national community.

- Israeli textbooks accurately naming Palestinian towns and villages, acknowledging Palestinian/Arab history and identity.

In the 1990s, Jordan's curriculum reform after its peace treaty with Israel included references to coexistence and removed passages depicting Jews solely as enemies – a small but meaningful model.

Cross-Border Educational Projects

Joint programs exist in Israel which bring Jewish and Arab children into the same classrooms, learning Hebrew and Arabic side by side. Graduates often report a stronger belief in the possibility of coexistence. In the Palestinian Authority, NGOs have piloted programs introducing students to global conflict-resolution stories (South Africa, Northern Ireland and others) to spark discussion about local application. These efforts help students understand that stubborn conflicts can change – and that compromise and mutual recognition are not signs of weakness.

Strategic Recommendations for Education

To embed the values outlined here in educational frameworks, and especially the acceptance and forgiveness necessary for coexistence, policymakers and educators should:

---

[77] https://www.templetonprize.org/laureate-sub/king-abdullah-ii-address-by-shaykh-hamza-yusuf/

1. Introduce dual narrative textbooks in history and civics that present Israeli and Palestinian experiences side by side.

2. Train teachers in conflict-sensitive pedagogy, so they model respect for multiple perspectives and do not humiliate or dismiss students who express the "other" narrative.

3. Support and require bilingual instruction, with Arabic and Hebrew taught as living, equal languages.

4. Create youth exchange programs for school visits across borders and within mixed cities.

5. Integrate peace-building skills – active listening, nonviolent communication, and empathy – into formal curricula.

As Egyptian diplomat Boutros Boutros-Ghali stressed, peace must be more than documents; it has to deliver tangible benefits. Mohammed gave the same logic a moral frame: *"Each of you is a shepherd, and each of you is responsible for his flock"* (Bukhari, Muslim). When the "flock" is the children of a nation, shaping them toward humility and acceptance may be the most strategic act of leadership possible.

2. Religion as a Bridge

In the Arab–Israel conflict, religion is often seen as a dividing line. Yet for centuries, the Abrahamic faiths have also been bridges, carrying shared values across communities. Gratitude and forgiveness are not political inventions; they are core religious obligations in Islam, Judaism, and Christianity. Anchoring them in religious life can make these values harder to dismiss as "concessions" and easier to embrace as acts of faith.

The Hebrew Bible stresses the importance of gratitude: *"Give thanks to the Lord, for He is good; His mercy endures forever"* (Psalm 136:1). As noted in chapter five, The Quran calls believers to gratitude as well. And both traditions make forgiveness a divine expectation: *"Let them pardon and overlook. Would you not like that Allah should forgive you?"* (Quran 24:22). *"Who is a God like You, who pardons iniquity and forgives transgression?"* (Micah 7:18).

<u>Religious Leaders as Gatekeepers of Moral Vocabulary</u>

Religious leaders shape the emotional climate of their communities more than most politicians. Sheikh Abdullah bin Bayyah has observed that religious discourse is the key to the hearts of the people; without it, political agreements may remain on paper. Rabbi Jonathan Sacks is reported to have said that forgiveness is the counterpoint to revenge, and gratitude is the counterpoint to resentment; without them, no society can heal.

When imams, rabbis, and priests publicly teach that gratitude and forgiveness are divine commands – not political weaknesses – they make space for these values to be part of public life.

Preaching Gratitude in Times of Conflict

In 1994, after signing the peace treaty with Israel, King Hussein of Jordan gave a Friday sermon in Amman thanking God for ending decades of war. He framed the treaty not as political capitulation but as a blessing from God and an occasion for national gratitude.

In Jewish tradition, post-war prayers of thanksgiving (*Hallel*) and the saying of Psalms have been used to mark moments of survival and peace – from the founding of the State of Israel in 1948 to the end of the Gulf War in 1991 and many other examples. By framing peace agreements, humanitarian cooperation, and even small acts of coexistence as occasions for gratitude to God, religious leaders can shift the moral conversation from suspicion to appreciation.

Preaching Forgiveness as Strength

Forgiveness can be presented as an act of moral courage, deeply rooted in prophetic example. The Prophet Mohammed, after returning to Mecca victorious, forgave his former enemies with the words: *"Go, for you are free"* (Ibn Hisham, *Sirah*). Rabbi Abraham Isaac Kook, the first Chief Rabbi of the Land of Israel, taught: *"The pure righteous do not complain about evil; they increase justice. They do not complain about heresy; they increase faith. They do not complain about ignorance; they increase wisdom."*

We saw how King Hussein personally visited the Israeli families of seven schoolgirls killed by a Jordanian soldier, kneeling before each grieving parent and asking forgiveness. That image became one of the most powerful demonstrations of moral leadership in the region's modern history.

<u>Practical Religious Initiatives</u>

1. Joint Sermon Exchanges – Imams and rabbis delivering sermons in each other's places of worship on themes of gratitude, forgiveness, and the sanctity of human life.

2. Sacred Text Study Groups – Bringing together religious scholars from Judaism, Islam, and Christianity to identify and publicize parallel teachings on mercy, thankfulness, and reconciliation.

3. Interfaith Days of Prayer and Service – Annual events tied to national or religious calendars where communities pray for peace and then engage in joint service projects, emphasizing shared (while distinct) religious values. (Americans can recognize this practice from ubiquitous joint services on Thanksgiving.)

4. Training Religious Leaders in Peace Messaging – Workshops to equip clergy with theological resources to preach reconciliation without being accused of betraying political commitments.

<u>Strategic Impact of Religious Engagement</u>

The religious basis for hatred is clear; if religious discourse is left to radicals, it can harden hostility for generations. But when rooted in gratitude and forgiveness, religion can make reconciliation seem not only possible but obligatory. The Jewish sage Ben Zoma asked: *"Who is mighty? One who conquers his own spirit"* (*Pirkei Avot* 4:1). As mentioned earlier, the Prophet Mohammed said: *"The strong man is not the one who can wrestle, but the one who can control himself when angry"* (Bukhari, Muslim).

If the religious leaders of all parties insist on even just on these two values – restraint and inner strength – it would carry political and social life forward in ways diplomacy alone cannot.

3. Governance and Purpose

Governance is the structural frame of a society – it gives structure and support to its values. We need to embed purpose into governance, to ensure that even noble agreements don't collapse under the weight of mistrust and shifting politics. In the Arab–Israel context, purpose must go beyond "ending conflict" to defining what peace is *for.*

The Quran teaches that leadership is a trust (*amānah*): *"Indeed, Allah commands you to render trusts to whom they are due and when you judge between people to judge with justice"* (Quran 4:58). The Hebrew Bible places the same duty on rulers: *"He shall write for himself a copy of this law… and he shall read in it all the days of his life, that he may learn to fear the Lord… and not turn aside from the commandment, to the right or to the left"* (Deuteronomy 17:18–20)

Governments throughout the region must pass legislation and enforce their laws promoting peace and outlawing violence (and the advocacy of violence), including throughout governmental agencies (not only but including religious, educational and media institutions supported by the state). The acceptance promoted here must be encouraged within a framework barring calls for others' death and destruction. (It's instructive to note here recent steps taken in the UK in late '25, banning the use of the call to "Globalize the 'Intifada'!" – recognizing how calls for violence lead to murderous attacks.)

In both traditions, governance is not just administration; it is a moral obligation to guide the community toward the common good.

<u>Defining Purpose in Peace Agreements</u>

Purpose in governance means peace agreements must contain constructive goals beyond security clauses to end the conflict.

The 1994 Israel–Jordan Peace Treaty tied political reconciliation to concrete shared purposes as noted above: water-sharing, agricultural trade, and tourism development. Although the 'purpose' of the treaty remained to achieve peaceful relations, these collaborative endeavors gave the treaty a constituency that benefited directly from its success.

Boutros Boutros-Ghali is quoted widely as having said, plainly: *"People do not eat peace. They eat bread. Peace must give them bread."* In Islamic thought, this mirrors the *maqāṣid al-sharī'ah* (higher objectives of law), which include the preservation of life, intellect, dignity, property, and religion. Peace that serves these ends is not just a political option or even a religious duty; it is life-giving.

<u>The Israeli Side of Purpose</u>

For Israel, embedding purpose into governance means ensuring that peace is not just an abstract "security achievement" but a platform for mutual prosperity. Former Israeli President Shimon Peres often spoke of a "New Middle East" where cooperation in technology, water, and agriculture could redefine the region's future, insisting that economic borders are the most important borders that should be open.

Governance can make this vision tangible by allocating resources and political capital to cross-border projects in health, environment, and commerce, and by making sure that citizens see concrete benefits – jobs, cleaner air and water, safer borders – flowing from cooperation.

<u>The Palestinian Side of Purpose</u>

For Palestinians, embedding purpose into governance means defining state-building not solely as resistance, but as creating the institutions and infrastructure that make self-determination viable.

Palestinian-American scholar Ziad Asali noted, as mentioned earlier, that if we define ourselves only by what we oppose, we will have nothing left when the opposition ends. Purpose here means that ministries, local councils, and economic plans must serve the construction of a functioning, accountable society – rule of law, transparent finances, independent courts – regardless of the pace of final-status negotiations.

<u>Institutional Mechanisms for Purpose</u>

Concrete governance tools that embody shared purpose should include:

1. Joint Economic Zones – Like the Jordan Gateway Industrial Park, where both sides benefit from investment and job creation.

2. Bilateral Infrastructure Councils – Permanent bodies managing shared resources such as water, energy, and transportation corridors.

3. Peace Implementation Budgets – Dedicated funding lines for projects that tie peace to visible, shared benefits.

4. Impact Evaluation Units – Shared teams that track whether

cooperative projects are meeting agreed goals, making purpose measurable and accountable.

5. Democracy tools and institutions including anti-corruption mechanisms to ensure responsible governing with accountability.

The Quran sets a cooperative standard: *"And cooperate in righteousness and piety, but do not cooperate in sin and aggression"* (Quran 5:2). Jewish tradition similarly urges responsible leadership: *"In a place where there are no men, strive to be a man"* (*Pirkei Avot* 2:5). By rooting cooperative governance in these shared values, leaders can frame purpose not as compromise, but as obedience to divine command.

<u>Political Core Issues in a Purpose Framework</u>

Even with the acceptance required above, any realistic roadmap still has to address the familiar "core issues" – borders, Jerusalem, refugees, security. And of course, now, the reconstruction and rehabilitation of Gaza and its population. A purpose-driven framework does not replace these important matters, but it changes how they are approached:

- Mutual recognition: Each side acknowledging the other's right to exist and its legitimate attachment to the land.

- Borders and sovereignty: Negotiated lines that allow each side to govern itself with security.

- Jerusalem: Shared or special-status arrangements that recognize its centrality to Jews, Muslims, and Christians.

- Refugees: A joint council addressing Jewish and Palestinian refugee claims with dignity, and with compensation when deemed appropriate, and a declared end to refugee status.

- Security: Mechanisms that protect civilians on both sides and reduce incentives for violence, in particular including the dismantling and disarming of Hamas and other Islamist terror groups.

- Governance and accountability structures, as above, to ensure adherence to agreements and fulfillment of obligations – likely with international oversight.

Purpose promotes specific areas of liability, and ensures these issues are not treated as zero-sum games, but as problems to be solved in a way that preserves life, dignity, and the long-term future of both peoples.

<u>The Strategic Payoff</u>

Purpose-driven governance changes incentives. When water, power, or health systems depend on cooperation, political actors have a reason to protect peace. It makes the costs of breaking agreements immediate and visible to the public.

This is also true in the realm of security. For instance, in December '25 it was revealed that a major strategic defense deal was finalized between UAE and Israel to develop an advanced sensitive security system. Though valued at $2.3 billion, as Dr. Salem Alketbi (a prominent UAE political analyst) said at the time, "The meaning of this deal is not really in the money. It is in its sovereign nature and what it shows: a high level of trust in sharing technology and building long-term security systems. Countries do not bring short-term partners into the heart of their defense structure. They only bet on this level of cooperation with parties that have proven they can commit and last."[78]

As quoted earlier, Sheikh Abdullah bin Bayyah exhorts us *"to build what will endure after us."* Purpose embedded in governance is exactly that: building something that will endure after leaders, after elections, and even after the memory of the negotiations that created it.

4.   Media and the Public Mind

If governance is the skeleton of peace, media is its bloodstream – carrying ideas, emotions, and narratives through the body of society. In the Arab–Israel conflict, like in the Rwanda genocide, media has often carried toxins: fear, resentment, and dehumanization. But it can also carry the nutrients of peace – humility, acceptance, gratitude, forgiveness, and purpose – if given the right direction.

Proverbs (18:21) offers a warning: *"Life and death are in the power*

---

[78] https://www.jpost.com/opinion/article-881200

of the tongue." The Quran similarly cautions about the power of information: "*O you who believe, if a corrupt person brings you news, investigate, lest you harm people in ignorance and become regretful for what you have done.*" (Quran 49:6)

When words and images can inflame a population within minutes, ethical media is not just good practice – it is a moral necessity.

The Problem: Conflict as Content

In both Arab and Muslim media – and in international coverage – the most extreme voices and images often dominate. And this is true even, sometimes, in Israel. Violence gets breaking-news banners; cooperation gets buried in the features section, if at all.

Palestinian journalist Daoud Kuttab has argued that the issue isn't only bias but the lack of stories that show the other side's humanity. Israeli media critic Rami Livni is reported to have put it even more bluntly: "*We are addicted to drama, and peace is not dramatic until it's dying.*"

Religious and Ethical Mandates for Speech

The Talmud links speech directly to moral responsibility: "*The tongue is like an arrow: once it is released, it cannot be recalled*" (Arachin 15b). Islamic tradition similarly teaches; Mohammed said, "*Whoever believes in Allah and the Last Day, let him speak good or remain silent*" (Bukhari, Muslim).

If religious leaders, journalists, and educators reinforce this ethic, the public can learn to demand higher standards from media.

Shifting the Discussion

To align with the five elements, media can:

- Model Humility by admitting errors, correcting misinformation quickly, and giving space to multiple perspectives.

- Show Acceptance by portraying the other side's legitimacy, not just their existence.

- Highlight Gratitude with stories of cooperation that benefit both peoples – shared medical projects, environmental work, trade.

- Tell Forgiveness Stories that show individuals breaking cycles of revenge.
- Frame Purpose by covering joint initiatives that create a better future, not just temporary ceasefires.

<u>Practical Media Models</u>

1. Joint Newsrooms – Collaborative projects like earlier Israeli–Palestinian reporting initiatives that train journalists together and require them to cover each other's communities with nuance.

2. Peace Correspondents – Reporters specifically assigned to cover cooperation, problem-solving, and intercommunity dialogue.

3. Shared Media Platforms – Social media pages or channels co-run by Israelis and Palestinians, where both post in Arabic and Hebrew.

4. Fact-Checking Partnerships – Cross-border teams that investigate and debunk false claims circulating in both communities.

5. Enforcement of laws regarding incitement to hatred/violence.

<u>The Power of Cultural Storytelling</u>

Television dramas, films, and music often shape perceptions more deeply than news. Earlier Egyptian TV series portrayed Israelis only as villains; more recent productions, though rare, have shown more complex characters. Israeli filmmakers such as Eran Riklis (*The Syrian Bride*) have explored cross-border relationships with empathy.

The Quran uses storytelling as a moral tool: *"Indeed in their stories there is a lesson for those of understanding"* (Quran 12:111). The Hebrew Bible does the same, from the reconciliation of Jacob and Esau to the parables of the prophets. If popular culture can retell the stories of this land in ways that make empathy possible, political peace will have richer soil to grow in.

<u>Strategic Recommendations for Media</u>

- Establish cross-border journalist training programs focusing on conflict-sensitive reporting.

- Create funding incentives for media outlets that meet diversity and accuracy benchmarks.

- Support cultural exchange productions in film, music, and theater that humanize both sides.

- Launch social media campaigns in Arabic and Hebrew that highlight the five elements in everyday life.

Sheikh Abdullah bin Bayyah has suggested that by changing our language we can change how people think and act. Rabbi Jonathan Sacks offered a parallel truth: *"Words create worlds."* The world we live in tomorrow will be shaped by the words we speak today.

6.   Grassroots and Daily Life

Diplomats can sign treaties, and leaders can make speeches, but the real test of peace is whether people live it on the street corner, in the market, on the bus, and at the school gate. The grassroots level is where abstract values either take root or wither. If humility, acceptance, gratitude, forgiveness, and purpose cannot be practiced in daily life, they will remain political ornaments instead of social foundations.

We see this in the contrast between the failure of the top-down process of the Oslo Accords and the bottom-up development of personal and business relationships as part of the Abraham Accords.

The Quran frames peace as an active personal duty: *"And if they incline to peace, then incline to it [also] and rely upon Allah"* (Quran 8:61). Jewish tradition echoes it as a constant quest, as noted above: *"Seek peace and pursue it"* (Psalm 34:14).   These verses do not assign peacemaking only to rulers. They call ordinary people to make peace part of their daily conduct.

Humility in Daily Encounters

Humility at the grassroots level means treating others as equals in dignity, even when political realities are unequal. In practice, this can be as simple as Israeli and Palestinian shopkeepers treating customers as guests, not intruders. Simple gestures of shared humanity go a long way in creating an environment of mutual respect – in public transportation, at government offices or interactions with officials, on the street and even on the telephone.

Imam Ali ibn Abi Talib's advice applies directly: *"People are of two types: your brothers in faith or your equals in humanity."* Israeli writer Amos Oz often put it in more modern terms, suggesting that true patriotism is the ability to see the other's point of view, even when you disagree with it.

<u>Acceptance in Shared Spaces</u>

Acceptance means recognizing that the other side's presence is not temporary or illegitimate. Municipal projects can model this – such as the bilingual street signs in Arabic and Hebrew, already the practice in Israel since its founding – as can mixed sports leagues as exist now in Jerusalem, Haifa, and Galilee towns. Similarly, joint business zones in industrial areas have been seen as a crucial element in peace-building efforts.

Jordan's King Abdullah II has said that *"Humanity is strongest when we walk together in mutual respect and harmony"* (UN General Assembly, 20 September 2016). When neighbors attend each other's weddings, shop at each other's markets, and send children to common extracurricular programs, they reinforce acceptance without waiting for a final-status agreement.

<u>Gratitude in Community Relationships</u>

Gratitude is cultivated through recognizing benefits that come from the other side. This can be as small as thanking a colleague from across the divide for help, or as large as celebrating joint harvests in agricultural cooperatives.

In Jewish tradition, the *Birkat HaGomel* blessing is recited after surviving danger – and this attitude, if not the actual blessing, can be adapted in communal life to give thanks for moments of cooperation that preserve life or avert harm. Mohammed said, *"He who does not thank people does not thank Allah"* (Abu Dawud). Expressions of appreciation – in behavior and in action – are hallmarks of polite society and good citizenship and should be encouraged throughout the region's culture(s).

<u>Forgiveness as Social Courage</u>

Forgiveness at the grassroots can be dangerous – families may see it as betrayal. Yet stories of grassroots forgiveness are among the most powerful.

Palestinian peace activist Bassam Aramin, whose daughter was killed by an Israeli soldier, meets with bereaved Israeli families in the Parents Circle–Families Forum. He says, *"I cannot forgive the bullet, but I can forgive the hand, because I will not let hatred own me."* Israeli bereaved mother Robi Damelin, whose son was killed by a Palestinian sniper, chose to join the same forum. Her words mirror Aramin's: *"I will not take revenge in my son's name."*

These are not sentimental anecdotes; they are practical demonstrations that forgiveness can break the cycle that keeps the conflict alive.

<u>Purpose as a Shared Horizon in Daily Life</u>

Purpose in grassroots work means building projects where both communities have a stake in success. Examples include:

- Environmental cooperation in the Arava Desert, where Israelis and Jordanians grow crops using shared water technology – something pioneered by the Arava Institute at Kibbutz Ketura and already in practice for decades, including joint educational projects between Israelis, Palestinians and Jordanians (and others).

- Medical partnerships like Save a Child's Heart, where Israeli doctors already today carry out live-saving surgeries for Palestinian and Arab (and many other) children.

- Tech incubators bringing together Israeli and Palestinian entrepreneurs in Ramallah and Tel Aviv – also already underway by groups like Tech2Peace and Alliance for Middle East Peace.

Palestinian businessman Sam Bahour describes this as "future-building", insisting that we can't wait for politicians to agree before we start building the society we want to live in. (This author worked with one of the first Israeli companies to purposefully employ Palestinian software engineers in the PA and in Jordan, TaskMail, led by my friend Jacob Ner David and his Jordanian partner, Omar Salah, back in 2000.)

<u>Practical Steps for NGOs and Local Leaders</u>

1. Community Dialogue Circles – Regular small-group meetings in mixed or neighboring communities to build trust.

2. Shared Public Service Projects – Road repairs, park clean-ups, or food drives done jointly.

3. Cultural Exchange Events – Food festivals, music nights, and art exhibitions sharing traditions.

4. Youth Mentorship Programs – Pairing Israeli and Palestinian teens for skill-building and leadership training.

5. Collaborative NGO activities abroad, for the benefit of vulnerable communities around the globe – for instance bringing renewable energy technologies, financing and know-how from across the region to Africa under the auspices of this author's US nonprofit, Gigawatt Impact.

<u>The Ripple Effect</u>

Grassroots initiatives may seem small compared to the scale of the conflict, but like drops in water, they create ripples that touch distant shores. Sheikh Abdullah bin Bayyah is also quoted as saying: *"If you cannot bring peace to the whole world, bring it to the space you stand in."* Rabbi Abraham Joshua Heschel gave a parallel challenge: *"In a free society, some are guilty, but all are responsible."*

When individuals take responsibility for embodying the five elements in their daily lives, they create a civic culture where peace is not just negotiated in conference rooms, but lived in marketplaces, classrooms, and kitchens.

The Horizon: A Land at Peace with Itself

Some horizons are mirages. Others are distant but real. Standing on a high ridge in the Galilee or the hills of Samaria, you can see the Mediterranean to the west, the Jordan Valley to the east, and the desert stretching south. The horizon of peace in this land is like that – visible, even beautiful, but only reached by long and deliberate steps.

The Hebrew Bible speaks of such a horizon: *"They shall sit every man under his vine and under his fig tree, and none shall make them afraid"* (Micah 4:4) The Quran offers its own parallel: *"And Allah invites to the Home of Peace and guides whom He wills to a straight path"* (Quran 10:25). The below is a description of our vision of peace, with forgiveness, acceptance and purpose bringing new meaning to all our lives. It is not imaginary or a fantasy; it is a presentation of what might be – what must be – a **new reality**.

Streets Without Fear

In this vision, a Jewish grandmother in Sderot walks to the market without worrying about rockets. A Palestinian father in Khan Yunis drives his children to school without worrying about military incursions or Hamas shootings. At crossings between Israel and the Palestinian Authority, between Israel and the Egyptian Sinai and Jordan and Syria and Lebanon as well, traffic moves at the pace of commerce, not suspicion.

It is not utopia. It is simply normal life – and in this region, normal is extraordinary.

Governance That Serves

Israel and Palestinian Authority have reinstated the shared water and energy councils that used to meet monthly – not under foreign pressure, but because shared infrastructure is the lifeline of both peoples. Ministries on both sides budget for peace implementation the way they budget for defense – because it is now understood that peace is a form of defense.

Boutros Boutros-Ghali also said: *"Peace is built day by day, choice by choice."* And so, in this vision, peace has become a policy habit.

Virtually all Arab and Muslim nations have joined the Abraham Accords, having established full and warm relations with the Jewish State. A Council of Abraham has been established as a coordinating mechanism for furthering economic, social, cultural, religious, academic and political relationships, enhancing the bonds already created across the region, including security cooperation against shared threats.

Schools That Teach Two Stories

In Bethlehem, Hebrew is taught alongside Arabic as a living language, just as Arabic is Israel's second official language. In Haifa, Jewish and Arab children learn two histories – their own and their neighbor's – and write essays on how both can be true without cancelling each other out. Teachers from both communities, and from neighboring Arab and Muslim countries, attend annual workshops on conflict-sensitive education, supported by ministries of education on both sides.

Faith That Unites

On Friday, an imam in Nablus/Shechem delivers a sermon on the Quranic call to *"repel evil with what is better"* (41:34). On Saturday/Shabbat, a rabbi in Jerusalem speaks of Joseph forgiving his brothers. On Sunday, a priest in Nazareth or Bethlehem quotes Jesus: *"Blessed are the peacemakers."* And the following Friday, the imam of the Grand Mosque in Gaza quotes all three. The four of them know each other's sermons because they met earlier in the week at an interfaith study circle – not to dilute their beliefs, but to strengthen them with the parallel calls to mercy and justice found in all.

Sheikh Abdullah bin Bayyah calls this *"building the jurisprudence of peace."*

Media That Reflects Humanity

Israeli and Palestinian news channels still cover politics and disagreements, but they also run nightly segments on cooperation: a joint tech startup in Ramallah and Tel Aviv, a reforestation project in the Negev, a medical team operating on refugees. Social media influencers in Arabic and Hebrew trade jokes and recipes, not insults. And this is true throughout the Arab and Muslim world. As per Rabbi Sacks, we are all using "different words."

Grassroots That Lead the Way

Coexistence is not just an NGO buzzword. It is lived reality in shared markets, soccer leagues, and business ventures. Farmers from Jenin and kibbutzniks from the Jezreel Valley run joint cooperatives. Jews from Beit Shemesh and Be'er Sheva have returned to their dentists and car mechanics in Hebron, and Arab Muslims and Christians from Ramallah and Gaza have resumed their visits to the Mediterranean beaches, shops, hotels and restaurants of Tel Aviv, Netanya, Herzliya and Ashkelon.

Hospitals employ mixed teams. Young people join cross-border mentorship programs, not because donors fund them, but because they work. Sam Bahour's aphorism – "future-building in the present tense" – takes shape in the lives of all people in the region.

Steps from Here: A Phased Roadmap

Visions inspire; roadmaps guide. The horizon of peace will remain distant unless governments, civil society, and ordinary citizens know what steps to take now, next year, and in the decades ahead. What follows is a phased approach – beginning with what can be done immediately, moving to mid-term foundations, and ending with long-term transformations.

Phase One: Immediate Actions (0–2 Years)

Governments

- Reopen and expand direct communication channels between security, health, and infrastructure ministries on both sides.

- Agree on a mutual moratorium on inflammatory official rhetoric, monitored by an independent body.

- Begin or renew discussions on core issues (borders, security arrangements, economic cooperation) with clear commitments to non-escalation.

Civil Society & NGOs

- Launch rapid-scale "dual narrative" teacher-training programs.

- Expand joint community projects – market renovations, public garden restorations, and local infrastructure upgrades – in mixed or adjacent towns.

- Support dialogue initiatives that bring together community leaders, youth, and women's groups from both peoples.

Individuals

- Practice micro-interactions of humility and acceptance in daily life: greetings in each other's language, shared hospitality, and willingness to listen.

- Share at least one positive story about the other community each week on personal social media.

- Refuse to forward dehumanizing content about the other side.

Phase Two: Building Foundations (2–7 Years)

Governments

- Integrate cooperative clauses into trade agreements – water, energy, agriculture – so economic ties strengthen peace.

- Reform school curricula to include both perspectives, beginning with pilot programs in select districts and expanding over time.

- Establish mechanisms for joint security coordination that protect civilians and reduce friction.

Civil Society & NGOs

- Create cross-border media platforms in Arabic and Hebrew for peace journalism and fact-checking.

- Scale up interfaith initiatives to reach rural and underserved communities, not just urban centers.

- Develop joint professional associations (doctors, engineers, educators) that meet regularly.

Individuals

- Join or form local dialogue circles with neighbors across the divide.

- Participate in inter-community cultural events – food festivals, sports leagues, and music workshops.

- Visit sites of the other community's pain and memory (e.g., cemeteries, memorials), when invited, as acts of respect.

Phase Three: Deep Embedding (7–15 Years)

Governments

- Establish a joint Peace Implementation Fund, with equal Israeli and Palestinian oversight, to finance cooperative projects.

- Create a shared environmental authority to manage water, waste, and renewable energy.

- Normalize cross-border movement for trade, education, and tourism, subject to mutually agreed security arrangements.

Civil Society & NGOs

- Build permanent peace education centers in major cities for training teachers, journalists, and community leaders.

- Develop mentorship programs pairing Israeli and Palestinian youth in professional apprenticeships and leadership tracks.

- Support think-tanks and universities in both societies to conduct joint research on conflict transformation and shared regional development.

Individuals

- Travel to each other's cities, markets, and cultural sites to normalize familiarity.

- Support businesses and products that employ or benefit both Israelis and Palestinians.

- Integrate the five elements into family life: how children hear adults speak about "them," how holidays are framed, how news is discussed at the dinner table.

Deepening Theological and Cultural Transformation

Alongside these phased steps, a deeper theological and cultural process is needed – particularly where Islamist political ideology has distorted Islam itself, and where Jewish or Israeli discourse can also occasionally harden into dehumanization.

Key directions include:

- Distinguishing Islam from Islamism – clarifying the difference between Islam as a faith and Islamism as a political ideology, and amplifying Muslim scholars who reject violence and supremacism.

- Encouraging *ijtihad* (independent reasoning) – supporting Islamic scholars who draw on classical tools to reinterpret texts in light of contemporary realities, emphasizing mercy, justice, and coexistence.

- Curriculum reform in religious education – in both Islamic and Jewish settings, integrating teachings that stress human dignity, freedom of conscience, and peaceful coexistence.

- Interfaith and intra-faith dialogue – building bridges not only between Jews, Muslims, and Christians, but also within each community (e.g., Sunni–Shia dialogues; secular–religious Jewish conversations) to marginalize radical voices.

- Empowering moderate role models – elevating imams,

rabbis, scholars, activists, and especially women who embody moderation, courage, and compassion.

- Connecting theology to policy – showing how Islamic concepts like *maslaha* (public interest) and *maqāṣid al-sharīʿah* (higher objectives of law), and Jewish concepts like *pikuach nefesh* (saving life), support compromise and peace.

These efforts must grow from within communities, not be imposed from outside. External actors can support with resources and protection, encouraging change but not dictating doctrine. The goal is not to Westernize Islam (or Judaism), but to recenter both on their own deepest teachings of mercy and justice.

<u>Leadership and Grassroots Together</u>

History shows that grassroots support is essential to the success of top-down peace, and that political frameworks are crucial to grassroots peace struggles' success. The roadmap must therefore be two-handed: one in government halls, one in the streets.

King Hussein often warned that unless we reach people's hearts, agreements won't last. Sheikh Abdullah bin Bayyah teaches that the best reconciliation is that which is grounded in cooperation.

The Realistic Path to This Horizon

The five elements – Humility, Acceptance, Gratitude, Forgiveness, and Purpose – are not new ideas. They echo through the Hebrew Bible and the Quran, through Arab poetry and Jewish wisdom, through the lives of leaders and ordinary people who chose a harder but better path. What is new here is the attempt to weave them together in a cohesive strategy for peace, as well as the insistence that these values cannot remain abstract. They must be fused into governance, media, education, and daily life until they become the common sense of society.

The Quran warns: *"Indeed, Allah will not change the condition of a people until they change what is in themselves"* (Quran 13:11). The Hebrew Bible offers a powerful analogous command: *"Choose life, so that you and your children may live"* (Deuteronomy 30:19).

Change begins inside, but it survives only when it is built outside – in systems, laws, schools, pulpits, newsrooms, and neighborhoods. The vision described above is not a dream plucked from the air. It is built on existing seeds. But we have to move from principle to policy, and then to practice. In governance, purpose must be written into agreements and budgets so that peace produces visible benefits. In media, the moral obligation is to tell the truth and to amplify stories that humanize rather than demonize. In education, humility and acceptance must shape how history is taught and how children learn to see "the other". In religious life, gratitude and forgiveness must be preached as obligations of faith. And in grassroots daily life, individuals must embody the five elements in markets, classrooms, and streets.

When these layers reinforce each other, peace stops being a fragile exception and becomes the default mode of society.

<u>Shared Moral Foundations</u>

As we have insisted and demonstrated throughout this work, Arab, Islamic, Jewish, and Israeli traditions share more than they often admit:

- Humility: Imam Ali's teaching that all people are "equals in humanity" aligns with Jewish teachings that every person is created in the divine image.

- Acceptance: The Quran's command to *"know one another"* (49:13) mirrors the Jewish idea that all humans are created *b'tzelem Elohim* – in the image of God.

- Gratitude: The Prophet Mohammed taught that *"He who does not thank people does not thank Allah,"* just as the Psalms overflow with thanksgiving.

- Forgiveness: Mohammed's pardon of his enemies at Mecca stands beside Joseph's forgiveness of his brothers in Genesis.

- Purpose: The *maqāṣid al-sharīʿah* (higher objectives of law) in Islamic thought and the prophetic call for Israel to be "a light unto the nations" both demand a constructive vision for the future.

These shared roots make the five elements not a foreign imposition, but a return to the best of each tradition.

Peace is often spoken of as a political project; to avoid collapse at the first political storm it must also be a personal and cultural project. With the five elements embedded deeply in the civic and moral life of the people, the appetite for peace will outlast the appetite for revenge, even if agreements may fail, leaders may fall, and violence may flare.

Sheikh Abdullah bin Bayyah says: *"Reconciliation is the restoration of the human being before it is the restoration of the treaty."*

Rabbi Jonathan Sacks echoed this when he wrote: *"The greatest single antidote to violence is conversation, speaking our fears, listening to the others', and in doing so, realising that they too are human."*

In sum, what is needed is scale, political will, and the steady cultivation of the five elements in each sphere.

Rabbi Abraham Isaac Kook wrote: *"The old will be renewed, and the new will be sanctified."*

Mohammad, reflecting Rabbi Tarfon's famous dictum about not avoiding crucial work, said: *"If the Hour is about to be established and one of you has a seedling in his hand, let him plant it"* (Musnad Ahmad).

The horizon of peace will not be reached in one lifetime. But every seed planted – in governance, in schools, in pulpits, in headlines, in homes – brings it closer.

A Call to Begin

No phase can begin without the first step. Mohammad said: *"The most beloved of deeds to Allah are those that are continuous, even if small"* (Bukhari, Muslim).

The work of peace is measured not in grand declarations, but in steady acts – planting seeds, tending them, and teaching others to continue watering them after us.

Chapter Nine: Conclusion – Putting it All Together

When Islam is understood in its classical sense as submission to God, it offers a profound pathway to humility, acceptance, gratitude, forgiveness and purpose.

Submission requires humility – the acknowledgment that human power is limited and that ultimate judgment does not belong to us. It requires acceptance – of reality, of history, of the existence of others created by the same God. It promotes appreciation for our blessings and the uprightness of forgiving others. And it certainly yields purpose – not the purpose of domination or revenge, but the purpose of living in alignment with divine attributes: mercy, restraint, justice, and care for life.

Where submission is replaced by grievance, or humility by supremacism, Islam is not being expressed but distorted.

Hiking the Trail, I discovered that peace begins when resistance to reality ends. I could not argue with the terrain; I had to submit to it – adjust my pace, carry my water, accept my limits. True also in life, with the humble acceptance of divorce and other hardships. Islam's notion of submission points to a similar wisdom at the national level. Peace will not come from insisting the world conform to our wounds, but from submitting to the truth that we must live together, or not live at all.

There comes a moment at the end of any long journey – whether walking across a rocky desert, navigating the collapse of a marriage, or trying to understand a generations-deep conflict – when motion slows and the heart finally speaks. Those moments came quietly when I was on the trek: on wind-swept ridges above the Negev, in olive-scented valleys shaped by ancient hands, at dawns where the sky blushed pink, and in nights so silent the stars seemed close enough to touch. Nothing dramatic happened. The insight was simple: every step, every ache, every doubt had brought me deeper not only into the land, but into understanding.

Purpose, I realized, is not a destination. It is a way of walking.

Nations also walk. Sometimes they stumble, defend old wounds, and guard grievances as if they were fragile bones. This is walking in place – or even walking backwards. Yet nations, too, long to move forward. The Arab–Israel conflict, steeped in history, myth, identity, and pain, has shown repeatedly that power alone cannot guarantee peace, and grievance alone cannot sustain identity.

Real peace – peace that reshapes futures rather than suspending hostilities – demands inner transformation before it yields outward change. It requires humility and empathy to see the other, acceptance to acknowledge their story, gratitude to recognize what remains good, forgiveness to release the grip of the past, and purpose to guide the steps that follow and give meaning to the national endeavor.

These five elements are not abstractions; they are tools, muscles, and discipline. I learned them from dust and sweat, from the rebuilding of a life, from Israeli and Palestinian friends, from wars endured, from teachers and texts, from conversations in synagogues and mosques and quiet kitchens. They are as old as Abraham and as urgent as tomorrow morning. But virtues alone do not build nations. Values without institutions are wind without sails.

That has been, in many ways, the thread through this book: not only what these elements mean, but how they manifest – in personal life, in communities, and in the hardest arena of all, the political realm between Arabs and Jews, Muslims and Israelis, neighbors and adversaries.

For Jews and Israelis – as in my own life, on the trek and healing from divorce – the sequence is clear. Humility enables acceptance; acceptance allows gratitude; gratitude opens the door to forgiveness; and forgiveness leads to purpose, even if purpose already lies under everything and gives meaning to life.

For a people with a well-defined historical mission like the Jews, rooted in covenantal identity and the moral imperative embedded in commandments, purpose is not merely the last element; it permeates the entire narrative. Why walk the *Shvil* except to discover meaning, to feel the Land, to reconnect with our history and people? Why endure and rebuild after divorce unless guided by purpose – hope, renewal, the desire to love again? Why has Israel sought peace so persistently, despite repeated rebuffs, if not because our sense of purpose itself commands it? The historical Jewish goal to bring light and goodness to humanity remains the calling of the people of Israel, of which our ongoing contributions to the world are proof.

In contrast, within much of the Arab and Muslim world, the order of the five elements must differ, as the history and ideologies involved present their own challenges.

This is true because, for over a millennium, mainstream Islamic thought – Shiite and Sunni alike – has emphasized expansion, dominance, and the subjugation or conversion of others. This does not negate the original moral richness of Islam; any informed observer knows its profound ethical teachings. Nor does it dismiss the vital spiritual contributions of Sufism, the Druze, Ismaili and other traditions, or the modern Wasatia movement, which may point toward a better future. But it does acknowledge a historical reality: that Arab and Muslim societies have not, on the whole, focused their collective purpose on human flourishing, peace, or individual dignity in the way Judaism and Christianity have largely evolved to do. [79]

It is essential to recognize this – not to condemn, but to understand. The Christian world has grappled with its violent Crusades and coercive conversions. Western civilization has its colonial sins. Jews have their own ancient chapters of conquest. But modern Christianity and Judaism have undergone deep moral and theological transformations, turning their energies toward benevolence, humanitarianism, and self-critique. And these revolutions in theology informed the political revolutions and ideological developments which led to the evolution of western civilization and the values entrenched across the free world.

Much of the Islamic world has not yet gone through an

---

[79] There is no point engaging in an intellectual discussion whether creating a global Caliphate by the sword and bringing humanity under the canopy of Islam through forced conversions might generate a sort of "peace and harmony" in the world. Our perspective is based on the moral compass of the modern, free, democratic world, which though it can thrive even in traditional or hierarchical societies like Japan or Azerbijan, Singapore or India, is not compatible with the repressive, autocratic and intolerant mentality associated, unfortunately, with traditional expressions of political Islam to date.

equivalent internal reckoning. Until it does, neither forgiveness nor gratitude nor true acceptance can take meaningful root, and it will be impossible for the Muslim world to move ahead.

Thus, they need to carry out the elements in a different order.

Humility must still come first; but for Arabs and Muslims, the next stage must be *purpose*. A renewed, reinterpreted, self-generated dedication to goals that align with peace, human dignity, and the Quranic aspirations for mercy and justice. This cannot be dictated by outsiders or Western leaders. But it can be encouraged, supported, and modeled by reformers whose voices call courageously for cultural and theological transformation.

Only after clarity of purpose emerges can forgiveness follow: forgiveness of Israel, of the West, of historical disappointments, of imagined slights and genuine wounds. Gratitude can come next – gratitude for progress, for partnership, for the potential of shared prosperity. And acceptance will come last: the acceptance of Israel's legitimacy, permanence, and indigeneity; acceptance that Jews are not colonial intruders but a people returning home.

This reordered sequence may be more successful than the original order, but that will be up to the leaders who pursue these ideas. For some, acceptance may be first, not least as the recognition of the Jews' connection to their ancestral homeland and the legitimacy of the establishment of Israel has been one of the leading messages of moderates in the past decade, not least as the theme of the Abraham Accords. (Though without forgiveness and the purpose of peace and coexistence, mere acknowledgement of Israel's "right to exist" has been proven to be insufficient.) At base, irrespective of the order in which these steps are carried out, the combination of all the components is the ultimate imperative.

Yes, it all seems ambitious; because it is. But peace will not come through half-measures. If we all need to apply and put into practice the five elements to better ourselves and get unstuck from where we are stuck, it is all the more crucial for Muslims and Arabs. The five elements can be a roadmap to their theological transformation, back to their peaceful roots.

How might this look in practice? In essence, three steps on each side.

For Arabs and Muslims:

- Courageous declarations by leaders proclaiming peace as their purpose and acknowledging Israel's legitimacy and their own people's need for renewal;
- Reformed education, media, and culture that teach coexistence and diminish grievance; and
- Genuine negotiations with a now-recognized Israel.

These three steps would by definition involve a tremendous intellectual, cultural, religious and political shift in the Arab and Muslim world; the suggestion is not made lightly. But as demonstrated above, that's what Mohammed Dajani is calling for; that's what Houssein Aboubakr advocates; that's what Ayaan Hirs Ali dreams of. And these measures can be promoted, and supported, by Christian leaders in Arab society and around the world.

Altering the priorities of their societies, leaders in their communities will focus their people on the Islamic aspirations for peace, fostering an environment which encourages acceptance, gratitude and forgiveness. This will include, not least, forgiveness of the West and Israel, Christians and Jews, for their unwillingness to embrace Islam and their success in developing their intellectually and economically thriving nations. And it will require forgiveness for both real and perceived injuries and insults. This is a call for a radical change in mindsets, no less.

For Israel:

- Declarations by leaders across the ideological spectrum reaffirming the moral imperative of peace, announcing a new era with real partners for peace, and calling to trust the process;
- A broad national-unity approach that includes Arab citizens and centrist Jewish factions in governing coalitions and increases interactions in civil society; and
- Sincere negotiations to achieve comprehensive regional agreements.

These Israeli steps are hardly hypothetical. For over a century, from Herzl onward, Jews and Israeli leaders have consistently pursued compromise. They accepted the division of the land in 1922, the Peel Plan of 1937, the UN Partition Plan of 1947, countless armistice and negotiation proposals, and every genuine peace initiative thereafter, withdrawing from the Sinai and from Gaza and more, up to and including the 2025 Gaza peace plan. The historical record is clear: compromise, concessions, and conciliation have defined Jewish political behavior.

When both societies embrace a parallel sense of purpose – one rooted not in conquest but in progress – then real peace becomes possible.

Reality must be recognized. The Jews are indigenous to this land. Israel has acted almost exclusively in self-defense. No nation in history has taken greater care to protect innocents, even in enemy populations, in wartime. Yet these truths have been buried under layers of propaganda. The primary barrier to peace has never been "settlements" or borders, or Israeli policy. It has been the continuous refusal of Arab and Muslim leadership to accept Israel's existence and the legitimacy of its founding, and the systematic radicalization of their societies. Until this fact is faced, peace cannot begin.

This is where international actors – Americans, Europeans, policymakers, religious leaders –can truly be helpful. Not by pressuring Israel into dangerous concessions, but by encouraging real reformation within Arab and Muslim societies and holding their leaders accountable for their choices, in all ways – through political and diplomatic pressure, funding and economic activity, military support, and more.

Throughout my life – at home, in my private life, at work, and as a public servant – and of course in the course of the hike, I discovered how forgiveness lifted weight from my heart; that purpose – having a goal – makes suffering endurable; and that Frankl's insight that meaning is essential to survival applies to both individuals and nations. When combined with Gandhi's "Truth," Dajani's Wasatia, and the Rambam's "Golden Mean", these ideas began forming a framework far larger than my personal story.

Part of the thesis of this book is that peace is indeed possible. It is in no way guaranteed, but peace is possible – when people and nations cultivate the internal soil from which peace grows: humility, acceptance, gratitude, forgiveness, and purpose. Especially purpose. Without a shared horizon – even loosely shared – every noble step risks falling; it just won't work.

Here is where the more lyrical truth joins the analytic one: The *Shvil* taught me that journeys are walked step by step, often in silence, often without applause. Peace is the same. It is not conjured; it is cultivated. It is the quiet decision, repeated daily, to choose generosity over suspicion, curiosity over certainty, hope over cynicism. Cynicism predicts chaos and calls it clarity; hope, when disciplined and realistic, becomes strategy.

So let us imagine – not naively, but with moral imagination – what purposeful peace might look like. Imagine leadership built on humility rather than defiance; education that teaches others' perspectives and promotes tolerance and peace; religious sermons that elevate compassion over rage; media that recognizes words as sparks capable of igniting flames or as water capable of cooling passions; economic partnerships that bind destinies rather than deepen dependencies; environmental collaborations that unite communities because climate ignores borders; families teaching strength without hatred; activists insisting that dignity is indivisible.

These are not dreams. They are designs – blueprints awaiting courageous builders.

In this blueprint our five elements form an interlocking framework for human and national flourishing: humility opens the mind, acceptance opens the heart, gratitude nurtures resilience, forgiveness frees the spirit, and purpose directs energy toward creation, healing, and coexistence. Applied across the divides of the Arab–Israeli conflict – or any deeply rooted conflict – they offer a moral, psychological, and practical roadmap.

The picture painted here may seem childishly naïve in its depiction of such a peaceful world. Indeed, we have seen more violence, not less, in recent decades, across the globe. But what I have suggested is a best-case scenario; advancing towards that target will improve lives regardless of whether we achieve all our aims at once. Any form of progress along these lines will be transformative.

Consider a comparison between our world and that of just two centuries ago. Note the free societies living in peace with each other today; the accomplishments of individuals and states in health, longevity, economics and technology; the eradication of slavery and misogyny (mostly) and the like. We must believe that humanity can and will continue to evolve. It seems – objectively – that we are closer to the perhaps over-used cliché of "world peace" than we ever have been, as a human society.

History further shows that the virtues needed to bring about change are not utopian either; they are embodied in the actions of real leaders. Sadat and Rabin risked all in carrying them out. Leaders and ordinary citizens, drawing on the wisdom of Judaism, Islam, and Christianity, can transform cycles of grievance into cycles of meaning and cooperation. In cultivating humility, acceptance, gratitude, forgiveness, and purpose, nations learn not merely to survive, but to thrive together – discovering that the deepest human longing, across cultures and faiths, is for peace grounded in understanding, justice, and shared purpose.

We can recognize that the idea of reforming Islamic theology and political philosophy is a sensitive one which must respect the autonomy and diversity of Muslim and Arab communities. The focus should be on fostering dialogue, empowering moderate voices, and addressing socio-political factors that contribute to extremism. Change, when driven from within and supported by thoughtful engagement, is more likely to be sustainable and authentic.

Our approach is a mandate for both philosophical and practical change; the specifics of "solutions" to the Arab-Israel conflict are not the focus here. As mentioned in the chapter on purpose, there are a variety of alternatives to consider, many of which provide reasonable answers to the most pressing challenges faced in the region. But they all require the acceptance, forgiveness, humility and sense of purpose described here.

This promised land has seen countless crossroads. Armies have marched through its valleys; prophets have walked its hills. Treaties have been signed, broken, and signed again. In every generation, men and women have had a choice – to answer conflict with more conflict, or to take the harder path of peace.

We stand there again. Still.

The Hebrew Bible commands it plainly, and it is worth repeating: *"Seek peace and pursue it"* (Psalm 34:14).

The Quran calls us to that choice, as also noted in our prologue: *"Repel [evil] by that [deed] which is better; and thereupon the one whom between you and him is enmity will become as though he were a devoted friend"* (Quran 41:34).

As referred to earlier, peace is not built in negotiation rooms. It is built in kitchens, markets, classrooms, buses, and social media feeds. Every person who chooses humility over pride, acceptance over rejection, gratitude over entitlement, forgiveness over revenge, and purpose over aimlessness contributes to the fabric of peace — even if they never meet a president or prime minister.

Rabbi Hillel asked: *"If I am only for myself, what am I?"* (*Pirkei Avot* 1:14)

The Prophet Mohammed said: *"The believer is not the one who eats his fill while his neighbor is hungry."* (Musnad Ahmad)

Both teachings remind us that peace begins in the refusal to live only for one's own side.

We know that choosing peace is rarely comfortable. It will draw criticism from one's own community. It will require patience with small steps, and persistence through setbacks. But moral courage — the courage to humanize the other in a time of dehumanization — is the engine that moves history toward justice.

As King Hussein told grieving Israeli parents in 1997: *"Your loss is my loss, my personal loss."* And as Israeli Prime Minister Yitzhak Rabin said before his assassination: *"You don't make peace with friends. You make it with enemies."*

As an almost final note, let's acknowledge that this book is not a manual for governments alone. It is a mirror for individuals. If you are reading these words in Jerusalem or Ramallah, in Amman or Cairo, in New York or London — you are part of the story. Your conversations, your posts, your votes, your purchases, your prayers — they all tilt the balance toward either deeper division or deeper reconciliation.

The question is not whether the path to peace is open. The

question is whether enough people will choose to walk it.

Our children are watching. They are learning from what we say, what we teach, and what we post. They are absorbing our grudges or our grace. One day, they will write the next chapter of this land's history. It will either begin with another cycle of "we suffered; therefore we strike," or with "we suffered; therefore we heal."

Sheikh Abdullah bin Bayyah has been quoted as urging us not to bequeath hatred to our children, but rather to bequeath them hope. Rabbi Jonathan Sacks, as quoted above, asserts that the world we build tomorrow is born in the words we speak today.

On the *Shvil*, it was obvious that you do not need to see the end of the journey to take the first step. We know that if the work is too great to finish, Rabbi Tarfon taught, we must do it anyway; if the Hour were to come and you held a seedling, Mohammed said, plant it.

The path is here. The horizon is visible. The choice is ours. The choice is yours.

And so we return, one last time, to the Trail. At the end of a long hike, there is no finish line – only a horizon. And at the end of a book like this, there really is no prescription – only an invitation.

- If you are a policymaker, craft policy rooted in dignity as much as deterrence.
- If you are a teacher, teach compassion with the same rigor as mathematics.
- If you are clergy, teach that God is not honored by hatred and murder.
- If you are a parent, tell your children stories not only of suffering but of strength.
- If you are a young person weary of the old arguments, bring new ones.
- If you are a leader, focus your people on acceptance and forgiveness, not conquest and control.

And if you are simply a human being – Jewish, Muslim, Christian, Israeli, Arab, or anything else – know this: peace begins not in treaties, but in people. It begins with the stories we tell and the choices we make.

Peace is not a miracle. Peace is a discipline.

Like every discipline, peace begins with a single act – done not once, but again and again – until one day, without knowing exactly when, we find ourselves living in a new world, full of hope and promise.

Acknowledgments

If *it takes a village to raise a child…* then it takes a neighborhood to write a book (at least one like this). My 'neighborhood' includes all those with whom I have talked/argued and learned from over the past decade while conceiving and then working on this book, and in particular those who have taken the time (and had the patience) to contribute to my understanding and to review this work.

First and foremost, I thank Miriam, my wife and partner in all things, for her encouragement, her forbearance, and her outstanding editing skills.

I am grateful to all my friends and mentors whose comments have enriched my arguments (and have corrected many errors), especially Mohammed Dajani, Khaled Abu Toameh, Gil Troy, William Daroff, Daniel Pipes, Michael Oren, and my brother-in-law, Yitzy Fischer.

I am indebted to many others, most of whom I also know personally, whose thought and works have influenced my thinking greatly over the years, and though I have not included a bibliography, nor quoted them all in the book, it is important to mention them by name.

They include Natan Sharansky, Einat Wilf, Bernard Lewis, Irshad Manji, Ayaan Hirsi Ali, Jonathan Spyer, Dore Gold, Yoram Hazony, Ishmael Khaldi, Yossi Klein Halevi, Brigette Gabriel, Daniel Pipes, Mordechai Kedar, Ephraim Karsh, Einat Wilf (& Adi Schwartz), Walid Salem, Martin Gilbert, Benny Morris, Daniel Gordis, Dennis Ross & David Makovsky, Yehoshafat Harkabi, David Shipler, Jean Bethke Elshtain, Michael Walzer, Robert Kagan, John Bolton, Melanie Phillips, Fareed Zakaria, Timothy Mitchell, Elie Kedourie, H.A.R. Gibb, Albert Hourani, Elan Journo, Fouad Ajami, Alan Dershowitz, Simon Sebag Montefiore, Rabbi Jonathan Sacks and, last but certainly not least, Mark Juergensmeyer.

And I want to express my gratitude, also, to my friend and consultant Yedidya Brauner, whose sage advice helped me to move ahead with the project when the process seemed stuck.

Of course, all errors, and all opinions expressed here, remain mine.

Last though certainly not least, I very much appreciate the support of my wider family – my mother, Joan, and all of Miriam's and my children – Yonatan, Shira, Michal, Harel, Moriyah, Tani, Naomi, Tal, Chagit, Navah, T'mima and Yehudah – and I forgive with great humility and gratitude your teasing over the years.

We can and we will change the world, together – for your children's sake.

Aryeh Green is a celebrated writer, speaker, and policy expert with decades of experience in Middle East affairs, regional cooperation, democracy promotion, and civil society development. A former senior advisor to Natan Sharansky, head of MediaCentral in Jerusalem, and longtime advocate for human rights and freedom, he has worked extensively across Israel and the Middle East and the broader Arab world. An Israeli/American thought-leader, strategic consultant and business executive, today Aryeh works to bring renewable energy to Africa from Israel as co-founder of Gigawatt Impact and as chief strategy officer of EnergiyaGlobal, and serves on the boards of a number of respected nonprofits including the Maaleh Film School in Jerusalem. He is a frequent lecturer on the Arab–Israel conflict, media issues, democracy, personal growth and spirituality, and his first book, *My Israel Trail,* inspired thousands with its message of resilience and transformation (www.myisraeltrail.com).

In *Finding Peace in the Promised Land,* he brings together personal knowledge, moral insight, and political analysis to propose an uplifting and pragmatic vision for reconciliation in the region.

Scan to learn more:

www.aryehgreen.com

aryeh.green@gmail.com

www.ingramcontent.com/pod-product-compliance
Lightning Source LLC
Chambersburg PA
CBHW031643170726
47990CB00019B/2104